Joseph Johnson

An Appeal to Impartial Posterity By Madame Roland...

Vol. I Containing Part I and II

Joseph Johnson

An Appeal to Impartial Posterity By Madame Roland...
Vol. I Containing Part I and II

ISBN/EAN: 9783744793544

Printed in Europe, USA, Canada, Australia, Japan

Cover: Foto ©ninafisch / pixelio.de

More available books at **www.hansebooks.com**

AN APPEAL TO IMPARTIAL POSTERITY,

BY

MADAME ROLAND,

WIFE OF THE MINISTER OF THE INTERIOR;

OR,

A COLLECTION OF TRACTS

WRITTEN BY HER DURING HER CONFINEMENT IN THE PRISONS OF THE ABBEY, AND ST. PÉLAGIE, IN PARIS.

IN FOUR PARTS.

TRANSLATED FROM THE FRENCH ORIGINAL,

Published for the Benefit of her only Daughter, deprived of the Fortune of her Parents by Sequestration.

SECOND EDITION, REVISED AND CORRECTED.

VOL I.

Containing PART I. and II.

May my last letter to my daughter fix her attention to that object which appears likely to become her essential duty; and may the remembrance of her mother attach her for ever to those virtues which afford us consolation in all circumstances.

Extracted from the piece entitled *My Last Thoughts,* in Part II. p. 120.

LONDON:

PRINTED FOR J. JOHNSON, ST. PAUL'S CHURCH-YARD.

1796.

ADVERTISEMENT

FROM THE EDITOR.

Royalism and Terrorism endeavour to excite doubts in the public mind concerning the authenticity of these writings. Both wish to suspend their sale: the former with the intention of favouring a counter-revolution, by aspersing a minister, whose firm and wise administration proved that France might be happy under a republican form of government; the latter, that they may not be held up to public view as the real authors of our present situation, and with the hope of being able to diminish the horror with which their crimes must necessarily inspire all those to whom they shall be faithfully narrated.

I request all good citizens, whose faith may have been staggered by their insinuations, to consider, first, that nobody but Madame Roland could detail an infinite number of circumstances, with which she alone could be acquainted; secondly, that every writer has his appropriate style, and that the manner of Madame Roland is sufficiently original to prevent its being easily confounded with that of another; in the third place, that my signature certifies the truth, and that all who please may come to my house and convince themselves, that the whole of the manuscript is in the hand-writing of my unfortunate friend.

BOSC.

Paris, 4th Floreal, 3d year of the Republic.

before was confined to a few intimates, but now when she was become the centre of a wider circle, the admiration of her friends, and the malevolence of her enemies, soon combined to give her a celebrity which she was still far from seeking.

Imprisoned, calumniated on all sides, and having nothing but a scaffold before her eyes, Madam Roland was naturally induced to seek the esteem of posterity as a consolation for the injustice of her contemporaries, and to aim at future glory, as a sort of compensation for an untimely death.

Then, and not till then, she appeared to separate her reputation from that of her husband: then, and not till then, she took up her pen to make herself known individually, and to furnish materials for history in her own name. It will be seen, however, that she was not actuated solely by the desire of vindicating her reputation, and acquiring fame: every page will show, that she was particularly anxious to repel the calumnious charges heaped upon her husband, and to revenge the memory of Roland, in case he himself should not have it in his power to write or publish his last justification.

The public, already prepossessed in her favour, will judge,

judge, from a perusal of her writings, whether she really merited the praise of her friends, and whether she did not deserve the hatred of the villains, who succeeded at last in bringing her to the block.

Malevolence, assuming the mask of criticism, will endeavour, no doubt, to depreciate this monument erected by a woman to the glory of her sex; but the impartial reader will acknowledge her powers. I will only say, as an excuse for some superfluous relations, and some negligences of composition, that Madam Roland composed the part entitled Historical Memoirs (two thirds of which, and those the most interesting, are lost) in the space of one month, and all the rest in two and twenty days, in the midst of sorrows and alarms of every kind; and that scarcely a passage in the manuscript is erased.

Many persons, whose characters Madam Roland has drawn, will have reason to complain; but it belongs to posterity alone to decide, whether she have done them justice. It was *my* duty to confine myself strictly to the office of an editor; and to make no alteration in the text, even when it was evident, that she had been mistaken. There is a passage, for instance, where she seems to throw reflections on citizen Dulaure, which I believe him far from deserving, and which every true republican will be eager to reject. It may not be amiss here to relate the cause of her error.

Dulaure, a patriotic journalist, and a bold assertor of truth, was a frequent visitor at Roland's, whose principles were analogous to his own, and whose conduct he deemed meritorious. But when Dulaure became a member of the convention, he thought it incumbent on him, as a matter of delicacy, to desist from going to the house of a minister, of whose actions he was constituted a judge. Madam Roland attributed this reserve to a change of political opinions, and to the instigation of the mountaineers: hence the ill-humour which seems to have predominated, when she wrote the article concerning him; but in which, notwithstanding, she does his character the justice it deserves. The courage with which citizen Dulaure printed all the complaints of madam Roland after the 31st of May; the honourable proscription he has undergone; and his last publication entitled, A Supplement to the Crimes of the late Committees of Government, render all farther justification unnecessary.

I could have wished to have given to the public the whole of the work at once; but the delays of the press at the present moment, and the observations of of some good citizens, have made me resolve to publish one part at a time. There will be four, which will follow each other, as speedily as circumstances will permit. The second will contain several detached pieces, respecting the events of the revolution, with the papers that relate to her death, or that immediately preceded it. The third and fourth will contain her private life, written precisely in the same manner, and with the same intention, as the Confessions of Rousseau: to which will be added some familiar letters, that I found among my papers. I much lament, that I have not a more complete series of her correspondence to publish *: it is in the effusions of friendship, that the mind displays itself fully, and that our opinions, inclinations, and acquirements, exhibit themselves naked to the eye. On this account I consider her letters, though at first view they appear to concern only our friendship, turn of mind, and our pursuits, as a necessary supplement to her private memoirs. Her republican ardour will appear from the very first of them; and certainly, on the 28th of August, 1792, she could not foresee, that France would become a republic;

---

* This correspondence, very active for several years, was frequently diurnal during her abode at Amiens. Imperfect traces remain in my memory of some interesting letters which I cannot now find: possibly they are with several others in the hands of Lanthenas, with whom that correspondence was frequently carried on in common. He then considered it, and with reason, as of great importance; but now!——

still

still less that she was destined to be a principal actor in that eventful scene.

Madam Roland was very fond of practising epistolary writing. She turned her pen to every subject with incredible facility, and with uncommon elegance of style. As a letter writer, she was superior, in my opinion, to a Sevigné or a Maintenon: because she was far better informed than those two celebrated women, and because her correspondence consisted of things, and not of words.

It is my wish to collect such of her letters, as may have been preserved; and I here request those who have them in their possession to send me the originals, as free from expence as may be; as I purpose publishing them at the end of several literary productions of madam Roland, which are known to me, and which I think worthy of seeing the light.

Roland during his retreat had also composed some historical memoirs; but they were consigned to the flames the moment the intrepid woman, who concealed him, was taken into custody. At the conclusion of his first ministry, he published a collection of pieces, calculated to make his conduct in office known to posterity; it is my intention to continue it, by getting together such as relate to his second ministry.

But that I may be enabled to accomplish this object, as well as the preceding one, it is requisite, that the national convention, either by a general law, solicited by all the friends of justice, or by a particular decree, desired by every true friend of liberty, restore to Roland's daughter the property to which she has a just claim. I must have liberty to search among the papers still under seal at Villefranche, and among those taken from the house at Paris, after the sale of the furniture by the agents of the national domains. It is incumbent on all true republicans, victims of tyranny, and persecuted for their virtues or talents like Roland and his wife, to favour my wishes with their influence, and to promote my engaging ward's restoration to her rights.

Let me be permitted to conclude with an observation, which perhaps is not unnecessary. This work is, at present at least, the sole fortune of Eudora, the beloved daughter, the only child of Roland. Woe to the villain who dares to pirate it! For certainly he would not be able to sell a single copy; and yet I should not fail to call down upon him all the vengeance of the law.

The portrait of madam Roland, engraved by the worthy Pasquier, the countryman of Roland, and the friend of them both, ought to be placed fronting the title page of the first part; but it cannot be got ready for delivery, till the publication of the last.

BOSC.

Paris, germinal 20, in the year of the republic 3 [April 9, 1795.]

HISTORICAL MEMOIRS.

Abbey Prison, June 1793.

To-day on a throne, to-morrow in a prison.

SUCH is the fate of virtue in revolutionary times. After the first commotions of a nation, weary of the abuses by which it has been aggrieved, have subsided, enlightened men, who have pointed out its rights, and assisted in regaining them, are called into places of authority: but they cannot long maintain themselves there; for the ambitious, eager to take advantage of circumstances, soon contrive to mislead the people by flattery, and set them against their real defenders, that they themselves may acquire consequence and power. Such has been the progress of things, particularly since the tenth of August. On some future day, perhaps, I shall recur to earlier times, to give an account of what my situation has enabled me to know: at present the sole object I have in view is to commit the circumstances of my arrest to paper: it is the kind of amusement most suitable to the solitary, to reflect on their personal concerns, and to express what they feel.

The resignation of Roland appeased not his enemies. He had quitted the ministry, in spite of his resolution to await there the laying of the storm, and to brave every danger;

danger; because the state of the council, when he became fully acquainted with it, and his want of influence, which kept continually increasing, and was particularly evident about the middle of January, no longer left him any thing to look forward to but faults and follies, of which he must participate the disgrace. He was not even allowed to enter his reasons or his opinions on the register of the proceedings, when they were contrary to the determination of the majority.

The consequence was, that from the day of that pitiful decree respecting the comedy intituled *l'Ami des Loix*, which he would not sign, because the second article was at best ridiculous, he no longer affixed his signature to any deliberation of the council. That was the fifteenth of January. The prospect held out to him by the convention was by no means encouraging. His very name was there become the signal of discord and disturbance; and could no longer be pronounced without producing an uproar. If a member ventured to answer the odious accusations gratuitously preferred against the minister, he was treated as an instrument of faction, and reduced to silence. In the mean time Pache was accumulating in the war department all the faults which his weakness and implicit submission to the jacobins enabled the perfidy, imbecility, and imprudence of his agents to commit; and yet the convention could not obtain the dismission of Pache; for the moment a single sentence was uttered against him, the bloodhounds of the mountain set up a howl against Roland. Thus the continuation of his courageous struggle in the ministry could no longer prevent the faults of the council, while it became an additional motive of disorder in the convention. He deemed it therefore

therefore prudent to give in his refignation. To prove that it was neceffary, it fuffices to remark, that the found part of the legiflative body, convinced as it was of the virtues and talents of the calumniated minifter, durft not make a fingle obfervation on the fubject. This was unqueftionably weaknefs; for it ftood in need of a firm and honeft man in the home department, who would have been its moft powerful fupport; and lofing this it could not do otherwife than fubmit to the yoke of the violent patriots, who were endeavouring to fet up and maintain an authority capable of rivalling the national reprefentation.

Roland kept a ufurping commune in awe. Roland gave to all the adminiftrative bodies a regular, uniform, and harmonious motion: he watched over the fupply of provifions of the great national family: he found means to re-eftablifh peace in all the departments; he diffufed throughout them that order which proceeds from juftice, and that confidence which is kept alive by a vigilant adminiftration; and he fet on foot between them a friendly correfpondence, and a ready communication of knowledge. Roland ought therefore to have been fupported: but fince weaknefs denied the means, he, to whom that weaknefs was well known, could not choofe but retire.

The timid Garat, an agreeable companion, a man of letters of moderate merit, and a deteftable minifter; Garat, whofe appointment to the judicial department proved the want of able men, a want which is inconceivable, and which none can tell but they who, occupying places of importance, have coadjutors to feek; Garat had not even fenfe enough to remain in that office, where there is leaft to be done, and where his bad health,

health, his natural indolence, and his incapacity for bufinefs, would have been leaft confpicuous; but removed
to the home department, without poffeffing the fmalleft
fhare of the requifite knowledge, not only where politics
are the queftion, but in regard to commerce, the arts,
and a multitude of adminiftrative operations, that come
within its cognizance. With all that ignorance, and with
all his inactivity, he ventured to take the place of the
moft active man in the republic, and the beft informed
in all the above particulars. The relaxation of the machine
foon occafioned the diflocation of its parts, and proved
the weaknefs of the regulator: the departments were
thrown into commotion, fcarcity began to be felt, the
flames of civil war were lighted up in la Vendée; the
authorities of Paris exceeded their powers; the jacobins
affumed the reins of government; and the puppet Pache,
difmiffed from the department, which he had thrown
into confufion, was raifed by a cabal to the mayoralty,
where his fupplenefs was wanted, while his place at the
council-board was filled by the idiot Bouchotte, as fup-
ple as he, and even furpaffing him in ftupidity.

 Roland gave a terrible blow to his adverfaries, by
publifhing, on his retirement, fuch accounts, as no
minifter before him had furnifhed. To have them examined and fanctioned by a report, was a piece of juftice, which he was doomed to folicit in vain; for that
would have been acknowledging the falfehood of the ob-
loquy thrown on him, the infamy of his detractors, and
the weaknefs of the convention, which had not dared to
undertake his defence.

 It was neceffary to perfevere in flandering him,
without coming to the proof; in order to perplex
               and

and mislead the public opinion, so as to be able to ruin him with impunity; and thus to get rid of a troublesome witness of so many atrocities, which must either be concealed, or justified, to preserve to the perpetrators the wealth and authority they helped them to acquire. In vain did Roland intreat, publish, and write seven times in four months to the convention, to demand an examination and a report on his conduct in the ministry. The jacobins continued to employ their satellites, to proclaim him a traitor: Marat proved to *his people* that the ex-minister's head was necessary to the tranquillity of the republic: conspiracies frustrated, set on foot anew, baffled again, and yet constantly carried on, ended at length in the insurrection of the 31st of May, when the good people of Paris, with a fixed determination to massacre no one, did every thing besides that their audacious directors, their insolent commune, and the revolutionary committee of messieurs the jacobins, grown mad or furious, or else become the hirelings of the enemy, were pleased to require. Roland had written the eighth time to the convention, which had not even deigned to read his letter; and I was preparing to get the municipality to sign passports, by means of which I might go with my daughter into the country, whither I was called by domestic business, by the state of my health, and by many good reasons beside. Among other things I considered, how much more easy it would be for Roland to escape alone from the pursuit of his enemies, should they proceed to the last extremities, than for the whole of his little family together: prudence pointed out the propriety of diminishing the number of points in which he was attackable*. My paſsports had been delayed at the ſection, through the chicanery of ſome zealous maratiſts, in whoſe eyes I was an object of ſuſpicion; and they were but juſt delivered to me, when a fit of the nervous colic, attended with violent convulſions, the only indiſpoſition to which I am ſubject, and to which the vehement affections of a ſtrong mind ruling a robuſt body expoſe me, obliged me to keep my bed. I paſſed ſix days in this ſtate, and purpoſed going out on Friday, to ſhew myſelf at the municipality; but the ſound of the alarm-bell informed me, that it was not a proper time. Every thing had long foretold an approaching criſis. It is true that the aſcendency of the jacobins made it very unlikely that its iſſue ſhould be favourable to the real friends of liberty: but energetic minds deteſt ſuſpenſe; and the debaſement of the convention, with its daily acts of weakneſs and ſlavery, appeared to me ſo diſtreſſing, that I hardly conſidered the worſt exceſſes as more lamentable, becauſe they would neceſſarily contribute to open the eyes, and determine the conduct of the departments. The alarm gun, and the commotions of the day, awakened in me that intereſt, which great events inſpire, without producing any painful emotion. Two or three perſons came to confer with us; and one, in particular, preſſed Roland to make his appearance at his ſection, by which

* That was not my ſtrongeſt inducement: for, tired of the courſe of affairs, I feared nothing for myſelf; innocent and courageous, injuſtice might reach, but could not degrade me; and to ſuffer it, was a trial, in the thought of braving which I felt pleaſure; but another reaſon, altogether perſonal, and which ſome day perhaps my pen will diſcloſe, determined me to depart.

he

he was esteemed, and of which the good disposition was the best warrant of his safety. It was agreed, however, that he should not sleep at home the following night: though, by the way, nothing was talked of but the good intentions of the citizens, who drew up under arms, in order to oppose every act of violence. It was not added, that they would permit preparations for every act of violence to be made.

The blood boils in my veins when I hear praises bestowed on the good-nature of the Parisians, who are determined not to have another day like the 2d of September. Why, good heavens! nobody wants you to execute another; you need only suffer it as you did before: but you are necessary to collect the victims, and you kindly lend your aid to apprehend them; you are necessary to give the appearance of a legitimate insurrection to the violence of the galleries* by whom you are governed, and you approve their undertakings: you obey their orders, you swear fealty to the monstrous authorities they create; you surround the legislative body with your bayonets, and you permit rebels to dictate to the national representation the decrees they wish to pass. Boast then no more of being its defenders; it is you who bind it in chains; you who deliver into the hands of oppression the members, the most distinguished for their virtues and their talents; you who with equal cowardice would see them brought to the block, by proceedings similar to those that destroyed Sidney; and you it is who will have to answer to indignant France for so many crimes; who

---

* Of the convention, which at this period were filled with ruffians from the jacobin club. *Tranf.*

serve the cause of her enemies, and who prepare the way for federalism. Think you, that the high-spirited Marseilles, and the enlightened department of la Gironde, will pass over the outrages committed on their representatives, or fraternise with a city polluted by such crimes? You are the destroyers of your country, and soon will you lament, in vain, your infamous pusillanimity in the midst of its ruins.

It was half after five in the evening, when six armed men came to our house. One of them read to Roland an order of the *revolutionary committee*, by virtue of which they were come to apprehend him. ' I know no law,' said Roland, ' which constitutes the authority you mention; nor shall I obey the orders which it issues. If you employ violence, I can only oppose to you such resistance as a man of my years is capable of; but I shall protest against it to the last moment of my life.'—' I have no order to employ violence,' replied the spokesman, ' I shall therefore go and communicate your answer to the council-general of the commune: in the mean time I will leave my colleagues here.'

It occurred to me immediately, that it would not be amiss to denounce these proceedings to the convention, in the most public manner, in order to prevent the arrest of Roland, or to obtain his prompt release, if it should have taken place. To communicate this idea to my husband, write a letter to the president, and set out, was the business of a few minutes. My servant being absent, I left a friend, who was in the house, to keep Roland company; and stepped alone into a hackney-coach, which I ordered to proceed as fast as possible to the Carouzel. The court-yard of the Tuileries was filled

with

with armed men. I croffed it, and flew through the midft of them like a bird. I was dreffed in a morning gown, and had put on a black fhaul, and a veil. On my arrival at the doors of the outer halls, which were all fhut, I found fentinels, who allowed no one to enter, or fent me by turns from door to door. In vain did I infift on admiffion; till at length it came into my mind to employ fuch language as a bigotted Robefpierian would have held. 'Why, citizens,' faid I, 'in this day of falvation for our country, and in the midft of the traitors, from whom we have fo much to fear, you do not know then of what importance fome notes may be which I wifh to tranfmit to the prefident. Send at leaft for an ufher, that I may entruft them to his care.'

The doors inftantly flew open, and I walked into the petitioner's hall. I then enquired for one of the ufhers, and was defired by a fentry, planted within the hall, to wait till one came out. A quarter of an hour had already paffed, when I perceived Rofe*, the very man who had brought me the decree of the convention, requefting me to repair to the bar, on account of the ridiculous accufation of Viard, whom I overwhelmed with confufion: I now folicited permiffion to appear there, and reprefented Roland's danger, as connected with the public weal. But circumftances were no longer the fame, though my rights were equally good: before, requefted refpectfully, now a fuppliant, how was I to obtain the fame fuccefs? Rofe took charge of my letter; conceived at once the fubject, and the greatnefs of my impatience;

---

* A Scotchman, who was ufher to the convention, as well as to each of the preceding affemblies. *Tranf.*

and

and left me, in order to lay it on the table, and to requeſt that it might be read without delay. An hour elapſed; I walked haſtily backwards and forwards; and every time the door was opened, my eyes were caſt towards the hall, but it was immediately ſhut by the guard, and from time to time a dreadful noiſe aſſailed my ears. Roſe made his appearance again.—'Well!'—'Nothing has yet been done. A tumult I cannot deſcribe prevails in the aſſembly. Some petitioners, at this moment at the bar, demand the confinement of the *twenty-two:* I have juſt aſſiſted Rabaud in getting out without being ſeen: they will not conſent to his making the report of the commiſſion of *twelve:* he has been threatened: ſeveral others are making off: nor can any one ſay what will be the event.'—'Who is preſident?'—'Héraut-Séchelles.'—'Ah! my letter will not be read. Send me ſome member or other with whom I may ſpeak a few words.'—'Whom?' —'Indeed I am little acquainted, or have little eſteem for any, but thoſe that are proſcribed. Tell Vergniaux I wiſh to ſee him.'

Roſe went in queſt of him; at the end of a very conſiderable time he came; and we talked together for ſeven or eight minutes. He then returned to the hall, came back, and ſaid: 'In the preſent ſtate of the aſſembly, I dare not flatter you: you have no great room for hope. If you get admiſſion to the bar, you may obtain a little more favour as a woman; but the convention is no longer able to do any good.'—'It is able to do any thing it pleaſes,' exclaimed I: 'for the majority of Paris only deſire to know how they ought to act. If I be admitted, I will venture to ſay, what you could not utter without expoſing yourſelf to an impeachment. As to me I fear

nothing

nothing in the world; and if I cannot fave Roland, I will fpeak fome home truths, which will not be altogether ufelefs to the republic. Inform your worthy colleagues: a courageous fally may have a great effect, or at leaft will ferve to fet a great example.'—I was indeed, in that temper of mind, which imparts eloquence: warm with indignation, and fuperior to all fear, my bofom glowing for my country, the ruin of which I forefaw, every thing dear to me in the world at ftake, feeling ftrongly, expreffing my fentiments with fluency, and too proud not to utter them with dignity, I had the moft important interefts to difcufs, poffeffed fome means of defending them, and was in a fingular fituation for doing it with advantage.—' But, at any rate,' faid Vergniaux, ' your letter cannot be read this hour or two: a motion of fix articles is going to be difcuffed; and petitioners, deputed by the fections, are waiting at the bar: only think what a tedious time you will have to ftay!'—
'I will go home, then, to know what has been paffing there; and will immediately return: you may tell our friends fo.'
—' Moft of them are abfent: 'they behave courageoufly, when they are here; but they are deficient in affiduity.'
—' That, alas! is but too true.'

I quitted Vergniaux, flew to Louvet's, wrote a note to inform him of what was going on, and what I forefaw would follow; threw myfelf into a hackney-coach, and ordered it to drive home. The wretched horfes did not get on to my mind; and we were foon met by battalions of national guards, whofe march ftopped the way. I jumped out of the coach, paid the coachman, rufhed through the ranks, and made off. This was near the Louvre, from whence I ran to our houfe, which was

in

in the *Rue de la Harpe*, oppofite the fchool of furgery. The porter whifpered me, that Roland was gone to the landlord's, at the bottom of the court; and thither I repaired, perfpiring at every pore. A glafs of wine was brought me, and I was told, that the bearer of the warrant having returned, without being able to procure a hearing at the council, Roland had perfifted in protefting againft his orders; and that thefe good people, after demanding his proteft in writing, had withdrawn; in confequence of which Roland had come to beg a paffage through their apartments, and had got out of the houfe by the back door. I did the fame in order to find him, to inform him of the attempt I had made, and of the fteps I meant to purfue. At the firft houfe to which I repaired, I found him not: in the fecond I did. From the folitude of the ftreets, which, by the way, were illuminated, I prefumed that it was late: I prepared neverthelefs to return to the convention, where I fhould have taken care to be ignorant of Roland's efcape, and fhould have fpoken as I had before intended. I was going to fet out on foot, without recollecting, that it was paft ten o'clock, and that I was out that day for the firft time fince my illnefs, which demanded reft and the bath. A hackney-coach was brought me. On approaching the Carrouzel, I faw nothing more of the armed force, except two pieces of cannon, and a few men, who were ftill at the gate of the national palace: I went up to it, and found that the fitting was at an end.

What! on the day of an infurrection, when the found of the alarm-bell fcarcely ceafes to ftrike the ear, when only two hours before forty thoufand men in arms furrounded the convention, and petitioners threatened its members

members from the bar, the assembly is not permanent!—Surely then it is completely subjugated! it has done every thing, that it was ordered! The *revolutionary power* is so predominant, that the convention dares not oppose it, and it stands itself in no need of the convention!

'Citizens,' said I to some sans-culottes collected round a cannon, 'has every thing gone well?'—'O wonderfully! they embraced each other, and sang the hymn of the *Marseillois*, there, under the tree of liberty.'—'What, then, is the right side appeased?'—'Faith, it was obliged to listen to reason.'—'And what of the committee of twelve?'—'It is kicked into the ditch.'—'And the *twenty-two*?'—'The municipality will have them taken up.'—'Ay, but can the municipality?'—'Why, body o' me, is not the municipality the sovereign? It is high time it should, to set those b——— of traitors to rights, and support the common-wealth.'—'But will the departments be well pleased to see their representatives * * * *'—'What are you talking about?—the Parisians do nothing but in concert with the departments: they said so to the convention.'—'That however is not quite so certain, for, to know their will, the primary assemblies were wanting.'—'Was there any want of primary assemblies on the 10th of August? Did not the departments approve what Paris did then? They will do the same now: it is Paris that is saving them.'—'Or rather, it is Paris that is ruining itself.'

I had crossed the court, and was returning to my hackney-coach, while concluding this dialogue with an old sans-culotte, who was well paid no doubt for tutoring the dupes. A pretty dog followed close at my heels:—'Is the poor brute your's?' said the coachman with a tone of sensibility very uncommon amongst his fellows,

lows, which struck me exceedingly.—' No: I am not acquainted with him:' answered I gravely, as if speaking of a man, but in reality thinking of something very different: 'you will set me down at the galleries of the Louvre.' There I meaned to call on a friend, with whom I intended to concert the means of conveying Roland out of Paris. We had not gone a dozen yards before the coach stopped. ' What is the matter?' said I to the coachman.—' Ah, he has left me; like a fool; for I wanted to keep him for my little boy. They would have been rare company for one another. Here! Here! my little fellow.'—I recollected the dog, and was highly pleased at having for my coachman, at such an hour, a good-natured man, possessed of a feeling heart, and a father. ' Endeavour to catch him:' said I: 'you shall put him into the coach, and I will take care of him.' —The honest fellow, quite delighted, caught the dog, opened the door, and gave him to me for a companion. The poor animal appeared sensible, that he had found protection and an asylum, and caressed me with great affection. I recollected the tale of Sandi, in which he describes an old man, who being weary of his fellow-creatures, and disgusted with their passions, retired to a wood; and there constructed himself a dwelling, of which he enlivened the solitude by the society of several animals, who repaid his cares with testimonies of affection, and with a species of gratitude, with which he contented himself, for want of meeting with its like among mankind.

Pasquier was just gone to bed. He rose; I submitted to him my plan; and we agreed, that he should call on me the next day a little after seven, when I would let him know where his friend was to be found. I stepped into

my

my coach again, and was proceeding home, when I was ſtopped by the ſentry, at the poſt of the *Samaritaine* *. 'Have a little patience:' ſaid the honeſt coachman in a whiſper, and turning round on his ſeat: 'it is the cuſtom at this time of night.'—The ſerjeant came, and opened the door. 'Who have we got here?'—'A woman.'—'Whence do you come?'—'From the convention.'—'It is very true:' ſaid the coachman, putting in his word, as if he were afraid I ſhould not be believed.—'Whither are you going?'—'Home.'—'Have you no bundles?'—'Nothing at all, as you may ſee.'—'But the aſſembly is broke up.'—'Yes: to my ſorrow, for I had a petition to preſent.'—'A woman! at this hour! it is extremely ſtrange: it is very imprudent.'—'It certainly is not a very common occurrence, nor is it with me a matter of choice. I muſt have had ſtrong reaſons for it.'—'But, madam, alone?'—'How, ſir, alone! Do you not ſee that I have *innocence* and *truth* for my companions? what would you have more?'—'Well! I muſt be contented with your reaſons.'—You are quite in the right:' replied I, in a gentler tone: 'for they are good ones.'

The horſes were ſo tired, that the coachman was obliged to pull them by the bridle, to get them up the ſteep part of the Rue de la Harpe. At length, however, I reached home, paid my coach, and had aſcended eight or ten ſteps, when a man, who had ſlipped in at the gate unperceived by the porter, and who was cloſe at my heels, begged me to conduct him to citizen Roland. —'To his apartment I will conduct you with pleaſure, if you have any thing advantageous to impart: but to *him* is impoſſible.'

---

* A fountain at one end of the Pont Neuf. *Tranſ.*

impossible.'—' Why, I came to let him know that they are absolutely determined to put him in confinement this very evening.'—' They must be cunning indeed if they accomplish their purpose.'—' I am very happy to hear it; for it is an honest citizen you are speaking to.'—' Well and good,' said I, and went up stairs, without well knowing what to think of the matter.

I may be asked, why, under such circumstances, I returned to the house? nor is the question irrelevant; for slander had attacked me too, and malevolence might direct its shafts against my bosom; but to give a proper answer to it, the state of my mind ought to be completely developed; and that would require details, which I reserve for a future period: their results will be all I shall notice at present. I have naturally an aversion to every thing inconsistent with the grand, bold, and ingenuous proceedings of innocence: an effort to escape from the hand of injustice would be to me more painful, than any thing it can inflict. In the last two months of Roland's administration, our friends often urged us to quit the hotel, and three several times they found means to make us sleep from home; but it was always contrary to my inclination. It was an assassination that was then apprehended; but I was of opinion, that no one would readily undertake to violate the asylum of a man invested with a public office; and if there were villains bold enough to attempt such a crime, it appeared to me, that its perpetration would not be altogether useless. At all events, it was incumbent on the minister to be at his post, for there his death would cry aloud for vengeance, and be a lesson to the republic; while it was possible to reach his life when abroad, with equal advantage to the devisers of the deed, but with less benefit to the public weal, and less glory to

the

the victim. Such reasoning, I am well aware, will be deemed absurd by those who prefer life to all things: but he, who sets any value on his existence in a period of revolution, will set none on virtue, on honour, or on his country. Accordingly I refused to leave the hôtel in the month of January; Roland's bed was in my chamber, that we might both undergo the same fate: and under my pillow I kept a pistol, not to kill those who might come to murder us, but to secure myself from their outrages, if they offered to lay hands upon my person.

When out of office the obligation was no longer the same, and I thought it right in Roland to shun the fury of the populace, and the clutches of his enemies. As to me, they had not an equal interest in doing me a mischief: killing me would be incurring an odium they did not desire; and my commitment to prison would be of little service to them, and to me no great misfortune. If they should feel any sense of shame, wish to proceed according to form, and begin the business by making me undergo an examination, I should find no difficulty in confounding them; and my answers might even serve to dispel more rapidly the delusion of those who were only misled in regard to Roland. If they should dare to go the length of another second of September, it could only be because all the honest members of the convention would be also in their power, and because all would be lost at Paris. In that case I should prefer death, to living a witness of my country's ruin; and glory in being comprehended among the glorious victims sacrificed to guilty fury. That fury, glutted by my destruction, would be less violent against Roland, who, if once saved from this crisis, might still render great services to the public in other parts of France.

France. Thus, of two things one was sure to happen: either I might only risque imprisonment and a trial, which would redound to my husband's and my country's good; or else, if I were doomed to perish, it would be under circumstances in which life itself would be a burthen.

I have an amiable daughter. I suckled her myself*. I have brought her up with the enthusiastic anxiety of maternal love. I have set before her such examples, as at her age will not be forgotten; and doubt not but she will make a good and accomplished woman. Her education may be completed without my assistance, and her father will derive consolation from her existence; but she will never feel my strong affections; she will never know my pains, nor my pleasures: and yet were I to be born again, and to have my choice of dispositions, I would not change my temper of mind, but would ask of the gods to make me such as I am. Since Roland's resignation, I had lived so secluded from the world, that I had scarcely the smallest intercourse with any human creature: the family at one house, in which I might have concealed myself, was gone into the country; in another there was a sick person, which rendered the admission of a new guest difficult; and that in which Roland lay hidden, could not accommodate me without the greatest inconvenience; it would besides have been suspicious, if not impolitic, for me to have been in the same place with him; and, in the last place, I should even have been sorry to abandon my servants. I therefore returned home, quieted their uneasiness, already excited to a considerable degree, kissed my

* In France it was unusual for any but women of the very lowest classes to suckle their children. *Transf.*

child,

child, and took my pen, to write a note, which I intended to dispatch early in the morning to my husband.

Scarcely had I sat down, when I heard a knock at the door. It was about midnight. A numerous deputation of the commune appeared, and inquired for Roland.—'He is not at home.'—'But,' said the person who wore an officer's gorget, 'where can he be? when will he return? You are acquainted with his habits, and can judge of the hour of his coming home.'—'I know not,' replied I, 'whether your orders authorise you to ask such questions; but this I know, that nothing can oblige me to answer them. As Roland left the house while I was at the convention, he had it not in his power to make me his confidante. This is all I have to say.'

The whole troop withdrew much dissatisfied; but I perceived that a sentry was left at my door, and a guard at that of the house. I therefore inferred, that I had nothing to do but to summon strength to support the worst that might happen. Being overcome with fatigue, I ordered supper, finished my letter, entrusted it to my faithful maid, and retired to bed. I slept soundly for about an hour, when a servant came into my chamber, to inform me, that some gentlemen of the section requested me to step into the adjoining apartment. 'I understand what it means,' replied I: 'go, child; I will not make them wait.' I sprung out of bed, and was dressing myself when my maid came in, and expressed her surprise at my being at the pains to put on any thing more than my bed-gown.—'When people are going abroad,' said I, 'they should at least be decent.'—The poor woman looked in my face, and the tears gushed from her eyes. I went into the next room.

'We come, *Citoyenne*, to take you into cuftody, and to put feals upon your property.'—'Where is your authority?'—'Here,' faid a man, taking out of his pocket a warrant from the revolutionary committee *, ordering me to be committed to the Abbey, without fpecifying any motive for my arreft. 'I have a right to tell you, like Roland, that I know nothing of your committee, that I will not obey its orders, and that you fhall not take me hence, unlefs by violence.'—'Here is another order,' faid a little hard-featured man, in great hafte, and in a commanding tone of voice, reading to me one from the commune, which directed alfo, without alleging any charge, the commitment of both Roland and his wife. In the mean time I deliberated, whether I fhould carry my refiftance to the utmoft, or quietly refign myfelf into their hands. I had a right to avail myfelf of the law, which prohibits nocturnal arrefts; and if the law, which authorifes the municipality to feize fufpected perfons were urged, I might retort the illegality of the municipality itfelf, cafhiered and created anew by an arbitrary power. But then this power is in a manner fanctioned by the citizens of Paris; the law is no more than an empty name, employed for the purpofe of trampling more fecurely on the moft ackowledged rights; and violence prevails, to which, if I had compelled thefe brutes to refort, they might have preferved no bounds in its application. Refiftance therefore was vain, and could ferve only to expofe me to indignities and infult.

'How do you mean to proceed, gentlemen?'—'We

---

* The author means the committee of infurrection of the commune of the 31ft of May.

have sent for a justice of peace of the section, and you see here a detachment of his armed force.'—The justice of peace came, went into the parlour, and sealed up every thing, even to the windows and the drawers containing linen. One strange fellow would have had the *forte piano* sealed up too, but he was told it was a musical instrument; he then drew out a foot rule, and took its dimensions, as if he intended it for some particular place. I asked leave to take out my daughter's clothes, and made up a small packet of night-clothes for myself. In the mean time fifty or a hundred persons were passing backwards and forwards continually, completely filled two rooms, crowded every place, and might easily have concealed malevolent persons disposed either to deposit or to carry any thing away. The atmosphere became infected with noisome exhalations, and I was obliged to retire to the window of the anti-chamber for a little fresh air. The officer not daring to lay his commands upon this crowd, requested them now and then in gentle terms to withdraw, which only served to produce the exchange of one set of persons for another. Sitting down at my bureau, I wrote to a friend concerning my situation, and to recommend my daughter to his care. I was folding up the letter, when Mr. Nicaud, the bearer of the order from the commune, told me it was necessary I should read what I had written to them, and let them know to whom it was addressed.—'I have no objection to read it, if that will satisfy you.'—'No, it would be better to let us know to whom you are writing.'—'I shall do no such thing: the title of my friend is not of a nature, at present, to induce me, to name the person on whom I bestow it:' and on my saying this I tore the letter to pieces. While I turned myself from them, they gathered up the fragments, in order to seal them up: a stupid precaution, which tempted me to laugh; for the letter was without an addreſs.

At length, at seven in the morning, I left my daughter and my servants, after having exhorted them to be patient and calm, and feeling myself more honoured by their tears, than dejected by the oppreſſion of which I was the victim.—'You have people there, who love you:' said one of the commiſſioners.—'I never had any about me who did not:' replied I, while walking down stairs. From the bottom of the stair-cafe to the coach, which was drawn up on the oppoſite ſide of the ſtreet, I found two ranks of armed citizens; and proceeded gravely with meaſured ſteps, and with my eyes fixed upon theſe puſillanimous or deluded men. The armed force followed the coach in two files; while the wretched populace, deceived, and maſſacred in the perſons of its true friends, ſtopped as I paſſed by, attracted by the ſight, and ſeveral of the women exclaimed, '*Away with her to the guillotine.*'—'Shall we draw up the blinds?' ſaid one of the commiſſioners very civilly.—'No, gentlemen, innocence, however oppreſſed, never puts on the guiſe of criminality: I fear not the eye of any one, nor will I conceal myſelf from any perſon's view.'—'You have more ſtrength of mind than many men: you wait patiently for juſtice.'—'Juſtice! Were juſtice done I ſhould not be now in your hands: but ſhould an iniquitous procedure ſend me to the ſcaffold, I ſhall walk to it with the ſame firmneſs and tranquillity with which I now go to priſon. My heart bleeds for my country; and I regret my miſtake in ſuppoſing it qualified for liberty and happineſs: but life I appreciate at its due value; I never feared

feared aught but guilt; and injustice and death I despise.'—The poor commissioners understood but little of this language, and probably thought it very aristocratic.

We arrived at the Abbey, the theatre of those bloody scenes, the revival of which the jacobins have for some time preached up with so much fervour. Five or six field beds, with as many men stretched on them, in a dark and dreary room, were the first objects that struck my sight. After passing the wicket, every thing seemed in motion; and my guides made me ascend a dirty and narrow stair-case. At length we came to the keeper's apartment, and found him in a kind of little parlour, kept tolerably clean, where he offered me a seat. 'Where is my room?' said I to his wife, a corpulent woman, of an agreeable countenance.—'Madam, I did not expect you: I have no room as yet: but in the mean time you will remain here.' — The commissioners went into the adjoining room, directed an entry of their warrant to be made, and gave their verbal orders. These, I afterwards learnt, were very severe, and often renewed afterwards, but they durst not give them in writing; and the keeper knew his trade too well literally to observe what he was under no obligation to perform. He is an active, obliging, and civil man, and in fulfilling his official duties does every thing that humanity or justice can demand.—'What would you choose for breakfast?'—'A little capillaire and water.'

The commissioners withdrew, observing to me, that if Roland were not guilty, there could have been no occasion for him to abscond.—'It is so strange to suspect a man, who has rendered such important services to the cause of liberty; there is something so abominable in calumniating, and persecuting with such bitter rage, a minister whose conduct is so open, and whose accounts are so clear, that he is fully justified in avoiding the last outrages of envy. Just as Aristides, and severe as Cato, it is to his virtues he is indebted for his enemies. Their fury knows no bounds: but let them satiate it on me: I defy its power, and devote myself to death. It is incumbent on him to save himself for the sake of his country, to which he may yet be capable of rendering important services.'—An awkward bow, in which their confusion was evident, was the only answer the gentlemen thought fit to make me.

As soon as they were gone, I sat down to breakfast, and in the mean time a bed-chamber was hastily put in order, into which I was introduced.—'You may remain here, madam, the whole day; and if I cannot get an apartment ready for you this evening, as we are rather crowded, a bed shall be made up in the parlour.'—After saying this, the keeper's wife made some civil observations on the regret she felt whenever a person of her own sex arrived, ' for,' added she, ' they have not all your serene countenance, madam.'—I thanked her with a smile; and she locked me in.

Well, then, I am in prison, said I to myself, sitting down, and falling into the deepest reverie. The moments that followed I would not exchange for those which others may esteem the happiest of my life, nor will they ever be erased from my memory. In a critical situation, and with a stormy and precarious period in view, they made me sensible of the value of honesty and fortitude, in union with a good conscience,

ence, and firm temper of mind. Hitherto impelled by circumstances, my actions, in this crisis, had been the result of strong feelings, hurrying me away. How grateful to find their effects justified by the sober operation of reason! I recalled the past to my mind: I calculated future events: and if, while listening to a tender heart, I sometimes felt too powerful an affection, I did not discover one that could suffuse my cheek with a blush; not one, but what served to keep alive my courage, nor one that my reason was not able to subdue. I devoted myself, if I may so say, voluntarily to my destiny, whatever it might be: I defied its rigour, and fixed myself firmly in that state of mind, in which we only seek employment for the present, without giving ourselves any concern about the future. But this tranquillity with regard to what concerned me alone, I did not even endeavour to extend to the fate of my country, and of my friends: I waited for the evening paper, and listened to the noise in the street with inexpressible anxiety. I did not however neglect to make inquiry concerning my new situation, and what portion of liberty was left me.—' May I write? May I see any body? What will be my expences here?' were my first questions. Lavacquerie, the keeper, acquainted me with the directions given him, and the liberty he could venture to take with orders of that kind. I wrote to my faithful maid, to come and see me; but it was agreed that she should keep this indulgence a secret.

The first visit I received at the Abbey was from Grandpré, on the day of my arrival.—' You should write to the assembly,' said he: ' have you not yet been thinking of it?'—' No: and now you put me in mind,
I do

I do not fee how I fhall be able to get my letter read?'
—' I will do all I can to affift you.'—' Very well: then
I will write.'—' Do fo. I will return in two hours.'—
He left me, and I wrote as follows.

' Madame ROLAND to the National Convention.

Abbey Prifon, June 1, 1793.

"LEGISLATORS! I have juft been torn from
my home, from the arms of my daughter, a girl of
twelve years of age, and am detained in the Abbey,
by virtue of orders which affign no caufe for my confinement. Thofe orders were iffued by a revolutionary committee; and commiffioners of the commune, who
accompanied thofe of the committee, fhewed me others
from the council general, which were equally defective.*"
Thus am I placed in the light of a culprit before the
eyes of the public. I was dragged to prifon with great
parade, in the midft of an oftentatious guard, and of
a mifled populace, fome of whom were for fending me
to the fcaffold; without my conductors being able to affign to me or to any other perfon the reafon why I was
prefumed a criminal, and treated accordingly. This is
not all. The bearer of the orders of the commune made no
ufe of them except in regard to myfelf, and to make me
fign minutes of what paffed: as foon as I quitted my
apartment, I was delivered over to the commiffioners
of the revolutionary committee, who conducted me to
the Abbey; and on their warrant alone I was conftituted
a prifoner. An attefted copy of that warrant, figned by

---

* The words between double commas had been changed.

a fingle

a single individual possessing no office, is here subjoined. Every thing in my house has been sealed up; and while that was doing, which was from three o'clock in the morning till seven, a crowd of citizens filled my apartment. If, among the number, there were any malicious person, capable of privately slipping false evidence into a library open in every part, he could not want an opportunity.

'As early as yesterday, the same committee sought to put the late minister under arrest, though the laws render him accountable to you alone for the acts of his administration, and though he has been incessantly soliciting an enquiry.

'Roland had protested against the order, and the bearers of it had withdrawn. He had afterwards left his house, to spare Errour a crime, while I was on my way to the convention, to give it information of those attempts; but it was in vain that I procured the transmission of a letter to the president: it was not read. I went thither to demand *justice* and *protection*: I demand them again, and with stronger claims, for I too am oppressed. I demand of the convention, to order an account of the cause and the manner of my being apprehended, to be laid before it; and I demand its decision. If it confirm my arrest, I appeal to the law which ordains the declaration of the crime, and the examination of the prisoner within twenty-four hours from the time of his caption. And in the last place, I demand a report on the accounts of that irreproachable man, who exhibits an instance of persecution unheard of before, and who seems destined to give to all Europe the terrible

lesson

lesson of virtue proscribed by the blindness of infuriate prejudice.

'If to have shared the strictness of his principles, the energy of his mind, and the ardour of his love of liberty, be a crime; I plead guilty, and await my punishment. Pronounce sentence, legislators: France, freedom, the fate of the republic, and of yourselves, depend on this day's distribution of that justice, which it is yours to dispense.'

The agitation, in which I had passed the preceding night, made me feel extreme fatigue. I desired to have a chamber that very evening; and obtained one, of which I took possession at ten o'clock. When I entered it, and found myself surrounded by four dirty walls, in the midst of which was a bed without curtains; when I perceived a double-grated window; and when I was assailed by that smell, which a person accustomed to an apartment extremely clean, always finds in those that are not so, I was sensible that I was indeed an inhabitant of a prison, and that I had no pleasure to expect from such a situation. My room, however, was sufficiently spacious; there was a fire-place; the bed-clothes were tolerable; a pillow was given me; and estimating things, in themselves, without entering into comparisons, I deemed myself not altogether badly accommodated. I went to bed fully resolved to remain in it as long as I should find myself comfortable there; and was not up at ten in the morning, when Grandpré arrived. He did not appear less affected, but more uneasy, than the preceding evening; and cast a mournful look around the

wretched

wretched room, which already appeared tolerable to *me*, for I had flept in it.

'How did you pafs the night?' faid he with the tears ftanding in his eyes.—' I was repeatedly waked by the noife; but fell afleep again as foon as it was over, in fpite even of the alarm-bell, which I thought I heard this morning.—Ha!—is it not founding ftill?'—' Why I thought fo:—but it is nothing.'—' Be it as it pleafes heaven: if they kill me, it fhall be in this bed; for I am fo weary, that here I will expect my fate. Is any thing new brought forward againft the members?'—' No. I have brought back your letter. It is my opinion, as well as Champagneux's, that the beginning fhould be foftened. Here is what we propofe to fubftitute; and then you fhould write a line or two to the minifter of the home department, that he may tranfmit your letter officially, which would enable me the better to folicit its being read.'—I took the paper; looked at it; and faid to him, ' If I thought my letter would be read as it now ftands, fo it fhould remain, even were I fure of its being attended with no advantage to myfelf; for it is hardly poffible to hope for juftice from the convention. The truths addreffed to it are not for an affembly which is at prefent incapable of putting them in practice; but they fhould be uttered, that they may be heard by the departments.'

I perceived, that my exordium might prevent the reading of the letter, and that confequently it would be a folly to let it ftand: I therefore omitted the firft three paragraphs, and fubftituted what was propofed to me in their ftead. As to the minifter's interference, I was fenfible it would render the proceeding more regular:

gular: and though Garat scarcely deserved the honour of being written to, I knew how to do it without lessening myself, and addressed him in the following lines.

' To the Minister of the Interior Department.

' THE part of administration allotted to you, citizen, gives you a right to superintend the execution of the laws, and to denounce their violation by authorities that hold them in contempt. I am persuaded, a sense of justice will make you happy to transmit to the convention the complaints I have but too much occasion to make against the oppression, of which I am the victim.'

Rising about noon, I considered how I should arrange my new apartment. With a clean napkin I covered a little paltry table, which I placed near my window, intending that it should serve me for a bureau, and resolved to eat my meals on a corner of the chimney-piece, that I might keep the table clean, and in order, for writing. Two large hat-pins, stuck into the boards, served me as a port manteau. In my pocket I had Thomson's Seasons, a work which I was fond of on more than one account; and I made a memorandum of such other books as I should wish to procure. First, Plutarch's Lives of Illustrious Persons, which at eight years of age I used to carry to church instead of the Exercises of the holy week, and which I had not read regularly since that early period: then Hume's History of England, and Sheridan's Dictionary,

tionary, in order to improve myself in the English language. I would rather have continued to read Mrs. Macaulay; but the person, who had lent me some of the first volumes, was not at home; and I should not have known where to enquire for the work, as I had already tried in vain to get it from the bookfellers. I could not avoid smiling at my peaceful preparations; for there was a great tumult in the town: the drums were continually beating to arms, and I knew not what might be the event. At any rate, said I to myself, they will not prevent my living to my last moment: more happy in my conscious innocence, than they can be with the rage that animates them. If they come, I will advance to meet them, and go to death as a man would go to repose.

The keeper's wife came to invite me to her apartment, where she had directed my cloth to be laid, that I might dine in better air. On repairing thither, I found my faithful maid, who threw herself into my arms, bathed in tears, and half suffocated by her sobs. I could not avoid melting into tenderness and sorrow. I almost upbraided myself with my previous tranquillity, when I reflected on the anxiety of those who were attached to me; and when I described to myself the anguish first of one friend, and then of another, my heart was rent by the keenest sensations of grief. Poor woman! how many tears have I caused her to shed! and for what does not an attachment like her's atone? In the common intercourse of life she sometimes treats me roughly, but it is when she thinks me too negligent of what may contribute to my health or happiness; and when I am in distress, the office of complaining is her's,

and

and that of confoling mine. There was no getting rid of fo inveterate a habit. I endeavoured to prove to her that, by giving way to her grief, fhe would be lefs capable of rendering me fervice; that fhe was more ufeful to me without, than within the walls of the prifon, where fhe begged me to permit her to remain; and that, upon the whole, I was far from being fo unfortunate as fhe imagined, which indeed was true. Whenever I have been ill, I have experienced a particular kind of ferenity, unqueftionably proceeding from my mode of contemplating things, and from the law I have laid down for myfelf, of always fubmitting quietly to neceffity, inftead of revolting againft it. The moment I take to my bed, every duty feems at an end, and no folicitude whatever has any hold upon me: I am only bound to be there, and to remain there with refignation, which I do with a very good grace. I give freedom to my imagination; I call up agreeable impreffions, pleafing remembrances, and ideas of happinefs; all exertions, all reafonings, and all calculations, I difcard: giving myfelf up entirely to nature, and, peaceful like her, I fuffer pain without impatience, and feek repofe or cheerfulnefs. I find that imprifonment produces on me nearly the fame effect as difeafe: I am only bound to be in prifon, and what great hardfhip is there in it? I am not fuch very bad company for myfelf.

I foon learnt that I muft change my habitation. Victims were abundant, and the chamber into which I had been put would contain more than one bed. That I might be alone, I was obliged in the evening to be fhut up in a little clofet, and confequently to remove the whole of my eftablifhment. The window

window of my new apartment is, I believe, over the sentry, who guards the prison-gate. All the night I heard, *Who goes there?—kill him!—guard!—patrole!—* called out in a thundering voice. The houses were illuminated; and from the number and frequency of the patroles it was easy to infer, there had been some commotions, and that more were to be feared. I rose early, and employed myself in my household affairs; that is to say, in making my bed, in cleaning my little place, and in rendering my person and every thing about me as neat as I could. Had I desired these things to be done for me, I knew that I should not have been refused; but I was aware, I must have paid for them dearly, waited a long time, and had them done in a very slovenly manner at last. By taking the office on myself I was sure to be a gainer: I was sure that I should be better and sooner served, and that the trifling presents I might make would be rated the higher, because they would be altogether gratuitous. I waited with impatience to hear the massy bolts of my door opened, that I might ask for a newspaper. I read it: the decree of impeachment against the twenty-two was passed: the paper fell from my hands, and in a transport of grief I exclaimed, ' My country is undone!'

Firm and tranquil, while I imagined myself alone, or nearly alone, beneath the yoke of oppression, I formed wishes for the future, and was not without hope that the defenders of liberty would triumph. But guilt and error have obtained the ascendancy; the national representation is violated; its integrity is destroyed; every one in it remarkable for probity, spirit, and talents, is proscribed; the commune of Paris overawes the legislative body;

Paris is undone; the torch of civil war is lighted up; the enemy is about to avail himself of our divisions; freedom is loft to the north of France; and the whole republic is become a prey to the moſt dreadful diſſenſions. Farewell my country! ſublime illuſions, generous ſacrifices, hope, and happineſs, farewell! At twelve years old I lamented, in the firſt expanſions of my youthful boſom, that I was not born a citizen of Sparta, or of Rome; and in the French revolution I thought I ſaw the unhoped for application of the principles impreſſed upon my mind. Liberty, ſaid I, has two ſources; good manners, which produce ſage laws; and knowledge, which leads us to both, by making us acquainted with our rights: my ſoul will no longer be afflicted by the ſpectacle of mankind debaſed: the human race will improve; and the happineſs of all will become the foundation and the ſecurity of that of each individual. Splendid chimeras! dear deluſions, from which I reaped ſo much delight, you are all diſpelled by the horrible corruption of this vaſt city. I deſpiſed life: the loſs of you makes me deteſt it, and defy the utmoſt fury of the men of blood. Anarchiſts, ſavages, for what await you? You who have proſcribed virtue, why do you not ſpill the blood of thoſe who obey her laws? when ſhed upon the earth, it will make her open her devouring jaws, and ſwallow you up.

The courſe of things ought to have made me foreſee the event: but I could not eaſily bring myſelf to believe, that the bulk of the convention would not pauſe at the magnitude of the danger; nor could I help being aſtoniſhed at the deciſive act, which tolled its paſſing bell.

At

At present a sullen sort of indignation prevails over every other sentiment: as indifferent as ever to what concerns myself, my hopes for others are feeble; and I wait for events with more curiosity than desire: I no longer live to feel, but to know. It was not long ere I learnt that the revolutionary movement which was ordered on purpose to extort the decree of impeachment, had excited some uneasiness about the prisons. That was the cause of the strict and noisy guard during the night; and that the reason why the citizens of the section of Unity would not obey the beat of drum, which called them to the convention; but remained at home, to watch over their property, and the prison within their precinct. I discovered the motive of Grandpré's alarm and disquietude, and the next day he confessed his apprehensions. He had repaired to the assembly, to obtain the reading of my letter; and, during eight successive hours, he, as well as several of the members, had repeatedly requested it of the president in vain: it was therefore evident, that I should not be able to get it read at all. Finding by the *Monitor*, that my section (that of Beaurepaire) had expressed its sentiments in my favour, even after my imprisonment, it occurred to me to write to it; and I did so in the following terms.

'Citizens,

'THE public papers inform me, that you have placed Roland and his wife under the safeguard of your section. This I knew not when I was dragged from my family: on the contrary, the bearer of the orders of the commune represented the armed force, by which he was accompanied,

accompanied, as that of the section, granted him on his requisition, and so it was stated in the minutes that were taken down. The moment I was shut up in the Abbey, I wrote to the convention, and applied to the minister of the interior-department, to forward my complaint. I understand he complied with my request, and that the letter was delivered; but not read. I have the honour to transmit you an attested copy. If the section think it not beneath its dignity to plead the cause of suffering innocence, it will be easy to send a deputation to the bar of the convention, there to make known my just complaints, and to add weight to my reclamations. This point I submit to its *wisdom:* I add no *intreaty*, for *truth* has but one language, and that is the exposition of *facts*. Citizens who love *justice* are not fond of having *supplications* addressed to them, and *innocence* is incapable of assuming the character of a suppliant.

‘ P. S. This is the fourth day of my detention, and I have not yet been examined. I must observe, that the order of arrest assigned no reason for my confinement; but imported, that I should be interrogated on the following day.’

Several days elapsed without my hearing any thing, and still I underwent no examination. I had however received a great many visits from administrators with foolish faces and dirty ribbands, some of whom said they belonged to the police, others to I know not what; violent sans-culottes, with filthy hair, and strict observers of the order of the day, who came to know whether the prisoners were satisfied with their treatment. I had expressed

pressed myself to them all with the energy and dignity suitable to oppressed innocence; and had noticed among them two or three men of good sense, who understood me, without daring to take my part. I was at dinner, when five or six were announced to me all at once. One came a little forward: he, who assumed the office of speaker, appeared to me, before he opened his lips, one of those empty-headed babblers, who judge of their merit by the volubility of their tongue.—'Good morrow, *Citoyenne.*'—'Good morrow, sir.'—'Are you satisfied with this house? Have you any reason to complain of your treatment, or any particular demand to make?'—'I complain of being here; and demand my enlargement.'—'Is your health impaired? or does solitude affect your spirits?'—'I am in good health, and not at all out of spirits. *Ennui* is the disease of hearts without feeling, and of minds that have no resources in themselves. But I have a strong feeling of injustice, and protest against the lawless oppression, which took me into custody without cause, and has since detained me without examination.'—'Why, in a period of revolution, there is so much to be done, that there is not time to attend to every thing.'—'A woman, to whom king Philip made nearly the same reply, answered him: "if thou hast not time to do me justice, thou hast not time to be king." Take care you do not oblige oppressed citizens to say the same thing to the people, or rather to the arbitrary authorities, by which the people is misled.'—'Adieu, *citoyenne!*'—'Adieu!'—And away went the flippant gentleman, not knowing what answer to make to my reasons. These people appeared to me to have entered purposely to see how I looked in my cage; but they might

might go a great way, before they would find dolts like themselves.

I have already mentioned my having inquired into the way of living in these places. Not that I set any great value on what are called the comforts of life. I make no scruple of enjoying them when it can be done without inconvenience; but it is always in moderation; and when it is necessary there is no one of them that I cannot forego. It is from a natural love of order that I desire to know the amount of my expenses, and to regulate them according to the circumstances of my situation.

I was informed that Roland, when minister, thought five livres [4s. 2d.] a head, the daily allowance of the prisoners, a great deal too much, and reduced it to two [1s. 8d.]: but the excessive rise in the price of provisions, which within these few months has been tripled, renders this allowance scanty enough: for the nation allowing nothing but straw and the bare walls, twenty sous [10d.] are deducted in the first place, as an indemnification to the keeper for his expenses, that is to say, for the bed and trifling furniture of the room. Out of the twenty sous remaining, candles, fire, if necessary, and meat and drink, are to be provided. The sum is insufficient for the purpose; but every prisoner is free, of course, to make what addition he pleases to his expense. As I am not fond of spending much on myself; and take a pleasure in trying my strength at privation, I felt a desire of making an experiment how far the human will is capable of diminishing our wants: but to go any great length, it is necessary to proceed by degrees. At the end of four days, I began by retrenching my breakfast, and
substituting

substituting bread and water for coffee and chocolate: I desired to have for dinner one plain dish of meat, with a few greens; and vegetables for my supper without a desert. To break myself of drinking wine, I took first to beer, and then I left off that also. As this regimen, however, had a moral purpose, and as I have as much aversion as contempt for useless economy, I began by giving a certain sum for the use of the miserable wretches, who were lying upon straw; that, while eating my dry bread in a morning, I might have the satisfaction to reflect, that the poor devils would owe to me their being able to add something to their's at dinner. If I remain here six months, I will engage to leave the place with a healthy complexion, and a body by no means emaciated, having reduced my wants so far as to be satisfied with soup and bread, and deserved a few benedictions *incognito*. I made some presents also, but with quite a different view, to the servants belonging to the prison. When a person is, or appears to be, rigidly economical in point of expense, he ought to be generous to others, if he would wish to avoid blame, particularly when the people about him derive from that expense their only emolument. I require neither attentions to be paid me, nor purchases to be made on my account; I send out for nothing; I employ nobody: I should be consequently the worst of prisoners to the domestics, who make their little profits on what they are commissioned to provide or procure: it is fitting, therefore, that I should pay for the state of independence in which I place myself: by so doing I render it more perfect, and am moreover a gainer in good will.

I have received several visits from the excellent Champaneux and the worthy Bosc. The former, father of a numerous family, was attached to liberty from principle, and had professed its sound doctrines from the very commencement of the revolution, in a journal, intended for the information of his fellow citizens. A good judgment, gentleness of manners, and great industry, are the most prominent features of his character. Roland, when minister, placed him at the head of the first division of the home department; and it was one of the best appointments he made: though by the way he was not less happy in other principal clerks, such as the active and ingenuous Camus, the able Fépoul, and several more. Never were offices better filled; nor could any thing but their excellent organization enable Garat to support a burden so far beyond his strength. It is to the honesty and capacity of such agents that he is indebted for the tranquillity he is allowed to enjoy. Of this he is sensible; and he said with good reason, that he would give up his situation, if he were obliged to make any change in his official establishment. Notwithstanding this, he will be forced to quit his post, for no talents in assistants can compensate a minister's want of firmness: irresolution is the worst of faults in those who govern, particularly in the midst of jarring factions. Garat and Barrère, as private individuals, would not be deemed deficient in sense or honesty: but the one charged with the executive power, and the other empowered to legislate, would ruin all the states in the world by their half-measures: their rage for what they term conciliatory plans propels them in that oblique path, which leads directly to mischief

and

and confusion. There should be nothing conciliatory about a statesman but his manner; I mean his mode of behaviour to those whom he employs: he ought to avail himself of the very passions and faults of those whose conduct he directs, or with whom he transacts business: but rigid in his principles, firm and rapid in action, no obstacle, no consideration, should make him waver in the former respect, or alter his course in the latter.

Could Roland unite with his extensive views, his strength of mind, and his prodigious activity, a little more artfulness of manner, he would easily govern an empire: but his faults are prejudicial to himself alone, while his good qualities are infinitely valuable in the administration of public affairs.

Bosc, our old friend, a man of an ingenuous disposition, and enlightened mind, came to me the first day of my imprisonment, and lost no time in conducting my daughter to madame Creuzé-la-Touche, who gave her a kind welcome, and treated her like one of her own children, with whom it was settled that she should remain under her fostering care. To be fully sensible of the value of this step, it is necessary to be acquainted with the persons. It is necessary for a man to describe to himself the feeling and open-hearted Bosc, running to the house of his friends, taking possession of their child, and intrusting her of his own accord to the most respectable family, as a deposit which he felt himself honoured in confiding to their hands, and which he knew would be received with the pleasure experienced by delicate minds, when an opportunity is offered them of doing good. It is

necessary

necessary to have been acquainted with the patriarchal manners, the domestic virtues of Creuzé and his wife, and with the gentleness and goodness of disposition for which they are remarkable, to judge of the welcome they gave my girl, and to be sensible of what it was worth.

Who, then, is to be pitied in all this? Roland alone: Roland, persecuted and proscribed; Roland, to whom the examination of his accounts is denied; Roland, compelled to conceal himself like a criminal; to avoid the blind fury of men misled by his enemies; to tremble for the safety even of those who give him shelter; to drink in silence the bitter cup of his wife's imprisonment, and of the sequestration of all his property; and to await, in a state of incertitude, the reign of justice, which can never indemnify him for all that perversity will have made him suffer.

My section, actuated by the best principles, had come on the third of the month to a resolution, which breathed the spirit of justice, and which established the right of citizens, to protest against arbitrary imprisonment, and even to resist it if attempted. My letter was read there, and listened to with concern. The debate, that took place in consequence, having been prolonged to the next day, the mountaineers laid their heads together: the alarm was given to their party; and a whole host of furious deputies arrived from the other sections, with a view to disturb the proceedings, and deliberations, and, if possible, to pervert the spirit of mine, or else in the hope of terrifying it by menaces, and of engaging a majority of the sections to deprive it of its arms.

In the mean time, being urged by Grandpré to neglect
no

no means of shortening the term of my captivity, I wrote again to Garat, and to Gohier also. The latter, whom I scarcely ever saw or knew, with at least as much weakness as Garat, appeared to me inferiour to him in every other respect. I could not easily write to such men, without giving them lessons; and they were severe. Grandpré thinking them mortifying, though just, I softened some of the expressions; and contented myself with the following words.

'Madame ROLAND to the MINISTER of Justice.

Abbey Prison, June 8, 1793.

'I AM suffering oppression: I am therefore entitled to remind you of *my* rights and of *your* duties.

'An arbitrary order, without specifying any charge, has plunged me into this dungeon prepared for criminals. I have inhabited it a week, and as yet I have not been examined.

'The decrees of the convention are known to you. They direct you to visit the prisons, and to enlarge those who are detained without just cause. Another has also lately been passed, enjoining you to require the communication of all the warrants that are issued, to see that they be grounded upon some specific charge, and to take care that all persons in custody be examined.

'I transmit to you an attested copy of that warrant by virtue of which I was taken from my home, and brought hither.

'I demand the execution of the law, on my own account, and even on yours. Innocent and firm, injustice may reach, but cannot debase me, and I can submit to it with pride, at a time when virtue is proscribed*. As to you, placed as you are between the law and dishonour, your inclination cannot be doubted: and you are to be pitied, if you have not courage to act according to its dictates.'

‘ To the Minister of the Home Department.

June 8, 1793.

‘ I know that you have transmitted my complaints to the legislative body; but my letter has not been read. Have you fulfilled the whole of your duty by forwarding it at my request?—I have been apprehended, without the specification of any reason: and I have been detained a week, without examination. It behoves you, as a man in office, when you have not been able to save innocence from oppression, to endeavour at least to bring about its delivery.

‘ You are more interested, perhaps, than myself, in the task I request you to undertake. I am not the only victim of prejudice and envy: and their present attacks upon every one remarkable for the union of a firm mind with virtue and talents, renders the persecution honourable, of which I am the object, and for which I am indebted to my connexion with the venerable man, whose cause posterity will revenge. But you, who are now at the helm, if incapable of holding it with a firm hand, will

---

* Here followed originally : ‘ But it is incumbent on you, placed between the law and dishonour, either to fulfil the duties of your place, or resign it; you must otherwise incur that infamy, with which posterity will brand weakness like yours.'

not

not efcape the reproach of abandoning the veffel to the waves, the difgrace of having occupied a poft which you could not maintain.

'Factions pafs away, juftice alone remains unalterable: and of all the faults of men in place weaknefs is the leaft pardonable, becaufe it is the fource of the greateft diforders, particularly in troublefome times.

'I need not add any thing to thefe reflections, if they reach you in time for you and for myfelf, or urge their application to my own concerns; fince nothing can fupply the want of courage and of good-will.'

Moft certainly the minifters, who neglected and defpifed the decrees, that enjoined them to profecute the authors of the maffacre of September, and the confpirators of the 10th of March; men, whofe weak and unworthy conduct on thofe occafions emboldened guilt, favoured its enterprizes, and infured this new infurrection, in which blindnefs and audacity, prefcribing laws to the national convention, call forth all the evils of civil war; fuch men certainly will not be the impeachers of oppreffion. From them I expect nothing; and the truths I addrefs to them are rather intended to fhow them what they ought, and what they have failed, to do, than to procure me that juftice, which they are incapable of rendering, unlefs a little fhame fhould chance to produce a miracle.

Efop reprefents all the animals, who ufually trembled at the afpect of the lion, coming, every one in his turn, to infult him when he fell fick: in like manner the mob of little minds, actuated either by delufion or jealoufy, fall with fury upon thofe, whom oppreffion holds captive,

or

or whose means of defence it diminishes, by lowering them in the opinion of the world. Of this the Thermometer of the Day, for the 9th of June, No. 526, affords an example. Therein appears, under the title of examination of L. P. d'Orleans, a series of questions, amongst which the following charge is worthy of remark: 'of having been present at secret cabals, held by night in the apartment of Buzot's wife, in the Fauxbourg St. Germain, whither Dumouriez, Roland and his wife, Vergniaux, Brissot, Gensonné, Gorsas, Louvet, Pétion, Guadet, and others used to repair.'

What atrocious wickedness! and what excess of impudence! The deputies here named are precisely those, who voted for the banishment of the Bourbons. Those high-spirited defenders of freedom never considered d'Orleans as a leader possessed of capacity; but he always appeared to them a dangerous tool. They were the first to dread his vices, his wealth, his connexions, his popularity, and his faction; to denounce the latter, and to hunt down those, who appeared to be its agents. Louvet marked them out in his Philippic against Robespierre; a valuable piece, as is every thing from his pen. In that composition, which history will carefully preserve, he follows them step by step to the electoral assembly, whence d'Orleans issued a deputy. Buzot, whose persevering energy has procured him the hatred of the factious, embraced the first favourable opportunity, to demand the banishment of the Bourbons; a measure, which he looked upon as indispensable, from the moment the convention resolved to pass judgment on Lewis. Neither Roland, nor I, ever saw d'Orleans. I even refused to receive Sillery, though

he

he was mentioned to me as as a good and amiable man, becaufe his connexion with d'Orleans rendered him fufpicious. I remember two curious letters on the fubject; one of which was written by madame Sillery to Louvet, after he had fupported Buzot's motion. 'Here,' faid Louvet, communicating the letter to me, 'is a proof that we are not miftaken, and that the Orleans party is no chimera. Madame Sillery would not write in fuch terms, if it were not a thing agreed upon between her and the parties concerned. If they be fo much afraid of banifhment, it muft be becaufe exile will defeat fome of their fchemes.' In fact, the object of the ftudied letter of madame Sillery was to prevail upon Louvet to change his opinion; to perfuade him, that the republican principles, in which the children of d'Orleans had been educated, rendered them the moft zealous partizans of a commonwealth; and that it was both cruel and impolitic to facrifice individuals, who might certainly be made ufeful, to prejudices alike unjuft and abfurd.

The other letter was Louvet's anfwer: replete with wit and dignity, it fet forth the reafons on which he founded his opinion in terms equally forcible and polite. Among other things he faid, that the monarchical principles, the ariftocratical and other prejudices, which appeared in the works of madame Sillery herfelf, were far from fatisfying him with refpect to thofe of her pupils; and he perfifted with all the fpirit of a free man in an opinion which the love of his country infpired.

As to the pretended cabals at Buzot's wife's, nothing in the world can be fo ridiculous. Buzot, whom I had frequent occafions of feeing at the time of the conftituent affembly, and with whom I had remained in friendly intercourfe;

tercourse; Buzot, whose spirit, sensibility, purity of principles, and gentleness of manners, inspired me with infinite esteem and attachment, came frequently to the *Hôtel de l'Interieur*: his wife I have visited only once since they came to Paris on the meeting of the convention; nor had they ever the slightest connexion with Dumouriez.

Indignant at these absurdities, I took up my pen to write to Dulaure, the editor of the *Thermometre du jour*, a worthy man, with whom I lived on friendly terms until the moment he was seduced by the mountaineers*.

Madame ROLAND to the Deputy DULAURE, Author of the *Thermometre du jour*.

Abbey Prison, June 9, 1793.

' IF any thing could add to the astonishment of innocence, when it finds itself under the yoke of oppression, I should tell you, citizen, that I have just read with the greatest surprise the absurdities contained in your paper of this day, under the title of examination of Philip d'Orleans, which chance has thrown in my way. It would appear very strange, had not experience proved it to be only very impudent, that those persons who first feared, denounced, and watched the manœuvres of the faction of d'Orleans, should be represented as having formed it themselves.

---

* I have since learnt, that the late excesses of the mountain have opened his eyes, and brought him to a proper sense of its principles.

' Time

'Time will unqueſtionably clear up this myſtery of iniquity: but while waiting for *its* juſtice, which may be tardy in the midſt of ſuch dreadful corruption, it appears to me incumbent on *your's*, when publiſhing the queſtions of an interrogatory calculated to excite ſuſpicions, to publiſh at the ſame time the anſwers, which muſt have been made, and which may ſerve to ſhow the degree of credit they deſerve.

'This act of juſtice is the more ſtrictly requiſite, as calumny and perſecution cloſely purſue the perſons named in thoſe queſtions; and as moſt of them are faſt held in the toils of a decree, extorted by audacity and prejudice from the hands of weakneſs and error. I myſelf have been confined a week, by virtue of a mandate which ſpecifies no reaſon for my arreſt. I have never been examined: I have not been able to obtain a hearing of my complaints from the convention; and when they were told, that thoſe complaints had been ſuppreſſed, they paſſed to the order of the day, under the pretence of its not being their concern. What! then new authorities act in the moſt arbitrary manner, while the conſtituted powers bow before them, and the acts of injuſtice they commit are not to be repreſented to the convention! It is not then to the legiſlative body that complaints ſhould be addreſſed, when there remains none other to hear them! It can intereſt itſelf in favour of perſons confined by order of the tribunal of Marſeilles; while I, who am confined here by a revolutionary committee, have no longer any rights! —And the commune makes the newſpapers repeat, that the priſons of Paris contain nothing but aſſaſſins, thieves, and counter-revolutioniſts!—Citizen, I have known you: I believe you honeſt: how will you grieve on ſome future

future day!—I tranfmit to you fome notes, which I beg you to perufe: and I requeft you to infert in your paper that letter, which I could not get read at the convention. You owe me this piece of juftice, as circumftances fufficiently demonftrate; and if your own feelings do not tell you fo, I fhould urge the matter in vain.

‘P. S. Neither Roland nor I ever faw Philip d'Orleans: and I can moreover fay, that I have always heard the deputies mentioned in the interrogatory, as quoted by the Thermometer of this day, profefs for him a contempt fimilar to that with which he infpired me. If, in fhort, we ever talked of him at all, it was to fpeak of the fears which the true friends of liberty might feel on his account, and of the confequent neceffity of banifhing him from the republic.'

As circumftances have led me to mention Dumouriez, I will fay what I know of him, and what I think: but this carries me back to Roland's firft adminiftration, and leads me to relate here how a man fo auftere in his manners came to be nominated to a place, which kings feldom fill with fimilar characters. I fhall take up the thread of my narrative at a period fomewhat remote; and fhall be indebted to my captivity for leifure to record facts, and recollect circumftances, which otherwife, perhaps, would never have employed my pen.

Roland executed the office of infpector of commerce and manufactures in the *generality* * of Lyons, with that

---

* Certain provinces, fubject to the *general* laws of the empire, were called *generalities*, in contradiftinction to the *Pays d'Etat*, or Provinces annexed to France with the referve of their particular privileges. *Tranf.*

knowledge and those administrative views, that ought to have distinguished the body of inspectors, if government had known how to keep up the spirit of the institution, of which Roland was almost the only example. Superior to his place in every respect, fond of employment, and not insensible to the allurements of fame, he digested in the silence of the closet the materials with which his experience and activity had furnished him; and continued the Dictionary of Manufactures for the new Encyclopedia. Some of Briffot's works were sent to him from the author, as a testimony of the esteem with which he had been inspired by the principles of liberty and justice, that appeared in Roland's writings. That testimony was received with the usual sensibility of authors, and with the feelings natural to a man of worth, who finds himself praised by a person of congenial mind. It gave birth to a correspondence at first very unfrequent; but afterwards supported by that of one of our friends, who became acquainted with Briffot at Paris, and spoke of his habits of life in a very favourable manner, as presenting a practical proof of the philosophical and moral theory contained in his writings. This correspondence was still further encouraged by the revolution of 1789; for events, succeeding each other with rapidity, called forth the most vigorous exertions of the minds and souls of philosophers prepared for liberty; and produced interesting communications between those, whose bosoms were enflamed with the love of their fellow-creatures, and the hope of seeing the universal reign of justice and happiness arrive. Briffot having at this juncture begun a periodical paper, that will be often consulted on account of the excellent reasoning it contains, we sent him every thing, of which circumstances seemed to make the publicity useful. Ere long our acquaintance received its last degree of improvement; and we became intimate and confidential friends, without ever having seen one another's faces.

Amid those struggles unavoidable in a period of revolution, when principles, prejudices, and passions, raise insurmountable obstacles between persons, who had before appeared well disposed to agree, Roland was elected a member of the municipality of Lyons. His situation in life, his family, and his connexions, were such as might be supposed to attach him to the aristocracy: while his turn of mind and reputation rendered him interesting to the popular party, to which he was naturally led to devote himself by his philosophy, and the austerity of his manners. No sooner had he taken a decided part, than he made himself many enemies, so much the more violent, as his inflexible integrity laid open without reserve the numerous abuses that had crept into the administration of the finances of the town. They exhibited an epitome of the dilapidations of those of the state, the debt of the city of Lyons amounting to no less than forty millions of livres [£1,666,667]. It was become indispensably necessary to solicit assistance, for the manufactures had suffered in the first year of the revolution, and twenty thousand workmen had been out of bread during the whole of the winter. It was therefore resolved to send a deputy extraordinary to the constituent assembly, to make known the circumstances, and Roland was the person chosen. We arrived at Paris the 20th of February, 1791. I had been five years absent from the place of my nativity; I had watched the progress of
the

the revolution, and the labours of the assembly; and had studied the characters and talents of its leading members, with an interest not easily to be conceived, and scarcely to be appreciated except by those who are acquainted with my ardent and active turn of mind. I hastened to attend their sittings; and there I saw the powerful Mirabeau *, the astonishing Cazalés, the daring Maury, the artful Lameths, and the frigid Barnave: I remarked with vexation that kind of superiority on the side of the *blacks* †, that dignified habits, purity of language, and polished manners, give in large assemblies; but the strength of reason, the courage of intregity, the lights of philosophy, the fruits of study, and the fluency of the bar, could not fail to secure the triumph of the patriots of the *left*, if they were all honest, and could but remain united.

Brissot came to visit us. I know nothing so pleasant as a first interview between persons, who have grown intimate by means of an epistolary correspondence, without being personally acquainted. They gaze upon each other, curious to observe whether the features of the face accord with the physignomy of the mind, and whe-

* The only man in the revolution, whose genius could guide the others, and sway the whole assembly. Great from his talents, little from his vices, but always superior to the multitude, and always master of himself, when he would take the pains to command his passions. He died soon after: I thought seasonably for his fame, and for freedom: though events have instructed me to regret him. The counterpoise of a man of such weight was wanting, to check the action of a pack of curs, and preserve us from the domination of ruffians.

† The court party, so called. The uniform of the emigrants assembled at Coblentz with the princes was black. *Transf.*

ther the person's outside confirm the opinion of him that had been previously entertained. The simple manners, natural negligence, and frankness of Brissot, appeared to me in perfect harmony with the austerity of his principles; but I found in him a sort of levity of mind and disposition, which was not equally suitable to the gravity of a philosopher. This always gave me pain, and of this his enemies never failed to take advantage. In proportion as I became more acquainted with him, I esteemed him the more. It is not in human nature to combine more complete disinterestedness with greater zeal for the public welfare, or to pursue the general good with more entire forgetfulness of private interest: but his writings are better fitted to effectuate it than his person; for *they* carry with them all the authority, which reason, justice, and intelligence can give; while in person he can assume none, for want of dignity. He is the best of men. A good husband, an affectionate father, a faithful friend, and a virtuous citizen, his company is as agreeable, as his temper is easy: confiding even to imprudence, and as gay, as simple, and as ingenuous, as a boy of fifteen, he was formed to live with the wife, and to be the dupe of the wicked. Learned in the science of law, and devoted from his youth to the study of social duties, and the great means of human happiness, he judges well of man, but of men he has no sort of knowledge. He knows, that vice exists; but he cannot believe any one vicious, who speaks to him with an open countenance: and when he has discovered a man to be so, he treats him as an idiot, who is to be pitied, without harbouring the least mistrust. Of hatred he is incapable: one would suppose that his mind, with all its sensibility, possesses not sufficient strength for a sen-

timent

timent of such energy. Extensive in his knowledge, he writes with extreme facility, and composes a treatise, as another would copy a song: hence the discriminating eye discerns in his works the hasty touch of a quick, and often light mind, though the groundwork itself is excellent. His activity and good-nature, which make him ready to do any thing, which he conceives may be of use, have given him an appearance of interfering in every thing; and have drawn upon him the charge of intriguing, from those who are in want of a subject of accusation. What a curious intriguer is a man, who never attends to himself, or those belonging to him; who is alike incapable of, and averse to, consulting his own interest; and who is no more ashamed of poverty, than afraid of death, looking upon both of them as the usual rewards of public virtue. I have seen him dedicating his whole time to the revolution, for no other end than to forward the triumph of truth, and promote the welfare of the public; and assiduously employed in the composition of his journal, which he might easily have made a matter of speculation, if he had not chosen to be content with the moderate recompence made him by his partner. His wife, as humble as himself, with a great deal of good sense, and some strength of mind, judged more properly of things. Ever since their marriage her views had been turned towards the United States of America, as the abode most suitable to their taste and manners, and a place where it was easy to settle with very slender means. Brissot had made a voyage thither in consequence; and they were on the point of embarking for that distant shore, when the revolution came and chained him to his native land.

Born

Born at Chartres, and a school-fellow of Pétion, who is a native of the same town, Briffot became still more intimate with him in the constituent assembly, where his labours and information were often of use to his friend. He made us acquainted with him, as well as with several other members, whom old habits of friendship, or the mere similitude of principles, and zeal for the public good, brought often together to compare their views. It was even agreed upon, that they should meet at my apartment four evenings in the week, because I was a very domestic, and could afford them good accommodations, and because my lodgings were so situated, as to be at no great distance from any of the persons who composed this little club.

This arrangement suited me perfectly: it made me acquainted with the progress of public affairs, in which I felt myself deeply interested; and favoured my taste for pursuing political speculations, and studying mankind. I knew what part became one of my sex, and never stepped out of it. The political debates passed in my presence, without my taking any part. Sitting at a table without the circle, I employed myself in working at my needle, or writing letters, while they were deliberating; and yet if I dispatched ten epistles, which was sometimes the case, I did not lose a single syllable of what was saying, and more than once bit my lips, to restrain my impatience to speak.

What struck me most, and distressed me exceedingly, was that sort of light and frivolous chit-chat, in which men of sense pass three or four hours, without coming to any conclusion. Taking things in detail, you would have heard excellent principles maintained, good ideas
started,

started, and some good plans proposed; but upon bringing the whole together, there appeared to be no path marked out, no fixed result, nor any determinate point, towards which it was agreed upon that each person should direct his views.

Sometimes for very vexation I could have boxed the ears of these philosophers, whom I daily learnt to esteem more and more for the honesty of their hearts, and the purity of their intentions: excellent reasoners all, and all philosophers, and learned politicians in theory; but being totally ignorant of the art of managing mankind, and consequently of swaying an assembly, their wit and learning were generally lavished to no end.

And yet I have known some good decrees thus planned, which have afterwards passed. But soon the coalation of the minority of the nobility completely weakened the *left side*, and produced the evils attendant on a revisal of the constitution. There remained but a small number of inflexible men, who durst contend for principles; and towards the conclusion these were reduced to little more than Buzot, Pétion, and Robespierre.

At that time Robespierre had to me the semblance of an honest man; and for the sake of his principles I forgave the defects of his language, and his tiresome way of speaking. I had, however, remarked, that he was always reserved in these committees, hearing the opinions of all, and seldom giving his own, or when he did, not being at the pains to set forth the reasons on which it was grounded. I have been told, that the next day he was the first to mount the tribune, and to avail himself of the arguments which the evening before he had heard delivered

by

by his friends. When he was sometimes gently reproved for this conduct, he would get off by a joke; and his artifice was forgotten, as the effect of that devouring self-love, by which he was so cruelly tormented. This however was in some degree destructive of confidence; for if any expedient were to be devised, any mode of proceeding to be determined upon, and any cast of parts to be adopted in consequence, there could never be any certainty that Robespierre would not come, as it were in a freak, and thwart the business; or else with a view of ascribing the honour to himself, bring forward the affair inconsiderately, and by so doing ruin all. Persuaded at that time that Robespierre was passionately fond of liberty, I was inclined to attribute his faults to an excess of fiery zeal. That kind of reserve, which seems to indicate either the fear of being seen through, because we can get nothing by being known, or the distrust of a man who can find no reason in his own bosom, for giving others credit for virtue; that kind of reserve, for which Robespierre is remarkable, gave me pain; but I mistook it for modesty. Thus it is that, with a favourable prepossession, we transform the most untoward indications into symptoms of the most amiable qualities. Never did the smile of confidence rest on the lips of Robespierre, while they were almost always contracted by the malignant grin of envy, striving to assume the features of disdain. His talents, as an orator, were below mediocrity; his vulgar voice, ill chosen expressions, and faulty pronunciation, rendering his discourse extremely tiresome. But he maintained principles with warmth and perseverance; and there was some courage in continuing to do so, at a time when the defenders of the

cause

cause of the people were greatly diminished in number. The court detested and calumniated them: to support and encourage them, was therefore the duty of a patriot. I esteemed Robespierre on this account; I told him as much; and even when he was not very assiduous at the little club, he occasionally came to take his dinner at our house. I had been much struck with the terror that seemed to have taken possession of his mind on the day of the king's flight to Varennes. That afternoon I found him at Pétion's, where he said with great alarm, that the royal family would never have taken such a step, without having a coalition in Paris, to direct a massacre of the patriots; and that he did not expect to live four and twenty hours. Pétion and Brissot on the contrary said, that the flight would be the king's ruin, and that it ought to be turned to good account: they observed that the people were perfectly well disposed, and would be more clearly convinced of the treachery of the court by this step, than they would have been by the ablest publications: that this single fact rendered it evident to all, that the king was adverse to the constitution, which he had sworn to maintain; that this was the moment to secure a more homogenous form of government; and that it would be proper to prepare men's minds for a republic. Robespierre, with his usual sneer, and biting his nails, asked what was a republic? The plan of a paper entitled the Republican, of which two numbers only were published, was then devised. Dumont of Geneva, a man of considerable abilities, was the editor; du Châtelet, an officer in the army, lent his name; and Condorcet, Brissot, and others, were preparing to give their assistance. The seizure of the king's

person

person gave Robespierre great pleasure; he saw in it the prevention of much mischief, and laid aside the fears he entertained on his own account; but the rest of the party were sorry for the event: they were of opinion that it was bringing back a pest into the government; that intriguing would revive; and that the effervescence of the public mind, allayed by the pleasure of seeing the culprit detained, would no longer serve to second the efforts of the friends of freedom. They judged aright; and with the less risk of being mistaken, as the reconciliation of Lafayette with the Lameths proved the existence of a new coalition, which could not have the public good for its foundation. It was impossible to counterbalance it, unless by the force of opinion displayed in a powerful manner; for which the patriots never had more than their pens, and their voices; but when any popular commotion came to their aid, they welcomed it with pleasure, without inquiring how it was produced, or giving themselves much trouble about it. There was behind the curtain a party, whom the aristocrats accused with so much vehemence, that it was impossible for the patriots not to be tempted to forgive him, so long as they perceived nothing, but what might be made to contribute to the public advantage: besides, they could not persuade themselves that the person in question was any way formidable.

It is not easy to command our passions in the time of a revolution: there is indeed no instance of one accomplished without their assistance. Great obstacles are to be overcome; and this cannot be effected without an ardour, and a devotion to the cause, bordering upon enthusiasm, or tending to produce it. Hence it is that we grasp

grasp with avidity at every thing that seems to serve our purpose, and lose the faculty of perceiving what may prove injurious. Hence that confidence, that eagerness to avail ourselves of a sudden movement, without tracing it to it's origin, in order to know how to direct it aright: and hence the indelicacy, if I may use the expression, of suffering the co-operation of agents whom we do not esteem, but whose proceedings we tolerate, because they appear to tend the same way as our own. D'Orleans standing singly was surely not to be feared; but his name, his connexions, his wealth, and his advisers, gave him great influence; and he unquestionably acted a secret part in all popular commotions. Men of pure intentions suspected him : but all this they considered as a fermentation necessary to set the inert mass a working: they contented themselves with taking no share in them, and flattered themselves, that they should make every thing turn to the advantage of the public: they were, besides, more inclined to ascribe to d'Orleans the desire of revenging himself on a court, by which he had been despised, and which he was inclined to humble, than any design of his own elevation.

The jacobins proposed a petition to the assembly, requesting it to pass judgment on the traitor who had fled, or to take the sense of the nation concerning the treatment he might deserve; and in the mean time to declare, that he had lost the confidence of the people of Paris. Laclos, that Laclos so remarkable for the powers of his mind, whom nature formed for the management of great affairs, but whose vices had made him dedicate all his faculties to intrigue; Laclos, devoted to d'Orleans, and of great weight in his council, made this proposal to the jacobins,

jacobins, who entertained it favourably, and among whom it was abetted by some hundreds of motion-makers * and strollers, who came thronging from the Palais-Royal into the place of their meeting at ten o'clock at night. I saw them arrive. The society deliberated in the presence of that mob, who were also allowed to give their votes; settled the fundamental points of the petition; and appointed a committee to draw it up, of which Laclos and Brissot were members. They were busied about it till a late hour of the night: for it had been resolved, that a deputation of the society should on the following day carry it to the Champ-de-Mars, there to be shown to all, who might wish to examine or to sign it. Laclos pretended that he had a head-ach proceeding from want of sleep, which would not suffer him to hold the pen: he therefore requested Brissot to take it; and, while conversing with him about the composition, proposed, for the last article, some clause, I know not what, which called for the restoration of royalty, and opened a road for d'Orleans to the throne. Brissot rejected it with warmth and astonishment; and the other, like an able politician, gave it up, under the pretence of his not having sufficiently considered its consequences: well aware, that he should still find means to get it foisted in; which in fact he did, since it made part of a printed paper that was dispersed as the plan agreed upon by the jacobins. But when the society which assembled the next morning to examine the draught of

---

* In the early part of the revolution, the garden of the *Tuileries*, and the interior of the Palais Royal, were filled with groups of twenty or thirty people, in the midst of each of which a demagogue called a *motionnaire* was holding forth. *Transl.*

the

the petition, and fend it away, was informed, that the national affembly had decided on the fate of the king, it difpatched its commiffioners to the Champ-de-Mars, to inform the people, that the decree refpecting the king having paffed, there was no longer any occafion for the intended petition. My curiofity had carried me to the *Champ-de-la-federation* *, where there were not more than two or three hundred perfons fcattered about the environs of the national altar, upon which deputies of the cordeliers, and of the fraternal focieties, bearing pikes with pompous infcriptions, ftood haranguing fmall groups, and exciting their indignation againft Lewis XVI. It was faid, that as the jacobins had fuppreffed their petition, it was proper that fuch citizens as were zealous in the people's caufe fhould draw up another, and affemble for that purpofe on the enfuing day. Then it was that the partifans of the court, feeling the neceffity of employing terror, concerted the means of ftriking a decifive blow. They prepared their meafures accordingly; and the unexpected proclamation of martial law, and its prompt execution, produced what has been juftly called the *maffacre of the Champ-de-Mars*. The terrified people durft not ftir, while part of the national guard, feduced or deceived, feconded Lafayette, either out of obfequioufnefs to the court, or blind confidence in his pretended patriotifm, and ferved as a rampart againft their fellow-citizens; the ftandard of death was difplayed from the town-hall; and the revifion of the conftitution was effected under its influence. The formation of the club of *Feuillans* had been planned much about the fame time, to weaken the jacobins; and moft affuredly

---

* The new name of the Champ de Mars. *Tranf.*

the whole proceedings of the coalition at that period proved, how much the court and its partisans were superior to their adversaries in weaving a tissue of intrigues.

I never knew affright comparable to that of Robespierre under these circumstances. There was indeed a rumour of putting him on his trial, which was probably meant only to intimidate him; and it was said, that there was a plot at the Feuillans both against him, and the committee, who drew up the petition at the jacobins. Roland and I were really uneasy on his account, and drove to his house, at the farther end of the *Marais*, at eleven at night, to offer him an asylum: but he had already quitted his habitation. Thence we proceeded to Buzot's to tell him, that perhaps it would not be amiss, if without leaving the society of the jacobins, he were to enter into that of the feuillans, in order to see what was going forward, and to be ready to defend those whom they might wish to persecute. 'There is nothing I would not do,' said Buzot after some hesitation, and speaking of Robespierre, ' to save that unhappy young man; though I am far from entertaining the same opinion of him that many others do: he thinks too much of himself, to be greatly in love with liberty; but he serves its cause, and that is enough for me. The public must nevertheless take place of him; and I should be inconsistent in my principles, and exhibit them in a false point of view, if I went to the Feuillans. I have too much repugnance to act a part that would oblige me to put on two different faces. Grégoire is gone thither: he will let us know what is going on; but after all, nothing can be done to affect Robespierre, without the intervention of the assembly, and there I shall at all times be ready to undertake

undertake his defence. As to the Jacobins, where I have been little of late, becaufe my regard for our fpecies makes me grieve to fee it more than ufually hideous in that noify affembly, I fhall be conftant in my attendance, as long as the perfecution is kept up againft a fociety, which I believe to be ufeful to the caufe of freedom.' Thefe words of Buzot were exactly defcriptive of the man: he acts, as he fpeaks, with truth and rectitude, the ftricteft probity, adorned with the pleafing forms of fenfibility, being the leading feature of his character. He had diftinguifhed himfelf in our little committee, by the foundnefs of his underftanding, and by that decided manner which befpeaks a man of integrity. As he lived at no great diftance from our houfe; and his wife, though fhe did not appear to poffefs a mind congenial to his, was an affable woman; we vifited each other frequently. When the fuccefs of Roland's miffion with refpect to the debt of the commune of Lyons allowed us to return to Beaujolois, we kept up a correfpondence with Buzot and Robefpierre. That with the former was the more regular: there was a greater familiarity between us, a wider foundation for friendfhip, and a rich ftock of materials to keep it from flagging. Our friendfhip became intimate and unalterable. Elfewhere I fhall fay how this connection grew clofer ftill.

Roland's miffion having detained him feven months at Paris, we quitted that city in the middle of September, after his obtaining every thing for Lyons that it could defire; and fpent the autumn in the country, employed in the vintage.

One of the laft acts of the conftituent affembly was the fuppreffion of infpectors. We confidered, whether we fhould should determine to remain in the country, or whether it would be better to go and pass the winter in Paris, where Roland might prefer his claim to a pension, as a reward for forty years service; and at the same time continue his labours for the Encyclopedia, which he would be sure to find more easy in the focus of science, amidst artists and men of letters, than in the depth of a desert.

We came back to Paris in the month of December. As the members of the constituent assembly had returned to their several homes; and Pétion, who had been chosen mayor, was wholly occupied with the cares of that office, we no longer had any rallying point, and saw Brissot himself much less frequently than before. The whole of our attention was concentrated at home. Roland's active mind inspired him with the idea of establishing a journal of useful arts; and by the charms of study we endeavoured to divert our attention from public affairs, which seemed to be in a lamentable state. Several deputies of the legislative assembly used however to meet sometimes at the apartments which one of them occupied in the *Place Vendôme*; and Roland, whose patriotism and knowledge were held in high esteem, was invited to make one of the party: but he disliked the distance, and seldom went. One of our friends, who was frequently there, informed us, about the middle of March, that the court, full of alarm and perplexity, was desirous of doing something to regain its popularity; that it would have no great objection to appoint jacobin ministers; and that the patriots were busied in endeavouring to make the choice fall upon men of steadiness and ability; which was of the more importance, as it might only be a snare on the part of the court, which

would

would not be sorry to have wrong-headed persons forced upon it, who might become just objects of complaint or derision. He added, that several persons had turned their thoughts towards Roland, whose rank in the republic of letters, administrative knowledge, and reputation for justice and vigour of mind, afforded a prospect of stability. Roland at that time went frequently to the jacobin society, and was one of the persons employed in its committee of correspondence. The idea however seemed to me to be visionary, and made but little impression on my mind.

The 21st of the same month, Brissot called upon me in the evening, and repeated the same thing in a more positive manner; asking at the same time whether Roland would consent to take such a burden on him. I said in answer, that, having mentioned the matter to him in the course of conversation, when the idea was first started, it had appeared to me, that after taking all the difficulties and danger into the account, his zeal and activity would not object to such a field for exertion; but that it was a business which required further consideration. Roland did not shrink from the task: the idea he entertained of his own abilities inspired him with a hope of being serviceable to the cause of freedom and to his country: and such was the answer that was given to Brissot on the following day.

On Friday, the 23d, at eleven in the evening, I saw him walk into our apartment with Dumouriez; who came on the breaking up of the council, to inform Roland of his being appointed minister for the home-department, and to salute him as his colleague. They stayed a few minutes; and an hour of the following day

day was fixed for Roland to take the oaths. 'There goes a man,' said I when they went away, speaking of Dumouriez, whom I had never seen before; 'there goes a man of a subtle mind, and a deceitful look; against whom perhaps it will behove you to be more upon your guard than against any man whatever: he expressed great pleasure at the patriotic choice he was employed to announce, and yet I shall not be surprised if on some future day he bring about your dismission.'—Dumouriez, indeed, at the first glance, appeared to me so widely different from Roland, that I could not suppose it possible for them to act long in concert. On one side I beheld integrity and frankness personified, with rigid justice devoid of all courtly arts, and of all the dexterous manœuvres of a man of the world: on the other I fancied I could recognize a libertine of great parts, a determined adventurer, inclined to make a jest of every thing, except his own interest and fame. It was not difficult to infer, that such elements would act repulsively upon each other.

Roland's incredible industry, his readiness in business, and his methodical turn, soon enabled him, when minister, to make an arrangement in his head of all the various branches of his department. But the principles and habits of the chief clerks rendered his employment extremely laborious. He was obliged to be on his guard, and to contend most strenuously to prevent any thing contradictory from taking place in his official proceedings; he was engaged in short in one continued struggle with his agents. He strongly felt the necessity of changing them; but he was too prudent to do so, before he had become familiar with affairs, and secured proper persons to supply their places.

places. As to the council, its sittings rather resembled the chit-chat of a private party, than the deliberations of statesmen. Each minister brought with him ordinances and proclamations to be signed; and the minister of justice presented decrees to be sanctioned. The king read the gazette; questioned each of them about his private affairs, thus testifying with no small share of address that sort of kind concern, of which the great knew how to make a merit; talked like a plain man about affairs in general; and at every turn professed, with an air of frankness, his desire to put the constitution in force. For the first three weeks, Roland and Claviere appeared almost enchanted with the king's excellent disposition of mind, giving him credit on his bare word, and rejoicing, like honest men, at the turn that things were about to take. 'Good God!' said I: 'when I see you set out for the council with all that delightful confidence, it always seems to me that you are on the point of committing some egregious act of folly.'—I never could bring myself to believe in the constitutional vocation of a king born and brought up in despotism, and accustomed to exercise arbitrary sway. Lewis XVI must have been a man above the common race of mortals, had he been sincerely the friend of a constitution that restrained his power; and if such a man, he would never have suffered those events to occur which brought about the revolution.

The first time Roland appeared at court, the plainness of his apparel, his round hat, and his shoes tied with ribbands, were matters of astonishment and offence to all the court valets; to those beings, who, deriving their sole consequence from etiquette, believed that the safety of the state depended on its preservation. The master of the ceremonies, stepping up to Dumouriez with alarm in his countenance and a contracted brow, pointed out Roland by a glance of the eye: Oh dear! Sir, said he in a whisper, he has no buckles in his shoes!——Oh Lord! Sir, answered Dumouriez, with gravity truly laughable, we are all ruined and undone.

A council being held four times a week, the ministers agreed to dine on those days at one another's houses by turns; and every Friday I received them as my guests. *Degrave* was then minister of war. He was a little man, in every sense of the word: nature had made him gentle, and timid; his prejudices prompted him to be haughty, while his heart inspired him with the desire of being amiable; and in his perplexity to reconcile these jarring affections, he became nothing at all. I think I see him now, walking on his heels like a courtier, with his head erect on his slender body; turning up his blue eyes, which he could not keep open after dinner without the help of two or three cups of coffee; speaking little, as if out of reserve, but in reality for want of ideas; and at length so bewildered in the labyrinth of his official business, as to ask leave to retire. *Lacoste,* a true jack in office of the old order of things, of which he had the insignificant and awkward look, cold manner, and dogmatic tone, wanted none of those advantages which a man hackneyed in the routine of public business seldom fails to acquire; but his apparent reserve and discretion concealed a violence of temper, which he carried when contradicted to the most ridiculous excess. He was besides, deficient both in the extensive views, and activity, necessary for a minister. *Duranthon,* who had been sent

for

for from Bourdeaux to be made minister of justice, was an honest man, according to common report; but he was very indolent; his manner indicated vanity; and his timid disposition, and pompous prattle, made him always appear to me no better than an old woman. *Clavière*, whose coming into office was preceded by a reputation of great skill in finance, was, I make no doubt, well informed upon that subject, of which I am no judge. Active, industrious, of an irritable disposition, obstinate, as most men are who live much in the retirement of the closet, and cavilling and uncomplying in debate, he could not do otherwise than clash with Roland, who was dry and peremptory in dispute, and not less stiff in opinion than himself. These two men were made to esteem, without loving each other; and they have not belied their destiny. *Dumouriez* had more of what is called parts than all of them put together, and less *morality* than any one of the number. Diligent, brave, an able general, an artful courtier, writing well, speaking fluently, and capable of great undertakings, he wanted nothing but strength of mind proportioned to his genius, and a cooler head to execute the plans he had conceived. Agreeable in his commerce with his friends, and ready to deceive them all; attentive to women, but by no means calculated to succeed with those, whom a tender passion might seduce; he was made for the ministerial intrigues of a corrupt and faithless court. His brilliant qualities, and love of fame, gave room to hope, that he might be employed with advantage in the army of the republic: and perhaps he would have proceeded in the right path, if the convention had been prudent; for he is too wise not to act like an honest man, when his doing so is conducive to his interest and reputation.

Degrave was succeeded by *Servan*, an honest man, in the fullest signification of the term, of an ardent temper and excellent moral character, with all the austerity of a philosopher, and all the benevolence of a feeling heart; an enlightened patriot, a brave soldier, and an active minister, he stood in need of nothing, but a more sober imagination, and a more flexible mind.

The troubles on the score of religion, and the preparations of the enemy, calling for decisive decrees, the refusal of sanctioning them completely tore away the veil from Louis XVI, whose sincerity was already strongly suspected by such of his ministers as had before been inclined to believe it real. At first the refusal was not positive: the king being desirous of considering the subject, put off the sanction till the following council, when he always found reasons for deferring it still longer. This procrastination gave his ministers an opportunity of speaking out. Roland and Servan, in particular, remonstrated incessantly, and spoke the most striking truths with becoming spirit.

Their situation became critical: the public weal was in danger: and it was incumbent on ministers truly patriotic, either to provide the means of its salvation, or to retire, that they might not be assisting in its ruin. Roland proposed to his colleagues a letter to the king purporting as much; but Claviere cavilled at the expressions, and Duranthon, who was fond of his place, was unwilling to risk the loss of it, if he could possibly keep it, without being a confest traitor. Lacoste did not approve

approve of strong measures, and the will of the king appeared to him, upon the whole, the best of all possible rules; while Dumouriez left them to settle the matter among themselves, that he might be more at leisure to play his own cards, and to revenge what he considered as a vexatious affront. The fact was as follows.

That kind of rumour, which does not as yet amount to the opinion of the public, but which foreruns and announces it, was afloat against Bonnecarrere, whom Dumouriez had made director-general of the department of foreign affairs. He had the reputation, the talents, the disposition, and the manners of an intriguer: so at least I have been told by men of probity, who related various circumstances of his life, and lamented the choice that Dumouriez had made.

A report was spread of some place being bestowed or affair settled, by Bonnecarrere, on his receiving a consideration of a hundred thousand livres [£4167], part of which was to be given to madam de Beauvert. That lady was Dumouriez's mistress; and lived in his house, where she did the honours of the table, to the great displeasure of men of sense, the friends of morality and freedom; for such licentiousness in a servant of the public, charged with the conduct of affairs of state, too plainly indicated a contempt of decorum; especially as madam Beauvert, the sister of Rivarol, a man unfortunately but too well known, lived in the midst of the sworn friends of aristocracy, people little entitled to commendation in any point of view. Dumouriez's conduct, even if it had not been fundamentally wrong, was impolitic, and calculated to excite suspicion.

I was frequently visited by Brissot, and several other members

members of the legiflative affembly. They fometimes met the minifters at my houfe; and kept up that kind of intimacy with them, which is requifite among men who, being devoted alike to the caufe of the public, ftand in need of an intercommunity of views and information, in order to ferve it the more effectually. The ftory of Bonnecarrere was related to one of them; and the parties were mentioned by name, as well as the notary in whofe hands the money was depofited, or who was at leaft appointed to receive it; but thefe particulars have efcaped my memory. I only recollect, that two men of character came to my houfe and affirmed them in the prefence of three or four members of the legiflative body, one of whom, a friend of Dumourez, was defirous of hearing the whole ftory from their mouths. It was refolved to repeat to Dumouriez, with a degree of folemnity, the arguments that had already been urged to him in private, concerning the neceffity, both on the public account and his own, of making his conduct, and the choice of his agents, more conformable to the political principles which he pretended to entertain. The converfation confequently took place in the prefence of his colleagues and of three or four members of the affembly. Roland, availing himfelf of the authority given him by his years and character, pointed out to Dumouriez the neceffity of his conducting himfelf with more propriety and prudence; and every one agreed, that this laft trait of Bonnecarrere ought to open his eyes, and induce him to put fome other perfon in his place. Dumouriez, who turned Bonnecarrere's talents to good account, and gave himfelf little concern on the fcore of morality, treated the obfervations of his friends with great levity, and at length rejected them with anger,

anger. From that moment he discontinued all intercourse with the members, behaved with greater coolness to his colleagues, and, without doubt, no longer thought of any thing, but overturning those by whose gravity he was the most displeased. I foresaw the effect of this conference, and said to Roland: 'if you were an intriguer, and capable of conducting yourself according to the policy of the old court and government, I should tell you, that the moment to ruin Dumouriez is at hand, if you wish to prevent his playing you a trick.' But honest men understand not this petty warfare; and Roland was as incapable of having recourse to it, as he would have been ill-fitted to carry it on.

The postponement of the sanction was nearly become a refusal: the utmost limit of delay was at hand*. We were sensible, as the council was neither sufficiently unanimous nor energetic to speak out in a collective shape, that it became the integrity and courage of Roland to step forward alone; and between us two we determined on his famous letter to the king. He carried it with him to the council, with the intention of reading it aloud, the very day when Louis XVI, on being pressed anew for his sanction, required each of his ministers to give him his opinion written and signed, and proceeded rapidly to discuss other affairs. Roland returned home, added a few introductory lines to his letter, and delivered the whole into the king's hands, on the morning of the 11th of June.

The next day, the 12th, at eight in the evening, Servan

---

* By the constitution of 1789, the king was allowed to withhold his sanction during a certain number of months, at the end of which his neglecting to give his consent amounted to a refusal. *Transl.*

walked

walked into my room with a smiling countenance, 'give me joy', said he, 'I have just had the honour of being turned away.'—'That is an honour,' answered I, 'that my husband will soon share; and I am not a little mortified that you should get the start of us.' He then related to me, that, having been with the king in the morning on particular business, he had strenuously insisted on the necessity of the camp of twenty thousand men, if it were sincerely his intention to oppose the designs of the enemy; that the king had turned his back upon him in very ill-humour; and that Dumouriez, at the very same instant, was coming out of the war-office, whither he had been to take his portfolio from him, by virtue of an order, of which he was the bearer.—'Who? Dumouriez? He is acting a vile part; but I am not at all surprised at it.'— The three preceding days Dumouriez had been frequently at the Tuileries, and had held long conferences with the queen; with whom, it may not be impertinent to remark, that Bonnecarrere had some interest, by means of her women. Roland, being informed that Servan was in my apartment, quitted the persons to whom he was giving audience, and on hearing the news, requested his colleagues, Dumouriez excepted, to repair to the hotel.

It was his opinion, that they ought not to wait for their dismission; but that in consequence of Servan's being declared, it became all those who professed the same principles to give in their resignations; unless the king should recall Servan, and dismiss Dumouriez, with whom they could no longer sit at the council-table. Had the four ministers acted thus, the court, I have no doubt, would have been not a little embarrassed to replace them; it would have done honour to Lacoste and Duranthon, and the affair would have had a more striking effect upon the public

public mind: but it was deftined to have that effect afterwards in a different way.

. The minifters came and debated for a long while, without coming to any refolution, except that they would meet again the next morning at eight, and that Roland fhould prepare a letter in the mean time. I could never have believed, had not circumftances put me in the way of knowing it, that foundnefs of judgment, and a firm temper of mind, are things fo uncommon, and confequently that fo few men are fit for the tranfaction of bufinefs, particularly that of the ftate. Would you wifh to meet with the above qualities in conjunction with perfect difintereftednefs?—"That were indeed the Arabian bird," fcarcely feen once in a long fucceffion of ages. I no longer wonder, that men fuperior to the herd, and placed at the head of empires, commonly entertain a fovereign contempt for their fpecies: it is the almoft inevitable confequence of an extenfive knowledge of the world; and to avoid the errors, into which fuch a fentiment may lead thofe to whom the welfare of a nation is entrufted, requires a fund of philofophy and magnanimity very extraordinary indeed.

The minifters came at the appointed hour; expreffed their doubts about the letter; and at length concluded, that it would be better to go to the king, and declare their fentiments in perfon. This expedient appeared to me no better than an evafion; for certain it is, that a man never fpeaks fo boldly as he may venture to write, to a perfon, who, by virtue of his rank, and the force of cuftom, lays claim to particular refpect. It was agreed upon that they fhould take Lacofte, who had not yet made his appearance, along with them, or at leaft that they fhould invite him to be one of the party. But fcarcely had

thefe

these gentlemen assembled at the admiralty-office, when a messenger from the king brought Duranthon an order to repair to the palace immediately and alone. Clavière and Roland told him, that they would go and wait for his return at the chancery. They had not been there long before Duranthon made his appearance in solemn silence, with a long face, and a hypocritical appearance of sorrow, taking slowly out of his pocket an order from the king for each of the other two.—' Give it me,' said Roland, with a smile : ' I perceive already that our delays have made us lose the start.'—In fact he brought their dismissions.

' Well! I am turned out too,' said my husband on his return.—' I hope,' answered I, ' that it is better deserved on your part, than on that of any one else; but you should not by any means allow the king to announce it to the assembly: since he has not profited by the lesson given him in your letter, you ought to render that lesson useful to the public, by making it known. Nothing appears to me more consistent with the courage evinced by writing it, than the hardihood of sending a copy to the assembly : on hearing of your dismission, it will also be acquainted with the cause.'

This idea could not fail to be agreeable to my husband. It was adopted; and every body knows the approbation which the assembly gave to the letter, by ordering it to be printed and sent to the departments, as well as the honour they did to the three ministers by declaring that the regret of the nation attended them in their retreat. In my own mind I am convinced, and I think the event has proved it, that Roland's letter contributed greatly to enlighten the French nation; it exhibited to the king, with so much force and wisdom, what his own

interest

interest required of him, that it was easy to perceive he refused his compliance, out of a determined opposition to the maintenance of the constitution.

When I recollect, that Pache was in Roland's closet while we were reading the rough draught of that letter, and that he deemed it an adventurous step; when I reflect how often that man has witnessed our enthusiasm in the cause of liberty, and our zeal to serve it; and see him now at the head of that arbitrary authority, which oppresses and persecutes us as enemies of the republic: I ask myself, whether I be awake, and whether the dream must not terminate in the punishment of that infamous hypocrite.

Thus did we return to private life. Perhaps I may be asked, whether I never knew any further particulars concerning the manner, in which Roland was called into administration. I can safely say, I never did; and that I never even thought of inquiring about it: for it appeared to me to be brought about like many other things in this world; the idea occurs to some one person, many approve it, and with this support it attracts the notice of people capable of carrying it into effect. I perceived, that the business in question had struck some of the members; but I know not who it was that first proposed it; nor by whom it was transmitted to the court. Roland knew no more of it, and gave himself no more concern about it, than I. When a successor to Degrave was thought of for the war department, the ministers and patriotic members did not know whither to direct their views, almost all the officers of the army, of any repute, being looked upon as enemies to the constitution. Roland at last thought of Servan, a military man, who had earned the

cross

cross of St Lewis by his services; and whose principles were not doubtful, since he had displayed them before the revolution, in a publication, called the Citizen Soldier, which had been well received. We were personally acquainted with him, in consequence of seeing him at Lyons, where he enjoyed the well-earnt reputation of an active and sagacious man: he had besides, in the year 1790, lost a place at court, where his civism was not agreeable to Monsieur Guynard-St.-Priest. These considerations induced the members of the council to join in proposing him to the king, by whom he was accepted.

As soon as my husband was in the ministry, I came to a fixed determination, neither to pay nor receive visits, nor invite any female to my table. I had no great sacrifices to make on that head: for, not residing constantly at Paris, my acquaintance was not extensive; besides, I had no where kept a great deal of company, because my love of study is as great as my detestation of cards, and because the society of silly people affords me no diversion. Accustomed to spend my days in domestic retirement, I shared the labours of Roland, and pursued the studies most suited to my own particular taste. The establishment of so severe a rule served then at once to keep up my accustomed style of life, and to prevent the inconveniences which an interested crowd throws in the way of people occupying important posts. Properly speaking, I never received company in my hotel: twice a week, indeed, I gave a dinner to some of the ministers, a few members of the assembly, and the persons with whom my husband had any thing to talk over, or whose acquaintance he wished to preserve. Business was talked of of in my presence; because I had not the rage of interfering, and was not surrounded with such company as could excite distrust. Out of all the rooms of a spacious apartment, I had chosen, for my daily habitation, the smallest parlour, which I had converted into a study, by removing into it my books and a bureau. It often happened, that Roland's friends or colleagues, when they wanted to speak to him confidentially, instead of going to his apartment, where he was surrounded by his clerks or by the public, would come to mine, and request me to send for him. By these means I found myself drawn into the vortex of public affairs, without intrigue or idle curiosity. Roland had a pleasure in afterwards conversing with me about them in private, with that confidence which we ever placed in each other, and which established between us an intercommunity of knowledge and opinions; and it sometimes happened also, that friends, who had only some information to give, or a few words to say, being always sure of finding me, came and requested I would make the necessary communication to Roland as soon as an opportunity might occur.

It had been found necessary to counterbalance the influence of the court, the aristocracy, the civil list, and the ministerial papers, by information given to the people in the most public way. A daily paper, posted up in the streets, seemed well calculated for that purpose; but it was necessary to find a judicious and enlightened man, capable of following up events, and exhibiting them in their proper colours, to be the conductor. *Louvet*, already known as an author, a man of letters, and a politician, was pointed out, approved of, and undertook the task. Money was also wanting for its support; but that was a thing not quite so easily to be obtained. Petion himself was allowed none for the police; and yet in a town like Paris, and in such a state of things, when it was of importance to have people in pay, in order to gain timely information of every thing that happened, or that might be in agitation, it was indispensably necessary. To obtain any thing from the assembly would have been difficult; for the demand would infallibly have given the alarm to the partisans of the court, and would have met with many obstacles. At last it occurred, that Dumouriez, who had secret service money for the department of foreign affairs, might allow a certain sum monthly to the mayor of Paris for the police; and that out of that sum might be taken the expenses of the daily paper which was to be posted up, and which the minister of the home-department was to superintend. The expedient was simple, and was adopted. Such was the origin of the *Sentinel*.

It was in the course of the month of July, that perceiving affairs daily growing worse through the perfidy of the court, the march of the foreign troops, and the weakness of the assembly, we looked out for a place where liberty, threatened from so many quarters, might find an asylum. We frequently conversed with Barbaroux and Servan concerning the excellent spirit that prevailed in the south, the energy of the departments in that quarter of France, and the advantages its situation afforded for founding a republic, if the triumphant court should find means to subjugate Paris and the North. We took a map, and traced the line of demarcation; Servan studied the military positions it offered; we calculated its strength; we examined the nature of its produce,

and

and the means of circulating that produce; every one called to mind the places, or the persons, from whom we might expect to receive support; and every one repeated, after a revolution that had afforded such great hopes, we ought not to relapse tamely into slavery, but should strain every nerve to establish a free government in some part of France. 'That shall be our resource,' said Barbaroux, 'if the *Marseillois*, whom I accompanied hither, be not sufficiently seconded by the Parisians to subdue the court. I hope, however, they will succeed, and that we shall have a convention, which will give a republican form of government to all France.'

We understood very well, without his explaining himself farther, that an insurrection was projected. It appeared indeed inevitable, since the court was making preparations, that indicated a design of enforcing submission. It may be said, they were made in its own defence; but the idea of attack either would have occurred to no body, or if it had, it would not have been embraced by the people at large, if the court had really and truly enforced the constitution: for, though aware of all its defects, the most strenuous republicans desired nothing more for the present, and would have quietly awaited its improvement from the hands of time and of experience.

It is true, at the period of a revolution, there will always be found, particularly among a corrupt people, and in large cities, a class of men destitute of the advantages of fortune, covetous of her favours, and inclined to make any sacrifice to obtain them, or else accustomed to supply the want of them by illicit means. If a daring mind, a courageous disposition, and some portion of natural abilities, diftinguifh a man of that defcription, he becomes the chief, or the director, of a turbulent band, whofe ranks are foon filled up by all thofe who, having nothing to lofe, are ready to attempt any thing; by all the dupes, they have art enough to make; and laftly, by the individuals difperfed among them by domeftic politicians or foreign powers, interefted in fomenting divifions, in order to weaken them by civil difcord, that they may afterwards take advantage of their diftracted ftate.

The patriotic focieties, thefe collections of men affembled to deliberate on their rights and interefts, have exhibited to us a picture in miniature of what paffes in the great fociety of the ftate.

Firft we find a few men of ardent difpofitions, deeply impreffed with a fenfe of the public danger, and feeking fincerely to prevent it. Thefe men the philofophers join becaufe they conceive fuch a junction neceffary to overturn tyranny, and propagate principles beneficial to mankind. Accordingly, great principles are developed, and difleminated; generous fentiments are called forth and diffufed; and a vigorous impulfion is given both to the hearts and minds of men. Then come forward individuals, who, by affuming principles that do not belong to them, which they decorate with the moft captivating language, endeavour to gain the favour of the public, in order to acquire confequence or power. They pafs the bounds of truth, to render themfelves more remarkable; heat the imagination by falfe and exaggerated reprefentations; flatter the paffions of the populace, ever difpofed to admire the gigantic; urge it on to meafures, in which they have the means of making themfelves ufeful, in order to be thought neceffary upon all occafions;

sions; and employ themselves in the foul work of throwing suspicion upon those prudent or enlightened men, of whose merit they are afraid, and with whom they are not able to stand in competition. Calumny, at first employed without art, learns, from the humiliation it receives, to shape itself into a system; and at length becomes a profound science, in which they and their fellows alone can succeed.

Unquestionably many people of this character joined the popular party against the court; ready to serve the latter for money, and as ready to betray it, in case it should become the weaker party. The court affected to believe that all those who opposed its designs were of the above description, and was fond of confounding them under the appellation of the factious. The real patriots suffered this noisy pack to go their own way, like so many hounds; and perhaps were not sorry to make them serve as a forlorn hope, to receive the first fire of the enemy. In their hatred of despotism they did not recollect, that, if it be allowable in politics, to suffer good things to be effected by bad men, or to profit by their excesses for some useful purpose, it is infinitely dangerous to ascribe to them the honour of the one, or not to punish them for the other.

Every body is acquainted with the revolution of the 10th of August, of which I know no more than is known to the public; for, though well informed of the great outline of affairs while Roland was a servant of the public, and attending to it with interest when he was no longer in place, I never was a confidant of what may be called the manœuvring of parties; nor was he himself ever concerned in that sort of business.

Recalled to the ministry at that period, he re-entered it with

with renovated hopes. It is a great pity, we used to say, that the council should be contaminated by that *Danton*, who has so bad a reputation.—' What can we do ?' said some friends, to whom I whispered the same remark; ' he has been useful in the revolution, and the people love him: there is no prudence in making malcontents: it will certainly be better to make the most of him as he is.'—There was some reason in this; but still it is much easier to deny a man the means of influence, than to prevent his putting it to a bad use. There began the faults of the patriots: the instant the court was subdued, an excellent council should have been formed, all the members of which being irreproachable in their conduct, and distinguished for their knowledge, would have conducted the government with dignity, and have impressed foreign powers with respect. To take Danton into the administration, was to deluge the government with such men as I have described; who harass it, when not in employ, and corrupt and debase it, when they participate in its operations. But who was to make these reflections? who could have dared to announce and openly maintain them? The choice was made by the assembly, or its committee of twenty-one; among whom there were many men of merit, but not one leader; not one of those beings cast in the mould of *Mirabeau*, and made to command the vulgar, to condense into one focus the opinions of the wise, and to present them with that force of genius, which compels obedience the moment it appears.

As they were at a loss for a minister of the marine, Condorcet mentioned Monge, because he had seen him solve geometrical problems at the academy of sciences; and

and Monge was chosen. Monge is a kind of original, admirably calculated to play tricks in the manner of the bears that I have seen dancing in the ditches of the town of Berne. There cannot be a more awkward buffoon, or one who has less pretensions to wit and pleasantry. Formerly a stone-cutter at Mézières, where the abbé Bossut encouraged him, and set him to study mathematics; he got on by dint of industry, and ceased to visit his benefactor, as soon as he began to entertain hopes of becoming his equal. A good kind of man in other respects, or at least contriving to be so esteemed, in a small circle, of which the most satirical members had not wit enough to divert themselves by shewing that he was no better than a narrow-minded blockhead. But in short he passed for an honest man, and a friend of the revolution; and people were so tired of traitors, and so puzzled to find men of ability, that they began to put up with any body of whose good faith they were convinced. I need not speak of his ministry: the deplorable state of our navy too plainly evinces his imbecility and insignificance.

Roland's first care was to make that reform in his office, of which he had felt the necessity. He collected about him a set of men attached to the principles of liberty, of active dispositions, and of enlightened minds: and, had he accomplished nothing more, he would have done great service to that branch of administration. He hastened to write to all the departments, with that force which reason gives, that authority which belongs to truth, and that expression of sentiment that flows from the heart; shewing them the new order of things that must necessarily result from the revolution of the 10th of August; and the necessity for all parties to rally around justice, which prevents excesses; around liberty, which produces the happiness of all; around good order, which alone can insure it; and around the legislative body, which stands charged with the expression of the public will. Those administrative bodies which appeared to hesitate, were suspended, or cashiered. Great dispatch in business, and the most active and extensive correspondence, diffused a similar spirit through every part, restored confidence, and gave fresh life to the interior of the kingdom.

Danton scarcely suffered a day to pass without coming to our house. Sometimes it was in his way to the council; he would arrive a little before the hour, and step into my apartment; or else he would call in his return, most commonly accompanied by Fabre-d'Eglantine: at other times, he would invite himself to dine with me, on days when I was not accustomed to see company, in order that he might converse with Roland about some business.

No man could make a show of greater zeal, of a greater love of liberty, or of a greater desire to concur with his colleagues in serving it effectually. I contemplated his forbidding and atrocious features, and, though I used to say to myself, that no one should be condemned upon hearsay evidence, that I had no certain knowledge of any thing to his prejudice, that the honestest man in the world must needs have two different characters when party-spirit ran high, and that appearances were not to be trusted, I could not bring myself to associate the idea of a good man with such a countenance. I never saw any thing that so strongly expressed the violence of brutal passions,

passions, and the most astonishing audacity, half disguised by a jovial air, an affectation of frankness, and a sort of simplicity. My lively imagination represents every person, with whom I am struck, in the action that I conceive suitable to his character. I cannot see for half an hour a face not from the common mould, without arraying it in the garb of some profession, or giving it some part to play, the idea of which it revives or impresses on my mind. In this manner my imagination has often figured Danton, with a dagger in his hand, encouraging by his voice and his example a band of assassins, more timid or less ferocious than himself: or else, when satiated with his crimes, indicating his habits and propensities by the gestures of a Sardanapalus. I certainly would defy an experienced painter, not to find in the person of Danton all the requisites for such a composition.

Could I have confined myself to a regular path, instead of abandoning my pen to the wandering course of a mind, that ranges at large over the wide field of events, I would have taken up Danton at the beginning of 1789, a miserable counsellor, more burdened with debts than causes; and whose wife was known to say, that she could not have kept house, without the assistance of a louis-d'or a week which she received from her father. I would have exhibited him making his first appearance at the *section*, which was then called a *district*, and attracting notice by the strength of his lungs: a great sectary of the Orleans faction; acquiring a kind of competency in the course of that year, without any visible means of making money; and obtaining a little celebrity by excesses, which Lafayette was inclined to punish, but which he artfully found means to turn to his own advantage, by procuring himself the protection of the district, which he had rendered.

turbulent.

turbulent. I should describe him declaiming with success in the popular societies, setting himself up for the defender of the rights of all, declaring, that he would accept no place of profit, till the revolution should be at an end; and succeeding nevertheless to that of substitute to the solicitor of the commune; preparing his influence at the Jacobins upon the ruins of that of the Lameths; making his appearance on the tenth of August among those who were returning from the palace *; and entering into the administration, as a tribune in high favour with the people, whom it was necessary to satisfy by giving him a share in the government. From that period his progress was equally bold and rapid. He attached to himself by largesses, or protected by his influence, those greedy and miserable men, who are goaded on by vice and want; he marked out the formidable persons whose ruin it was necessary to effect; he paid the hireling scribes, and inflamed the minds of the enthusiasts, whom he intended to set upon them; he refined on the *revolutionary* inventions of headlong patriots, or artful knaves; he devised, promoted, and executed plans capable of striking terror, of removing numerous obstacles, of collecting great sums of money, and of misleading the public opinions concerning all these matters. He formed the electoral body by his intrigues, influenced it openly by means of his agents, and nominated the deputation from Paris to the convention, of which he became a member. He went to Belgium to augment his treasures; and had the hardihood to avow a fortune of 1400000 livres [£.58333], to wallow in luxury, whilst preaching up *sans-culolitisme*, and to sleep on heaps of slaughtered men.

* See Louvet's Narrative, p. 17. *Transf.*

As to Fabre d'Eglantine, muffled in a cowl, armed with a poniard, and employed in forging plots to defame the innocent, or to ruin the rich, whose wealth he covets, he is so perfectly in character, that whoever would paint the most abandoned hypocrite, need only draw his portrait in that dress.

These two men were very desirous of making me speak out, by vaunting their own patriotism. It was a subject on which I had nothing to conceal, or dissemble: I avow my principles equally to those, whom I suppose to participate in them, and to those, whom I suspect of not entertaining sentiments so pure: in regard to the former it is confidence—to the latter pride. I disdain to disguise myself, even under the pretence, or with the hope of being better able to fathom other people's mind. I form a first opinion of men intuitively, and judge them afterwards by their conduct compared at different times with the language they hold; but as to me, I lay open my whole soul, and never suffer a doubt to exist of what I really am.

As soon as the assembly had of its own accord passed a decree, allowing the minister of the home department 100,000 livres [£.4,167], to defray the expences of useful publications, Danton, and Fabre more particularly, asked me by way of conversation, whether Roland were prepared on that point, and if he had writers in readiness to employ. I answered, that he was no stranger to those who had already attained any celebrity; that the periodical works, composed according to right principles, would point out in the first place those whom it was proper to encourage; that it would be adviseable to see their authors; and sometimes to bring them together, that they might

might be informed of facts, the knowledge of which it would be useful to diffuse, and that they might agree on the most efficacious method of leading men's minds to the same point. That if either of them, Fabre or Danton, knew any in particular, they should mention and bring them to the minister; where they might converse, once a week for instance, on what in existing circumstances ought more especially to occupy their pens.

'We have the idea,' answered Fabre, 'of a paper to be posted up, entitled *Compte rendu au Peuple souverain**, which shall exhibit a sketch of the late revolution, and for which Camille-Desmoulins, Robert, and some others, will write.'—'Very well! introduce them to Roland.'— This he took care not to do, and said no more about the paper; which was however set on foot, as soon as the assembly had given the council two millions [£ 83,333] for *secret expenses*. Danton told his colleagues, that it was proper for each minister to make use of it in his own department; but that as those of the war department and foreign affairs had already similar funds, the above sum ought to be at the disposal of the other four, who would consequently have so many hundred thousands of livres each. Roland objected strongly to this proposal. He showed, that the intention of the assembly had been, to give the executive power, at this critical period, all the necessary means of acting with promptitude; that it was the council collectively that had a right to decide on the employment of the monies, on the demand being made, and the purposes specified, by the head of each department: and he declared, moreover, that, for his own part, he

---

* An account rendered to the sovereign people.

would

would never make any use of it, without producing vouchers to the council, to whose care the money was committed, and who had a right to watch over its expenditure *. Danton in reply, swore according to custom, and talked of the revolution, of decisive measures, of secrecy, and of freedom; while the others, seduced perhaps by the pleasure of *dabbling* each in his own way came over to his opinion, contrary to all justice, delicacy, and sound policy; and in spite of Roland's protest, and of his determined opposition, the harshness of which procured him ill-will. Danton quickly drew a hundred thousand crowns [£. 20,833] out of the public treasury, and disposed of them as he thought proper: which did not prevent his getting 60,000l. [£. 2,500] from Servan, and a still larger sum from Lebrun, out of the secret service money of their several departments, under various pretences. To the assembly he never gave any account; contenting himself with affirming, that he had accounted to the council: though he only told the council, at a meeting at which Roland was not present on account of indisposition, that he had given twenty thousand livres to one person, ten to another, and so of the rest, on account of the revolution, for their patriotism, or for reasons of a similar kind.

This is the way in which Servan related the story to me. The council, on being desired by the assembly to say, whether Danton had given them any account, answered simply *yes*. But Danton had acquired so much

---

* He expended of this fund only 1200l. [£. 50], in an order payable to Hell, formerly member of the constituent assembly, for the expense of a body of instruction for the people, in the german language, for the departments of the Rhine.

power, that these timid men were afraid of giving him offence.

Immediately after the brave Servan went out of office, Danton, no longer finding any opposition from the war-office, polluted the army with cordeliers *, as cowardly as they were avaricious, who promoted plunder and devastation; rendered the soldiers as ferocious to their countrymen as to their enemies; made the revolution odious to the neighbouring nations, by excesses of all kinds, which they practised in the name of the republic; and by preaching insubordination in every quarter, laid the foundation of the misfortunes that have since attended our arms.

After this no one will be astonished to hear, that Danton, wanting to send one of his creatures into Brittany, under pretence of visiting the sea-ports and examining the inspectors, prevailed on the minister of the marine to give him a commission. But commissions of this kind required the signature of all the members of the council, and Roland refused his. 'Either,' said he to Monge, 'your agents do their duty, or they do not; and of this you are competent to judge. If they do not, dismiss them without mercy: if they do, why damp their zeal and insult them, by sending a stranger among them, who has no connexion with your department, and would only prove your distrust. Such a proceeding by no means becomes the character of a minister; nor will I sign the commission.' The sitting of the council was unusually protracted, and towards the end of it the papers to be signed presented themselves in rapid succession.

* A faction which took its name from a particular club, that far outwent the Jacobins in revolutionary rage. *Transf.*

Roland perceiving, that he had juſt put his name, after thoſe of all his colleagues, to the rejected commiſſion, which had been ſlipt into his hand, cancelled it, and upbraided Monge. 'It is Danton who will have it ſo,' anſwered Monge in a whiſper, and with fear pictured in his countenance: if I refuſe, he will denounce me to the commune, and to the cordeliers, and get me hanged.'—'Well! in my mind, a miniſter ought to die, rather than give way to ſuch conſiderations.'

The bearer of this commiſſion was arreſted in Brittany, by order of an adminiſtration which took offence at his conduct, and to which the cancelled ſignature of Roland appeared a ſufficient reaſon to enter into a cloſe examination of his conduct. Heavy charges were preferred againſt him; but it was at the end of the year, when the cauſe of all anarchiſts was eſpouſed by the mountain, which obtained a decree, directing that Guermeur ſhould be ſet at large.

I have ſuffered myſelf to be hurried away by circumſtances; let me now reſume the chain of facts.

Danton and Fabre ceaſed to viſit me towards the latter end of Auguſt. No doubt they were cautious of expoſing themſelves to attentive eyes, while chanting the matins of September; and were well aware of the nature of Roland and the people he had about him. His firm temper of mind, his upright and ingenuous diſpoſition, the ſtrictneſs of his principles, diſplayed without oſtentation, and yet without conſtraint, and the uniform tenor of his conduct, are ſure to ſtrike every eye at the firſt glance. They concluded, that Roland was an honeſt man, who was not to be tampered with in undertakings like their's: that his wife had no weak ſide,

through

through which he might be affailed; and that, with an equal fhare of principle, fhe poffeffed perhaps more of that penetration peculiar to her fex, againft which deceitful people have the moft reafon to be upon their guard. Perhaps too they judged, that fhe could fometimes wield a pen; and that fuch a couple, endowed as they were with the faculty of reafoning, a firm temper of mind, and fome portion of talents, might ftand in the way of their defigns, and were fit only to be ruined. The events that enfued, illuftrated by a number of circumftances, which it would be difficult for me to detail at prefent, but of which a lively impreffion remains upon my mind, give to thefe conjectures all the evidence of demonftration.

It had been deemed expedient, as one of the firft meafures to be taken by the council, to difpatch commiffioners to the departments, for the exprefs purpofe of explaining the events of the 10th of Auguft, and ftill more for that of inducing the people to prepare for defence, and to be expeditious in raifing the neceffary recruits for the armies oppofed to the enemy upon the frontier of France. As foon as the felection of proper perfons, and the fending them upon their miffion began to be agitated, Roland defired a day's delay to confider whom he fhould propofe.—' I will take it all upon myfelf,' exclaimed Danton: ' the commune of Paris will furnifh us with excellent patriots.'—The indolent majority of the council accordingly intrufted him with the care of pointing them out: and the next day he came to the council with commiffions ready made out, fo that nothing more was neceffary than to fill them up with the names he recommended, and to affix the neceffary fignatures. The council made
little

little inquiry about them, and figned the commiffions without going into any debate. Thus did a fwarm of men fcarcely known; intriguers of fections, or bawlers at clubs; patriots from fanaticifm, and ftill more from views of intereft; people deftitute for the moft part of all kind of confequence, except what they had affumed, or hoped to acquire, in public commotions; but entirely devoted to Danton their protector, and enamoured of his manners and licentious doctrines; thus did thefe men, I fay, become the reprefentatives of the executive council in every department of France.

This bufinefs always appeared to me a great ftroke of policy on the part of Danton, and a moft egregious blunder on that of the council.

A man muft figure to himfelf the perplexity of each minifter in the midft of affairs of his own department, in thofe turbulent times, to be able to conceive that upright and able men could act with fo much inconfideration. The fact is, that the minifters of the home department, of war, and even of the marine, were overwhelmed with an excefs of bufinefs, and that official details fo completely engroffed their thoughts as to allow them no time to reflect on the general fyftem of politics. The council ought to be compofed of men employed folely in deliberating, and freed from all the cares of adminiftration. Danton was in the department that gives the leaft trouble; and cared little about fulfilling the duties of his place: he gave his *griffe* * to his clerks, who turned the wheel, and the machine went on its own way without his taking any concern in the matter. All his

* An iron ftamp ufed in France by people in office to repeat their fignature with greater difpatch. *Tranf.*

time and attention were dedicated to intrigues, and schemes, tending to promote his views of aggrandizement, fortune, and power. Continually haunting the offices of the war department, he procured appointments in the army for people of his own description; and found means to give them an interest in the contracts and purchases made on the public account. In short, he neglected no line in which it was possible to promote these men, the dregs of a corrupted nation, of which they become the scum in political fermentations, and over which they domineer for a short space of time: with these he augmented his credit, and composed a faction, that soon became powerful, and are now lords paramount of all.

The enemy advanced, and made an alarming progress on our territory. Men, who desire to govern the multitude, and who have studied the various means of working upon their minds, know terror to be one of the most powerful. This affection absolutely subjects those who experience it, to the men who allow it to hold no dominion over their minds; how much greater still are the advantages of those, who purposely inspire it by false rumours or pretences! That calculation had certainly been made by the instigators of the massacres of September; they must have had the two-fold object of producing a tumult, under cover of which, the violation of the prisons, and the murder of the prisoners, would afford them an opportunity of gratifying their private animosities, of executing schemes of plunder, the produce of which held out a pleasing prospect to their avarice; and at the same time of diffusing that kind of stupor, during which a small number of bold and ambitious men might lay the foundations

dations of their power. Inferior agents were easily brought over by the lure of profit: the pretence of immolating supposed traitors, from whom conspiracies were to be feared, could not fail to delude men of weak understandings, deceive the people, and serve to justify an action from which its directors would derive the blind obedience of their well paid satellites, the attachment of all who shared the profits with the leaders, and the submission of an intimidated people, surprised at the energy, or persuaded of the justice of an operation, which the perpetrators would find means to make it abet, by representing it as its own work. Accordingly whoever afterwards dared to reprobate those crimes was proclaimed a *calumniator* of the city of Paris, pointed out as such to the fury of a certain class of its inhabitants, and styled a *federalist*, and a *conspirator*. Such was the crime of the *twenty-two*, joined to the unpardonable guilt of superiority.

A loud and alarming report of the taking of Verdun got abroad on the first of September. The orators accustomed to harangue the groups collected in the streets, said that the enemy was in full march to Châlons: according to them three days more were sufficient to bring them to Paris; and the people, who calculated nothing but the distance, without taking into the account the various things necessary to the march of an army, for its sustenance, and the conveyance of its baggage and artillery, every thing, in short, that renders its progress so very different from that of an individual, already beheld the foreign troops triumphant amid the smoaking ruins of the capital.

Nothing was neglected, that could inflame the imagination, amplify objects, or augment the apprehension of danger; nor was it difficult to get the assembly to adopt measures calculated to promote such designs. Domiciliary visits, under the pretence of searching for concealed arms or discovering suspected persons, so frequent since the 10th of August, were resolved upon as a general regulation, and made in the dead of night. They gave occasion to fresh and numerous captions, and to vexations unheard of before. The commune of the tenth, composed in great part of men, who, having nothing to lose, have every thing to gain by a revolution; the commune already guilty of a thousand enormities, stood in need of more; for it is by the accumulation of crimes that impunity is secured. The misfortunes of the country were solemnly announced. The signal of distress, the black flag, was hoisted on the towers of the metropolitan church. The alarm-gun was fired. The commune proclaimed, by sound of trumpet, a general assembly of the citizens, on Sunday, the 2d, in the *Champ-de-Mars*, in order to rally round the altar of the nation those zealous patriots who would immediately set off for its defence. At the same time it directed the barriers to be shut, and yet no one was struck with these contradictory proceedings. There was a rumour of a plot hatching in the prisons by the aristocrats (or the rich), of whom great numbers were confined; and of the uneasy and repugnant feelings of the people at quitting their homes, and leaving behind them those ravenous wolves, who were about to break their chains, and would fall with fury upon their dear and defenceless relatives.

On the first symptoms of commotion, the minister of the interior, whose business it is to watch over the general tranquillity, but who has neither the immediate exercise of power, nor a right to employ the public

public force, wrote in an urgent manner to the commune, through the medium of the mayor, pointing out the vigilance that it became them to display. Nor did he content himself with this step; but applied also to the commandant general, exhorting him to strengthen the posts, and keep an eye on the prisons. He did still more; for hearing they were threatened, he called upon him in the most formal manner, to keep a strict guard over them, making his head responsible for events: and to give more efficacy to a requisition, to which his authority was confined, he had it printed and posted up at the corner of every street. That was hinting to the citizens at large, to be watchful themselves, in case the commandant should neglect his duty.

At five in the evening of Sunday, nearly at the very moment when the prisons were invested, as I have since been informed, about two hundred men repaired to the hotel of the home department, calling loudly for the minister, and for arms.

I was sitting in my own apartment, and as I thought I heard a noise, I rose, and perceiving the mob from the rooms that overlook the court, stepped into the antichamber, and inquired what was the matter. Roland was gone out; but the persons who asked for him not being satisfied with that information, insisted upon speaking with him at any rate. The servants refused to let them come up, and told them over and over again the real state of the case. Perceiving those assurances ineffectual, I sent out a domestic, to invite ten of them in my name to walk up stairs; they came in, and I asked them calmly what they wanted. They told me, they were honest citizens, ready to set off for Verdun, but being in great want of arms,

arms, they were come to afk the minifter for a fupply, and were refolved to fee him. I obferved to them, that the minifter of the interior never had arms at his difpofal; and that it was at the war-office, to the minifter of that department, they fhould addrefs their requeft. They faid in reply, that they had been there, and had been told there was no fuch thing; that all the minifters were rafcally traitors, and that they wanted Roland.—' I am forry he is gone out, for his folid arguments would have fome weight with you: come along with me, and fearch the hotel, and you will foon be fatisfied that Roland is not at home, and that there are no arms here; nor indeed ought there to be any, as upon reflection you muft needs fuppofe. Return to the war-office, or make your complaint to the commune: and if you wifh Roland to fpeak to you, repair to the hotel of the marine, where all the council is affembled.' —On their withdrawing, I went into the balcony over the court, and thence beheld a furious fellow in his fhirt, with his fleeves tucked up to his fhoulders, and a broadfword in his hand, declaiming againft the treachery of the minifters. The ten deputies difperfed themfelves among the crowd, and at length prevailed on it to retreat by beat of drum; but they carried the valet-dechambre away with them as an hoftage, made him follow them through the ftreets for an hour, and then let him return.

Immediately after I got into a coach, and haftened to the admiralty, to inform my hufband of what had juft paffed. The council was not yet fitting; but I found a numerous circle, in which were feveral members of the affembly. The minifters at war and of juftice not being

arrived,

arrived, the others were conversing in the council chamber like a private party. I related my story, on which each made his remark, most of them supposing it the fortuitous result of circumstances, and the effervescence of the public mind.

What was Danton doing all that time?—I knew not till several days after; but it is worth while to mention it here, in order that facts may be compared. He was at the *mairie* *, in the committee of vigilance, as it was styled, whence issued the orders of arrest that were become so numerous within the last few days. There a reconciliation had just taken place between him and Marat, after they had made a parade of a feigned quarrel for four-and-twenty hours. He went up to Pétion's apartment, took him aside, and said to him, in his customary language, interlarded with energetic expressions: 'Can you guess what they have taken into their heads? Why, may I die, if they have not issued a warrant against Roland?'—'Who do you mean?'—'Why, that madheaded committee, to be sure. I have the warrant in my possession: look, here it is. We can never suffer them to go on at this rate. What, the devil! against a member of the council!'—Pétion took the warrant, read it, and returned it to him with a smile: 'Let them proceed,' said he: 'it will have a good effect.'—'A good effect!' replied Danton, examining the mayor's countenance with an earnest eye. 'Oh! no, I can never suffer it: I'll find means to make them listen to reason.'—And so he did; for the warrant was never carried into execution. But who so blind, as not to see, that the two

* The residence of the mayor.

hundred men were sent to the minister of the home department by the devisers of the warrant? Who so dull, as not to suspect, that the failure of their attempt, by delaying the execution of the project, might give time to pause to those by whom it was conceived? And who so wanting in penetration as not to perceive, in Danton's conduct with the mayor, that of a conspirator endeavouring to discover what effect such a blow would produce, or to ascribe the honour of having parried it to himself when once it has failed, or been rendered dubious, by involuntary delay.

It was past eleven, when the ministers left the council; nor was it till the next morning that we learnt the horrors, of which the night had been witness, and which still continued to prevail in the prisons. Distressed beyond measure at these abominable crimes, the inability of preventing them, and the evident participation of the commune and the commandant general *, we agreed that there

* Grandpré, who by his office is bound to give an account of the state of the prisons to the minister of the home department, had found their sad inmates in the greatest affright, in the morning of the 2d of September. He had taken various measures to procure the liberation of many of them, and had succeeded with respect to a considerable number; but the rumours that prevailed, kept those who remained in the greatest consternation. That worthy citizen, on his return to the hotel, waited for the ministers at the breaking up of the council. Danton first made his appearance. He went up to him, told him what he had seen, related the steps he had taken, the requisitions made to the armed force by the minister of the home department, the little regard apparently paid them, the alarms of the prisoners, and the care which he, as minister of justice, ought to take on their account. Danton, vexed at this unlucky representation, cried out in his bellowing voice, and appropriate gestures: 'I don't care a d——n for the prisoners; let them take care of themselves!' and walked away in a rage.

there remained nothing for an honest minister to do, but to denounce them in the most public manner, to engage the assembly to put a stop to them, to rouse the indignation of all honest men, to do away in this manner the dishonour of consenting to them by silence, and to expose himself, if need be, to the daggers of the assassins, in order to avoid the guilt and shame of being in any way their accomplice.—' It is equally true,' said I to my husband, ' that a courageous determination is not more consonant to justice, than conducive to safety. Firmness alone can repress audacity. If the denunciation of these enormities were not a duty, it would be an act of prudence. The people who perpetrate them must necessarily hate you, for you have endeavoured to obstruct their proceedings: nothing remains for you now, but to inspire them with fear.'—Roland wrote to the assembly his letter of the third of September, which became equally celebrated with that he had addressed to the king. The

rage. That was in the second anti-chamber, in the presence of twenty people, who shuddered at hearing such a savage speech from the minister of justice. Danton enjoys the fruits of his crimes, after having attained successively the several degrees of influence; and persecuted and proscribed that probity, which declared war against him, and that merit, of which he dreaded the ascendency: Danton is become our master. His voice governs the assembly; his intrigues keep the people in motion; and his genius rules the committee, falsely denominated the committee of public safety, in which all the power of the government resides. Thus disorder every where prevails: the men of blood bear sway; the most rigid tyranny oppresses the people of Paris; and France, torn to pieces, and degraded, under such a master, can no longer change its oppressors. I feel his hand rivet the fetters that bind me, as I perceived his inspiration in the first attack made upon me by Marat. It is incumbent upon him to ruin those who know him, and resemble him not.

assembly

assembly were delighted, and ordered it to be printed, posted up, and sent to the departments: it applauded, as weak men applaud acts of courage they cannot imitate, but which affect their feelings, and inspire them with hope.

I remember to have read a little work, strongly aristocratic, published since that era at London, I believe by Pelltier: the author is greatly astonished, that the same person, who had been so audaciously wanting in respect to his king, should afterwards display so much justice and humanity. Either the spirit of party must render a man extremely inconsistent, or virtue is so scarce, that its very existence is become questionable. The friend of freedom and his fellow-creatures holds in the same thorough detestation, and denounces with equal energy, the tyranny of a mob, and the tyranny of a king, the despotism of a throne, and the disorders of anarchy, the wiles of a court, and the ferocity of a lawless banditti.

That same day, the 3d of September, a man, formerly a colleague of Roland, and to whom I had imagined I owed the civility of inviting him to dinner, took it into his head to bring with him the *orator of the human race*, without giving me any notice, or enquiring whether it would be agreeable. I considered his behaviour as attributable to the want of breeding of an honest man, imposed upon by the noisy fame of the orator. I gave a polite reception to *Clootz*, of whom I knew nothing but his bombast orations, and of whom I had heard nothing else unfavourable; but one of my friends on seeing him, whispered in my ear: 'Your guest has introduced to you an insufferable parasite, whom I am sorry to see here.'

The

The converfation turned on the events of the day. Clootz attempted to prove, that they were indifpenfable and falutary meafures; made many common-place obfervations on the rights of the people, the juftice of their vengeance, and its fubferviency to the happinefs of mankind; fpoke loud, and long; ate ftill more than he fpoke; and tired more than one of his auditors. Being foon after chofen a member of the convention, he returned occafionally of his own accord; feating himfelf in the firft place, and helping himfelf to the niceft difhes, without ceremony. My extreme and cold politenefs, accompanied with the care of always helping feveral perfons before him, was calculated to make him fpeedily perceive, that he had been " weighed in the fcale, and found wanting." He felt it, came no more, and revenged himfelf by calumnies. I fhould not have mentioned this contemptible fellow, but for the diftinguifhed part he acted amongft the flanderers of better men, and the art with which he contrived to make *federalifm* a fcarecrow for fools, and to fet it up as a title of profcription againft men of underftanding, who refufed to adopt his chimera of an univerfal commonwealth.

The laft time he came to vifit me he mounted his hobby-horfe, and rehearfed all his extravangancies concerning the poffibility of a convention formed of deputies from every corner of the world. Some of the company anfwered him with a jeft, while Roland, tired of the noife and pedantry, with which Clootz maintained his opinion, and attempted to make converts to it, had the goodnefs to affail him with a fyllogifm or two, and then turned away to another part of the room. The converfation cooled, and branched out into a variety of fubjects.

Buzot,

Buzot, whose solid understanding never amuses itself long with attacking castles in the air, was astonished, that federalism should be treated as a heresy in politics. He observed, that Greece, so celebrated and so prolific of great men and heroic actions, was composed of small confederate republics: that the United States, which in our own days exhibit the most interesting picture of a good social organization, are a composition of the same nature: and that Switzerland afforded a similar example. That at the present moment indeed, and in the actual situation of France, it was important for it to preserve its unity; because in this way it presented a more formidable mass to foreign powers, and a singleness of action which it was highly expedient to keep up for the completion of those laws, on which it depended for a constitution: that it could not however be denied, there would ever be a laxity in political bands, uniting a Fleming and a native of Provence; that it was difficult to diffuse that attachment, in which the strength of a republic consists, over a surface so extensive; because the love of our country is not strictly that of the land we inhabit, but of the citizens with whom we live, and the laws by which they are governed, without which the Athenians would never have transferred their existence from their city to their ships; that we can never thoroughly love any but those whom we know; and that the enthusiasm of men separated by a distance of six hundred miles can never be general, uniform, and lively, like that of the inhabitants of a little state.

These sage reflections, esteemed as such by most of those who heard them, were reported and denounced by Clootz as a conspiracy to federalize France, and to

detach

detach the departments from Paris. He reprefented Buzot as the moſt dangerous of the conſpirators, Roland as their chief, and the members who viſited me moſt frequently as abettors of this *liberticide project*. I know not whether a madman like Clootz may have been ſincere in his apprehenſions. I cannot perſuade myſelf of it; but rather, that he ſaw, in the fabrication of his lie, an opportunity of revenging his vanity, offended at not being admired; a ſubject for declaiming in his own way, extremely ſuitable to the turgidity of his ſtyle, and the diſorder of his imagination; the occaſion of injuring men, whoſe reaſon muſt neceſſarily diſpleaſe him, and of making a common cauſe with thoſe in whoſe vices he delights; even ſuppoſing him to have no ſecret miſſion to embroil France, by the help of extravagant patriots, in order to clear the way for his countrymen, the Pruſſians.

In the mean time the maſſacres continued; at the Abbey, from Sunday evening till Tueſday morning; at the Force, ſtill longer, and four days at Bicêtre. To my preſent abode, in the firſt of thoſe priſons, I am indebted for a knowledge of particulars, at which humanity ſhudders, and which I have not the heart to relate. One circumſtance, however, I will not paſs over in ſilence, becauſe it helps to demonſtrate, that it was a deep-laid ſcheme. It is this: the police having a receiving houſe in the Fauxbourg St. Germain, where it depoſits the priſoners which the Abbey cannot admit, when too much crowded, choſe Sunday evening for their removal, the very inſtant before the general maſſacre. The aſſaſſins were prepared, fell upon the carriages, which were five or ſix hackney-coaches, and with their ſwords and pikes

ſtabbed,

stabbed, and murdered, all that they contained, in the middle of the street, and unrestrained by their sad and heart-rending cries. All Paris witnessed these horrible scenes, perpetrated by a small number of cut-throats: so small indeed, that they scarcely exceeded a dozen at the Abbey, the gate of which was guarded by two national guards only, notwithstanding the requisitions made to the commune and the commandant. All Paris looked on—all Paris was accursed in my eyes; and I could no longer entertain hopes of the establishment of liberty among cowards, insensible to the last outrages that can be committed on nature and humanity, and coolly contemplating enormities, which the courage of fifty armed men could have prevented with ease.

The public force was badly organized, as it is still; for a lawless banditti, when determined to domineer, take care to oppose all kind of order, that may obstruct their proceedings. But is it necessary for men to know their captain, and march in battalion, when called upon to fly to the assistance of victims who have the knife of the assassin at their breast? The fact is, that the rumour of a pretended conspiracy in the prisons, improbable as it was, and the affected annunciation of the uneasiness and rage of the people, kept every one in a state of stupefaction; and made him believe, while trembling within doors, that it was the people who were the actors; whereas, it appears from the best accounts, that there were not two hundred villains concerned in the whole of those infamous proceedings. It is not the first night, therefore, that astonishes me: but four whole days!— and curious people went to the spectacle!—No! I

know

know of nothing in the annals of the moſt barbarous nations, comparable to thoſe atrocious acts.

Roland's health was impaired by it. The diſturbance of the nervous ſyſtem was ſo great, that his ſtomach rejected every thing, and the bile, obſtructed in its courſe, diffuſed itſelf over the ſurface of the ſkin. He grew yellow and weak, but retained his uſual activity; and while unable to eat, or ſleep, continued his labours without intermiſſion. He was ſtill ignorant of a warrant having been iſſued againſt him; for though it had come to my knowledge, I took great care to keep the ſecret, as it could only have tended to feed an affection that had already gained too much ground: ſomebody, however, I know not who, took it in his head to mention it the following week. It muſt be confeſſed, that it ſometimes happened to him to ſtate the particular fact in ſuch a way, that his enemies affected to believe, his inveighing againſt thoſe maſſacres aroſe only from the fears he had entertained of being comprehended in the number of the victims; while, in reality, to the juſt horror, with which they had inſpired him, he only joined his indignation, at having been included in the number of the proſcribed.

Danton was the man, who took the moſt pains to repreſent Roland's oppoſition to theſe events as the fruit of an ardent imagination, and of the cauſeleſs terror with which he was ſtruck. I always thought much might be inferred from that circumſtance.

Hiſtory will no doubt preſerve the infamous circular letter of the committee of vigilance of the commune, containing an apology for the September maſſacres, and an invitation to perpetrate the like throughout

France;

France; a letter of which great numbers were dispatched from the office of the minister of justice, and countersigned by his own hand.

Various circumstances concurring to shew that the prisoners from Orleans, whose removal had been ordered, and who were already on the road, could not be brought to Paris without danger, the minister of the interior gave orders, in conformity with the opinion of the council, to conduct them to Versailles; and a numerous escort was sent off for that purpose. Men who affected horror at the assassinations of Paris, contrived, by means of that disguise, to make part of it, and were the directors of the slaughter that took place on the arrival of the prisoners at Versailles.

The gold, silver, jewels, and other valuables, which abounded at that time in the prisons, in consequence of the wealth and condition of their inhabitants, were pillaged, as may be supposed.

And much more considerable still was the plunder collected by the members of the commune after the 10th of August, from the palace of the Tuileries, from the royal houses in the environs of Paris, to which it sent commissioners, and from the houses of private persons who were termed suspected, on whose property it had affixed its seal.

The commune had received considerable deposits, and had ordered the removal of considerable treasures, and yet no account appeared; nor could the minister of the interior obtain the information he had a right to demand concerning these matters. He complained to the assembly; as he did of the negligence of the commandant-general, from whom he requested in vain a more

numerous

numerous guard for the poſt of the *Garde-meuble*. In the mean time the *brigands* went every length, making a forcible ſeizure of watches, ſhoe-buckles, and ear-rings, upon the *boulevards*, and in the market-places, in open day. The aſſembly, as uſual, commended the miniſter's zeal; directed him to make a report of the ſtate of Paris; and took no meaſures whatever.

The robbery of the *Garde-meuble* was effected, and millions fell into the hands of perſons, who would naturally employ them to perpetuate that anarchy from which they derived their power.

On the day that ſucceeded this important theft, d'Eglantine called at our houſe at eleven in the morning; d'Eglantine, who had never made his appearance there ſince the matins of September; and who the laſt time he came, told me, as if from a deep conviction of the critical ſituation of France, that 'things would never go well without a concentration of powers: the executive council, ſaid he, muſt have the dictatorſhip; and the preſident muſt be the man to exerciſe it:'—D'Eglantine did not find me at home; for I had juſt gone out with madam Pétion. He waited two hours; and at my return, I found him in the court-yard. He walked up ſtairs with me, uninvited; and ſtayed an hour and half, without being aſked to ſit down. He lamented in a hypocritical tone the robbery of that night, which deprived the nation of ſo much real wealth; inquired, whether any information concerning the parties had been obtained; and wondered much at its not having been foreſeen. He talked afterwards of Robeſpierre and of Marat, who had begun their attacks upon Roland and myſelf, as of hot-headed men, who muſt be permitted to go on in their own way, who meant well, were extremely zealous, and took umbrage at every thing, but whoſe conduct ought to excite no alarm. I let him talk on, ſaid very little, and took care not to ſpeak out. At length he withdrew, and I have never ſeen him from that day to this; nor could I ever clearly comprehend the purpoſe of this ſingular viſit. It is a myſtery that time muſt unfold.

I have juſt ſaid, that Marat was beginning to ſlander us; and it ſhould be ſaid alſo, that, the moment the aſſembly had ordered a ſum to be left at the diſpoſal of the miniſter of the home department for printing uſeful works, Marat, who, the day after the 10th of Auguſt, had got *his people* to carry away four preſſes from the royal printing-houſe, by way of indemnifying him for thoſe which had been ſeized by the hand of juſtice, wrote to Roland for fifteen thouſand livres [£.625], to enable him to publiſh ſome very excellent things. Roland made anſwer, that the ſum was too great to be delivered, without knowing the purpoſe for which it was to be employed; but that if Marat would ſend him his manuſcripts, he would lay them before the council, who would determine whether it were proper to publiſh them at the expenſe of the nation. Marat replied in a bad ſtyle, a thing he is very capable of, and ſent a heap of manuſcripts, the very ſight of which was enough to frighten one. There was an eſſay on *the chains of ſlavery*, and I know not what beſides, bearing evident marks of the author's pen, which is characterizing them ſufficiently.

I had ſometimes doubted, whether Marat were not a fictitious a fictitious entity: but I was then convinced, that such a being really existed. I spoke of him to Danton, expressed a desire to see him, and begged he would bring him to our house; for monsters are deserving of attention, and I was desirous of knowing whether he were out of his wits, or a well-prompted actor. Danton declined it, as a thing perfectly useless, and even disagreeable, since it would be only making me acquainted with an original like nothing else in the world. Judging, from the manner in which he excused himself, that he would not gratify my longing, even if I insisted on it, I pretended not to have been serious in my request.

The council decided, that Marat's manuscripts should be put into the hands of Danton, who would find means to settle the matter in some way or other. This was cutting the gordian knot, instead of untying it. It did not become the minister of the home department to expend the public money in feeing a madman, nor was it prudent to make him an enemy: but a plain and direct refusal from the council would have set the question at rest. Entrusting this office to Danton was affording him fresh means of ingratiating himself with the mad dog in question, and of turning him loose upon every body he might wish him to worry.

Three weeks more had passed away, and the business of *Septembrizing* was at an end. Marat had the impudence to post up a demand of fifteen thousand livres from d'Orleans, complaining bitterly of the want of *civism* which Roland showed by refusing him that sum, and this when he had just stuck up a bill, in which I was attacked by name. I was not to be so deceived.—

' This,'

'This,' said I to my husband, ' is Danton all over: intending to attack you, he begins by prowling round your house. With all his sense he has the folly to imagine that I shall be hurt by his abuse; that I shall take up my pen to answer it; that he shall have the pleasure of bringing a woman forward upon the stage; and thus expose the man to whom she is allied to the shafts of ridicule. These people may form a tolerable opinion of my abilities, but are utterly incapable of judging of the temper of my soul. Let them continue their calumnies as long as they please—they will never make me stir a step, nor call forth my complaints, nor excite my uneasiness.

Roland made his report concerning the state of Paris on the 22d of September. It was exact and spirited: that is to say, it depicted the disorders that had been committed, and the impropriety of suffering any longer the want of subordination that prevailed among the constituted authorities, and their dangerous exercise of arbitrary power. He did justice to the zeal of the commune of the 10th, and acknowledged the great services it rendered to the revolution on that important day: but he shewed, that the prolongation of revolutionary measures produced precisely the reverse of what was hoped for; since tyranny was only destroyed with a view of introducing the reign of justice and order, not less averse from anarchy than from despotism itself; he concluded by pointing out the propriety and difficulty of obtaining accounts from the commune, from which he had repeatedly demanded them in vain.

The assembly, found in its intelect, but of a weak temper of mind, applauded the report, ordered it to be
printed,

printed, passed a few insignificant decrees, and rectified nothing. It is scarcely possible to conceive a situation more painful, than that of a firm and upright man, who, while at the head of an important department, appearing to possess considerable power, and lying under a heavy responsibility, is obliged to be the daily witness of shocking abuses, of which the denunciation alone belongs to him, and which the legislative authority either wants means or courage to repress. To cashier the commune, to order a new municipality to be elected according to the forms prescribed by law, to organize the public force, and to have a commander appointed by the sections; these were the only measures capable of restoring order, without which the laws would be appealed to in vain, and the convention would necessarily become subject to the municipal authority, which defied all restraint. In this state of things, I would rather have wished Roland to dedicate his talents to his country as a representative of the people, than as member of a council without energy, and minister of a government without power. I did not conceal this way of thinking from a few persons capable of estimating it properly; for as to the vulgar, they would never have been able to understand how any one could prefer a modest situation to the " pride, pomp, and circumstance," of a place in the ministry; and for want of seeing the matter in a proper light would have been apt to form very silly conjectures.

The department of the Somme, in which Roland had long resided, elected him a member of the convention. This choice excited almost universal regret. It appeared inconsiderate and absurd to take from the helm a man of integrity, courage, and understanding, whom it would

would be difficult to replace; in order to put him into an affembly, where fo many others might ferve the ftate by their votes as well as he, without poffeffing equal abilities. Roland faw no room for hefitation. He wrote to the affembly in confequence, requefting that his place might be filled up, and pointing out the perfon whom he thought beft qualified to fucceed him. This news occafioned extraordinary agitation: great was the outcry on all fides; and a motion was made, that he fhould be invited to remain in the miniftry. The convention had already formed itfelf into a body, compofed of the great number of members of the legiflative affembly who were re-elected, and of the new members who arrived firft from the country; or elfe the latter took their feats in the legiflative affembly. Which of the two was the cafe I do not perfectly recollect at this moment, when I have no documents by me: but Danton was prefent*, and rofe to oppofe this invitation with great warmth. His impetuofity betrayed his rancour, and led him to fay many ridiculous things: among others, that they ought to addrefs the invitation to me alfo, as a perfon by no means ufelefs to Roland's adminiftration. Murmurs of difapprobation repelled the invidious infinuation; but the decree did not pafs, though the general wifh was ftrongly expreffed. Neither was the offer of refignation accepted, and Roland remained ftill

---

* I remember that, for more than a month, he continued to officiate at the council, while he went and voted in the affembly. This concentration of power in one perfon appeared highly improper to Roland, who, during the laft fortnight that Danton proceeded in this manner, kept away from a council, influenced by a man who had no longer any right to fit there.

free

free to make his option. A crowd of members repaired to his houfe, to entreat him not to quit the miniftry. They preffed the matter home to him, as a facrifice he owed to his country, and affured him that the convention, when once complete, would bring the public affairs to a grand and decifive iffue, which his fpirit and activity would help to advance, and by which he would be fupported. Two days had paffed in thefe folicitations, when news was brought, that his election was void, becaufe made in lieu of another erroneoufly fuppofed to be null; and that confequently he had no reafon to quit the miniftry.

Accordingly he refolved to keep his place; and wrote to the affembly in a courageous and dignified ftyle, which was crowned with the plaudits of the majority, and made his enemies tremble. His election proved void in reality; but this was a circumftance that Danton's party endeavoured to conceal till he fhould have quitted the miniftry, in order that he might be thrown out of every fituation. That party no longer gave him any quarter: every day produced fome frefh attack: Marat's journal, pamphlets compofed for the purpofe, and denunciations at the Jacobins, kept repeating inceffant calumnies and accufations, each more ftupid or more atrocious than its predeceffor. But effrontery and perfeverance in things of this kind are fure to fucceed with a people naturally fickle and fufpicious. They even went fo far as to impute to him as a crime, what ought to have procured him praife; and had the art of infpiring honeft men of weak nerves with alarm at that very folicitude, which tended moft to the fafety of the republic; I mean his care to inform the public mind. It requires no profound skill in politics to know, that the strength of a government depends upon opinion; and accordingly all the difference that exists in this respect between a tyrannical administration, and one which takes justice for its guide, is, that the former is employed wholly in contracting the sphere of knowledge, and suppressing truth, while the latter makes it a rule to diffuse them as widely as possible.

The assembly rightly judged that the events of the 10th of August would produce different impressions, according to the prejudices or interests of individuals, and the manner in which they should be represented, directed a narrative of the facts to be drawn up, decreed that it should be printed, supported it by the publication of all the documents that tended to prove its accuracy, ordered the minister of the home department to dispatch them to every part of France, and enjoined him to promote the writing of pamphlets conducive to the same end.

Roland felt that, in the circumstances of the times, the art of diffusing information needed improvement, and that it was requisite to produce a stream of light, that might in some measure supply the want of public instruction, ever too much neglected. By means of the inquiries he set on foot in the departments, he found out and retained a small number of zealous and enlightened men, on whose fidelity, in distributing such writings as might be sent to them, he thought he could rely. He made it a rule to answer every body, and to keep up a correspondence with all the popular societies, country clergymen, and private persons, who might apply to him. He sent to the societies a circular letter, reminding

ing them of the spirit of their institution, and calling them back to the fraternal care of instructing and enlightening each other, from which they had but too great a tendency to depart, in order to debate on public measures, and interfere with the government. He selected from among his clerks three or four intelligent men to carry on this *patriotic correspondence*, and dispatch the printed tracts, intrusting the principal management to him among them who had most sensibility of heart, strictness of principle, and amenity of style; and this correspondence he frequently animated by his own circular letters, dictated by circumstances, and always breathing that morality, and couched in those terms of affection, which engage men's hearts. It is impossible to conceive the excellent effect that these things produced: troubles of every kind subsided; the administrative bodies executed their functions with regularity; and five or six hundred societies, and a considerable number of country clergymen, employed themselves with laudable zeal in diffusing instruction, and in attaching to the public weal men hitherto occupied in their manual labours, but at the same time lost in ignorance, and more disposed to hug their chains, than to maintain that freedom, of which they neither knew the extent, nor the limits, nor the duties, nor the rights.

This *patriotic correspondence* is a valuable monument, equally attesting the pure principles and enlightened vigilance of the minister, the good will of a great number of intelligent citizens, and the admirable fruits of wisdom, patriotism, and reason.

In the thing itself, and in its effects, suspicious and jealous men saw less the triumph of freedom, the maintenance

tenance of tranquillity, and the confolidation of the republic, than the fame and reputation that might accrue to the firſt mover. From that moment Roland was reprefented as a dangerous man, who had *offices of public spirit*; foon after as a corruptor of the people's opinions, and a man ambitious of the fupreme power; and laſt of all, as a confpirator.

All that was wanting was to read his writings, and examine his correfpondence. The departments, that received his letters, anfwered him with their warmeſt thanks; but the banditti of Paris, always calumniating, and never proving any thing, excited by means of a thoufand ſtratagems, a fort of diſtruſt in the public mind, which the jacobins feconded with all their power, for they were no longer fwayed by any body but the Dantons, the Robefpierres, and the Marats.

NOTE.

St. Pélagie, Auguſt 8, 1793.

MORE than two months have I been imprifoned, becaufe I am allied to a worthy man, who thought proper to retain his virtue in a revolution, and to give in exact accounts though a miniſter. For five months he folicited in vain the paſſing of thofe accounts, and the pronouncing of judgment on his adminiſtration. They have been examined: but, as they have afforded no room for blame, it has been deemed expedient to make no report on the fubject, but to fubſtitute calumny in its place. Roland's activity, his multifarious labours, and his inſtructive writings, had procured him a degree of confideration which appeared formidable; or fo at leaſt envious

vious men would have it, in order to effect the downfal of a man whose integrity they detested. His ruin was resolved upon, and an attempt was made to take him into custody at the time of the insurrection of the 31st of May; the epoch of the complete debasement of the national representation, of its violation, and of the success of the decemvirate. He made his escape, and in their fury they fastened upon me; but I should have been arrested at any rate; for though our persecutors know that my name has not the same influence as his, they are persuaded that my temper is not less firm, and are almost equally desirous of my ruin.

The first part of my captivity I employed in writing. My pen proceeded with so much rapidity, and I was in so happy a disposition of mind, that in less than a month I had manuscripts sufficient to form a duodecimo volume. They were intitled Historical Notices, and contained a variety of particulars relative to all the facts, and all the persons, connected with public affairs, that my situation had given me an opportunity of knowing. I related them with all the freedom and energy of my nature, with all the openness and unconstraint of an ingenuous mind, setting itself above selfish considerations, with all the pleasure which results from describing what we have experienced, or what we feel, and lastly with the confidence, that, happen what would, the collection would serve as my moral and political testament.

I had completed the whole, bringing things down to the present moment, and had entrusted it to a friend, who rated it at a high price. On a sudden the storm burst over his head. The instant he found himself put under arrest, he thought of nothing but the danger, he felt

felt nothing but the neceffity of averting it, and without cafting about for expedients, threw my manufcript into the fire. This lofs diftreffed me more than the fevereft trials have ever done. This will eafily be conceived, when it is remembered that the crifis approaches, that I may be murdered to-morrow, or dragged, I know not how, before the tribunal which our rulers employ to rid them of the perfons they find troublefome; and that thefe writings were the anchor to which I had committed my hopes of faving my own memory from reproach, as well as that of many deferving characters.

As we ought not, however, to fink under any event, I fhall employ my leifure hours in fetting down, without form or order, whatever may occur to my mind. Thefe fragments will not make amends for what I have loft, but they will ferve to recall it to my memory, and affift me in filling up the void on fome future day, provided the means of doing fo remain in my power.

PORTRAITS AND ANECDOTES.

BUZOT.

A MAN of an exalted mind, high spirit, and impetuous courage, endowed with great sensibility, ardent, melancholy, and indolent, cannot but sometimes run into extremes. A great admirer of nature, feeding his imagination with all the charms she has to offer, and his mind with the principles of the most amiable philosophy, he seems formed to taste and to confer domestic happiness: he would forget the whole world in the placid enjoyment of private virtues with a heart worthy of his own. But, thrown into public life, he attends to nothing but the laws of rigid equity, and defends them at all hazards. Easily roused to indignation against injustice, he assails it with ardour, and is incapable of entering into a composition with guilt. The friend of human nature, susceptible of the tenderest feelings, and capable of the sublimest flights and most generous resolutions, he loves his fellow-creatures, and, like a true republican, is ever ready to sacrifice himself for their good: but a severe judge of individuals, and cautious in selecting the objects of his esteem, he bestows his friendship upon few. This reserve, added to the energetic freedom with which he
expresses

expresses himself, has drawn upon him a charge of haughtiness, and made him many enemies. Mediocrity scarcely ever forgives merit; but vice detests and persecutes that courageous virtue, which sets it at defiance. Buzot is the gentlest man on earth with his friends, but the roughest adversary a knave can have to do with. While yet a young man, the ripeness of his judgment, and purity of his morals, obtained him the esteem and confidence of his fellow-citizens. Their confidence and esteem were justified by his devotion to truth, and by his firmness and perseverance in speaking it. Men of vulgar minds, who depreciate what they cannot attain, call his penetration a revery, his warmth passion, his strong remarks satire, and his opposition to all violent measures a revolt against the majority. He was accused of *royalism*, because he asserted, that morals were necessary in a republic, and that nothing should be omitted that may tend to maintain or correct them; of *calumniating Paris*, because he abhorred the massacres of September, and ascribed them to a handful of cut-throats hired by robbers; of *aristocracy*, because he wished to call upon the people to exercise its sovereignty by passing judgment on Lewis XVI; of *federalism*, because he insisted upon the maintenance of equality among all the departments, and opposed the municipal tyranny of an overweening commune. Such were his crimes. He had his errors also. Possessing a nobleness of countenance, and elegance of shape, he dressed himself with that care, neatness, and decorum, which bespeak a love of order, a sense of propriety, and that respect which a well-bred man owes to the public and to himself.

Thus, when the scum of the nation put the helm in the

the hands of men, who made patriotism consist in flattering the people, in order to mislead them; in overturning and invading every thing, by way of procuring consequence and wealth; in libelling the laws, that they might govern according to their own discretion; in protecting licentiousness, as a mean of procuring impunity for their crimes; in cutting throats, on purpose to perpetuate their power; and in swearing, drinking, and dressing like porters, in order to fraternise with wretches like themselves; Buzot still professed the morality of a Socrates, and retained the politeness of a Scipio.— What a villain!—Accordingly the *upright* Lacroix, the *judicious* Chabot, the *gentle* Lindet, the *modest* Thuriot, the *learned* Duroi, the *humane* Danton, and their faithful imitators, have declared him a traitor to his country: they have had his house razed, and his property confiscated, as in former days Aristides was banished, and Phocion condemned to die. I am astonished at their not passing a decree, making it felony to remember his name. It would have been more consistent with their views, than their attempts to preserve it coupled with epithets, that are disproved by the evidence of facts.

They cannot expunge from the page of history Buzot's conduct in the constituent assembly; nor suppress his judicious motions, and vigorous sallies, in the convention. However his opinions may be falsified by faithless journals, the principles by which they are supported are still to be perceived through the disguise. Buzot frequently spoke off-hand; was indolent in other respects; but never failed to stand up against all perverse systems of politics, and every plan that appeared prejudicial to liberty. His report on the departmental guard,

guard, a project so much decried, contains arguments that have never been answered. That concerning the law proposed against instigators to murder displays the soundest policy, and a spirit of philosophy, as true as it is natural, and as strong as the reason by which it is upheld. His proposal for the banishment of the Bourbons is developed with precision, supported by the most accurate reasoning, and written with equal elegance and feeling. His opinion on the judgment of the king, while it abounds with facts and arguments, is free from that declamation and irrelevance of matter, in which so many others indulged in their harangues upon that important subject. And lastly, his letters to his constituents, of the 6th and 22d of January, depict his mind with such truth, as will make them long an object of attention. A few combatants of his strength might have given the convention the impulsion which it wanted: but the rest of the men of talents, keeping themselves back as *orators* for great occasions, were too neglectful of the petty warfare which was carried on every day; nor were they sufficiently aware of the tactics to which their adversaries were forced by their mediocrity to resort.

PÉTION,

A TRULY honest and good-natured man, is equally incapable of doing the least thing repugnant to justice, of inflicting the slightest injury, or of giving the smallest uneasiness to any one. In regard to himself, he can neglect

glect many things, but knows not how to refuse a favour to any person in the world. The serenity of a good conscience, the mildness of an easy temper, with frankness and cheerfulness, are depicted in his countenance. He was a prudent mayor, and faithful representative: but he is too sanguine, and too peaceable, to foresee or to lay a storm. Sound judgment, good intentions, and what is termed justness of thought, are the characteristics of his opinions and writings, which bear stronger marks of good sense than of talents. As an orator he is cold; as a writer his stile is loose. An equitable minister, and a good citizen, he was formed for the practice of the social virtues in a republic, and not to found a republican government among a corrupt people, who for some time idolized him, and then rejoiced at his proscription, as at that of an enemy.

At the time of the constituent assembly, during the revision of the laws, I was one day with Buzot's wife, when her husband returned at a late hour from the assembly, and brought Pétion with him to dinner. It was at that period when the court affected to consider them as factious men, and described them as intriguers entirely occupied in exciting disturbances. After dinner, Petion, who was sitting on a large sofa, began to play with a young pointer, with all the earnestness of a child, till at length they both grew tired, and fell asleep *in one another's arms.* The conversation of four persons did not prevent Pétion from snoring. 'Do but look at that sower of sedition,' said Buzot, with a smile: 'we were eyed askance as we were quitting the hall; and our accusers, very busy about party intrigues themselves,

themselves, imagine that we are engaged in similar manœuvres.'

The circumstance, and the remark, have often recurred to my mind, since these unfortunate latter times when Pétion and Buzot are accused and proscribed as royalists, with as much reason as the court then had to charge them with intrigue. Always alone with their principles, or associating with none but men who professed the same, in order to discuss their opinions; they thought it would suffice to contend obstinately for justice, to speak the truth constantly, and to sacrifice themselves, or at least to run every hazard, rather than betray so good a cause.——And yet these are the men that are declared *traitors to their country*.

I will here record a fact of some consequence. It has been seen elsewhere, that during the first patriotic administration, it had been agreed upon, that the minister for foreign affairs should take from the fund allotted to his department for secret service money certain sums, which were to be put into the hands of the mayor of Paris, as well for the police, which was reduced to nothing for want of means, as for publications to counteract the influence of those of the court. Dumouriez having quitted that department, the matter was mentioned to d'Abancourt, that is to say, as far as regarded the money wanting for the police alone. D'Abancourt would do nothing in it himself; but pretended, that it was a business, which the king should be brought to approve, and of which his majesty would not fail to see the justice. The proposal was not at all to the taste of the king, who answered in direct terms,

terms, that he would not buy rods to whip himself. In this he spoke sensibly enough, as he was not a sincere friend to the constitution; and such an answer might have been expected. But a few days after, Lacroix, the present colleague of Danton, in concert with whom he is plundering Belgium; Lacroix, the persecutor of honest men, and the sovereign of the day, who then had a seat in the legislative assembly, and who was known to frequent the palace, called upon Pétion to promise him the free disposal of three millions of livres [£125,000] if he would employ them in such a way as to support his majesty; a proposition which must needs have been more offensive to Pétion, in his character of mayor, than the other could have been to Louis XVI. It was accordingly rejected, notwithstanding the peculiarly kind reception he met with at that very time from the king; for being sent for to the palace, instead of finding the monarch, whom he had never before seen alone, surrounded as usual, he was introduced into his closet, where there appeared to be no one else, and where Louis XVI. lavished upon him many marks of affability and regard, and even those little captivating cajoleries, which he had the art of distributing at will. A slight rustling of silk behind the hangings made Pétion imagine that the queen was present without being visible, and the caresses of Louis convinced him of his hypocrisy: he remained firm and honest, without yielding to the king, who was trying to corrupt him, in like manner as, without flattering the people, he wished to appeal to them on the trial of that very king; while Lacroix, who had served him, and had probably been well paid for his services, thought that he could not be too speedily condemned to die.

PACHE.

PACHE.

It has been said with reason, that the talent of knowing mankind is of the first importance to those who govern, their errors in that particular being always the most fatal. But the exercise of this talent, at all times so difficult, becomes infinitely more so in the time of a revolution; there is besides a degree of hypocrisy, by which it is no disgrace to be duped, since a man must be wicked himself to suspect its existence.

In my youthful days, I had met, at the house of one of my relations, a clerk in the post office, of the name of Gibert, who possessed that mildness of manners which generally accompanies a taste for the fine arts. Gibert, a man of a cultivated mind, and an affectionate father, amused himself with painting, made a study of music, and by his strict probity obtained the esteem of all his acquaintance. He was extremely attached to a man, his most particular friend, whose extraordinary merit he extolled with all the enthusiasm of an affectionate heart, and with all the modesty of a person who thought himself far his inferior. I was sometimes in company with this friend; in whom there was nothing remarkable at first sight, but his extreme simplicity. I had, however, no opportunity of forming a judgment of him, for I met with him but seldom, and did not often see Gibert himself; I only learnt, that his friend, who was *Pache*, being enamoured of a country life, the only one suited to his patriarchal manners, and in love with liberty, of which his well informed mind enabled him to estimate all the

advantages,

advantages, was about to resign a genteel place under the French government, to settle with his family in Switzerland. I afterwards leant, that having lost his wife, and perceiving that his children regretted Paris, and that the revolution was paving the way for our national emancipation, he had taken the resolution of returning; and that being satisfied with the independence he had derived from the sale of his former property, and the fortunate purchase of a national estate, he had sent back the grant of a pension to a quondam minister by whose interest it had been obtained.

It was not necessary to be often in Gibert's company, and to know his intimacy with Pache, to be informed of every thing that could be said to the latter's advantage. In the month of January, 1792, he brought him to our house, and I saw him from time to time. Pache, as I have already observed, wears an appearance of the utmost modesty. It is so great indeed, that you would be tempted to adopt the opinion he seems to entertain of himself, and take him for a thing of no great value. But credit is given him for that modesty, when it is discovered that he reasons well, and is by no means wanting in information. As he is extremely reserved, and never unbosoms himself freely, people soon suspect him to know more than he says, and end with ascribing to him more merit than he possesses, because they were very near committing the injustice of allowing him none. A person who talks little, listens with an air of intelligence to every subject of discussion, and ventures a few well-timed observations, easily passes for a man of sense. Pache had made an acquaintance with Meunieurs and Monge, both members of the academy of sciences;

sciences; and had helped them to form a popular society in the section of the Luxembourg, the object of which, they said, was the diffusion of information, and the encouragement of patriotic sentiments. Pache was very assiduous in this society; and appeared to dedicate to his country, as a citizen, all the time which he did not devote to his children, and which intervened between the public lectures, whither he attended them.

I have related elsewhere how Roland was called to the ministry at the end of March of the same year. The offices were filled with agents of the old government, little disposed to favour the new; but they were accustomed to the routine of business; and it would have been wrong to hazard unhinging the whole of a great machine, in those troublesome times, for the sake of changing a few clerks. Nothing more then was to be done but to keep a strict eye over them, and to make preparations for their removal in due time. But in the multiplicity of business, the daily current of which hurries a man in office along with inconceivable rapidity, it cannot be denied, that he may easily commit himself, if he do not pay the most scrupulous attention to every thing, an attention which becomes infinitely irksome, when the consequence of distrust. In this situation, Roland was desirous of finding a trusty man, whom he might have always with him in his closet, and whom he might get to read over a letter, or a report, on any urgent business, when other business still more urgent would not permit him to revise it himself: not to make any alteration in the composition, but merely to see that the adverse principles of the clerks had not influenced the manner of stating facts, or drawing conclusions; a man, in short, who might be be trusted to seek for a particular paper, in a particular office, or to deliver a verbal message on any matter of importance. The idea of Pache occurred. Pache had been a clerk in the admiralty; was well acquainted with the routine of office; possessed abilities, patriotism, morals, which would procure a man in office credit for his appointment, and that simplicity which never excites ill-will. The idea appeared excellent. It was mentioned to Pache, who immediately expressed the utmost eagerness to serve Roland, by making himself useful to the public weal; but on condition of preserving his independence, by taking neither title nor salary. This was beginning well. It was supposed that, when a new arrangement should take place in the office, it would be easy to see for what he was particularly fit; and Pache came to Roland's closet every morning at seven, with his morsel of bread in his pocket, and staid till three, without its being possible to prevail on him to take any thing: attentive, prudent, zealous, doing his duty diligently, making an observation, putting in a word, to bring the argument back to the point in question, and soothing Roland, who was sometimes vexed at the aristocratical contradiction of his clerks.

Roland, whose disposition was ardent, and his feelings strong, rated the mildness and complaisance of Pache very highly, and treated him as a valuable friend: while I, grateful for the service I supposed him to render my husband, lavished on him marks of esteem, and proofs of attachment. The style of Pache was a bad one: it did not do to set him about composing a letter: it was sure to be dry and flat; but he was not wanted for that purpose, and was useful on those occasions which had been supposed to require the superintendance of a trusty person. Our friend *Servan*, lately appointed minister at war, was alarmed at the complication and derangement of certain branches of his department, and envied us Pache. 'Let me have that honest man,' said he to Roland: 'you have no further occasion for him, you are above your business a hundred times over; and now that the chaos of the first outset has assumed shape and order, you no longer need the superintendance of another; but as to me, I am overwhelmed with business, and in the utmost want of persons in whom I can confide.'—These ministers were also of opinion, that some share of capacity was wanting to fill a place, and that a man ought not to be employed without reasonable grounds to suppose him possessed of the necessary qualifications. Roland consented, and Pache, upon being consulted, yielded with as good a grace, on the same conditions that he had made with Roland. After his being thrown into this situation, we scarcely ever saw him; but Servan spoke highly in his praise.

A change in the ministry took place. Roland kept himself secluded from the world; and Pache returned to his section. The tenth of August followed soon after; and the legislative assembly recalled the patriotic ministers. Roland arranged his offices; and as Pache persisted in his resolution to retain his independence, Roland appointed Fépoul, whom Pache had introduced; an intelligent, industrious, and careful man, very well calculated for the accomptant department, dexterous in his conduct, never setting himself up in opposition to any one, and ever adhering to the strongest party.

Roland,

Roland, elected a member of the convention, and disgusted at the horrors of September, was desirous of retiring from the ministry; and, knowing the extreme embarrassment the wisest heads would have been in to find him a successor, thought he should render an essential service to the public by mentioning Pache. This he did with all the franknefs that belonged to his character, and all the warmth of a feeling heart, proud of acknowledging merit, wherever it seems to reside.

Pache, to whom he had not hinted his intention, and who had a little before refused the superintendance of the jewel office, a place for which he proposed *Restout*, whom Roland appointed upon his recommendation, appeared well satisfied to remain his own master. He accepted, however, a mission from Monge for Toulon, repaired thither, and committed several acts of folly, as I was afterwards informed.

Servan's health obliging him to quit the war-office, the man whom Roland had recommended was appointed to fill that department, as the person on whom in point of principle the strongest dependance might be placed, and who, as to talents, could not but be sufficiently qualified for such a place. We wrote to Pache, to inform him of his appointment, and pressed him to accept it. But this was in all likelihood unnecessary; for, jealous as he was of his independence, he appeared not to have the least uneafiness concerning the burden about to be laid on his shoulders, and took it up without hesitation. On his return to Paris he came to see us, and we talked with him freely on the disposition of men's minds; of the party which the Parisian deputies were forming; of the enormities of the commune;
of

of the dangers that appeared to threaten the liberty of the convention, and particularly of thofe, which might arife from the predominance of immoral and guilty men, who only fought to acquire power in order to efcape punifhment or to gratify their paffions; of the order to be eftablifhed in his department, and of our joy at feeing him in the council, where his prefence would preferve a union of will and finglenefs of action. Pache liftened to the effufions of confidence with the filence of a man who conceals his own fentiments; oppofed every opinion of Roland at the council-table; and came to fee him no more.

At firft we imagined, that this conduct arofe from a movement of felf-love, a fort of fear of appearing the creature of Roland. But I learnt, that this man, who never accepted the invitations of his colleague, under pretence of the retirement in which the multiplicity of his bufinefs obliged him to live, received Fabre, Chabot, and other mountaineers at his table; that he paid his court to their friends; that he took their creatures into office, all of them, either as great knaves as the valet in a comedy *, or ignorant fellows, or intriguers like themfelves; and that honeft men began to murmur and defpair. I thought it right to try the only means that remained of opening his eyes, if he were merely mifled, or of pulling away the mafk if he were really acting with ill faith. I wrote to him then on the 11th of November, in a friendly ftyle, to communicate to him the murmurs that began to prevail, the caufes to which they were owing, and what his own in-

* In the old French comedies, the lackey is invariably a knavifh buffoon, who flicks at nothing. *Tranf.*

tereft

tereft feemed to require. I reminded him of what had been faid in confidence on his entrance into the miniftry; and I added a word or two concerning the unequivocal fentiments we had expreffed, the unanimity they promifed, and the prefent ftate of things, fo oppofite to what they would have led one to expect.

Pache made me not the fmalleft anfwer; and we foon after heard that his firft clerks Haffenfratz, Vincent, and the reft (miferable beings, whom I would not mention, had not their enormities already infured their names a place in the hiftory of the popular commotions of thefe latter times) were declaiming at the jacobins, and elfewhere againft Roland, and holding him up as the enemy of the people. There could no longer then be any doubt but that Pache was feeking his downfal. The atrocity and bafenefs of this conduct filled me with indignation and contempt: fentiments, in which I was beforehand with feveral who had become acquainted with Pache by means of us, and who were then inclined to charge me with levity, though their averfion to the man has fincé exceeded mine. The peculation, or the profufe expenditure at leaft, that took place in the war department during his adminiftration, was horrible; every thing was diforganifed, owing to the bad choice of the perfons employed; it was proved, that regiments reduced to a fmall number of men were paid as if complete; it was not only impoffible to furnifh an account, but even to imagine the means of doing fo, for more than 130 millions of livres [near five millions and a half fterling]. In the twenty-four hours that followed his difmiffion, rendered indifpenfable by fo much mifchief, he filled up fixty different places, with all the perfons he knew of who were base enough to pay their court to him, from his son-in-law, who from a curate became commissary-general with a salary of 19000 livres [£.792], to his hair-dresser, a blackguard boy of nineteen, whom he made a muster-master. These are the exploits which the people of Paris rewarded by calling him to the mayoralty, where, supported by the Chaumets, Heberts, and other tatterdemalions, he favoured the oppression of the legislative body, the violation of the national representation, and the proscription of all virtuous men, and thus helped to seal the ruin of his country.

And this was the man who was in search of a free country, who gave up pensions, and refused a place! But Pache went into Switzerland, where his family originally resided—(a circumstance that enabled his father to keep a great man's door at Paris *,) hoping there to lead a more agreeable life, than in a place which reminded him of the obscurity of his birth; and Pache received from *Castries* a pension, which bore witness to the state of dependence that he had lived in at his house, and might have excited suspicion, when the nobles and ministers of the old government were objects of persecution. This was a part of his history, which I was unacquainted with, and which is no way inconsistent with Pache returning to France after the taking of the Bastile, currying favour in a little popular society well contrived for the acquisition of influence, obstinately refusing second-rate places, but not hesitating a moment to become a member of the council, and

---

* The reputation of the Swifs for probity was so great in France, that all the noblemen had them in their service as porters. A porter and a Swifs became at last synonymous words. *Transf.*

take upon himself that department in the administration, which circumstances rendered most important. He is in politics the Tartuffe * of Moliere.

Whilst I am writing this, Biron is confined in the prison that I inhabit. Towards the end of Pache's ministry, Biron came to denounce him to the assembly, and was consequently provided with documents capable of proving his misdemeanours. Biron met with him; was seduced by his air of simplicity; persuaded himself that he had erred rather from unskilfulness than dishonesty; thought it cruel to bring a man to the block who might have been deceived; relinquished his design; and then mentioned it to Pache himself. Pache came to an explanation; contrived to wheedle Biron out of all the information and documents that related to the complaint of which he was the object; and then had him sent to the army of Italy, where he was left destitute of every thing. Biron obtained some advantages; they were never mentioned: he made complaints; no attention was paid to them: time ran on; the evils increased: he grew urgent; an order was sent him to repair to Paris: as soon as he arrived he was taken into custody, and confined at St. Pélagie. In this stroke he recognizes the hand of Pache, and has no doubt as to the tyrant by whom he is oppressed.

* A consummate hypocrite. *Transf.*

GIRONDE.

GIRONDE.

GUADET and GENSONNE

Love each other, probably because there is no resemblance between them. Guadet is as impetuous as Gensonné is cool: but the violent sallies of his fiery temper are never succeeded by malice; nor is his soul susceptible of an intention to offend. Nature has made Guadet an orator; Gensonné has made himself a logician. The one frequently loses, in deliberating, the time which should be employed in action: the other dissipates, in bold, but short and transient, flights, that warmth, which ought sometimes to be concentrated, and always to be longer supported, in order to produce a durable effect.

Guadet had brilliant moments in each of the two assemblies, the legislative and conventional: they were owing to the ascendency of honesty, seconded by talents: but possessed of feelings too strong to keep up a long struggle without tiring, he has drawn upon himself the hatred of the wicked, without exciting much of their fear; nor did he ever attain the degree of influence which his enemies were fond of ascribing to him, in order to render him an object of distrust. Gensonné, useful in debate, which, however, he has the fault of drawing out to too great a length, took an active part in the committees, and drew up part of the plan of the intended constitution. His speech on the business of the king is enlivened by sarcastic strokes, to which an apparent coolnefs gave an edge, and which the fons of the mountain will never forgive.

Both of them tender hufbands, good fathers, excellent citizens, virtuous men, and fincere republicans, they only funk under the accufation of the confpirators, becaufe they did not even know how to *coalefce* in favour of the good caufe, the only one for which they contended, and for which they deferved to live.

Vergniaux

WAS, perhaps, the moft eloquent man in the affembly. He did not fpeak without preparation, like Guadet: but his made fpeeches, of great argumentative ftrength, full of fire, abounding in matter, refplendent with the moft beautiful forms of oratory, and fupported by a dignified delivery, may ftill be read with the greateft pleafure.

And yet I love not Vergniaux: he appears to me a philofopher totally abforbed in felf. Difdaining mankind, no doubt becaufe he knows them well, he gives himfelf no concern on their account: but with this way of thinking, a man fhould keep out of all public employs; if he do not his idlenefs becomes a crime; and in this refpect Vergniaux is highly culpable. What a pity, that talents like his fhould not have been employed with the ardour of a man devoted to the public weal, and with the perfeverance of an active mind!

Grangeneuve

Grangeneuve

Is the best of men, with a countenance of the least promise. His understanding is of the common level; but his soul is truly great: and he performs noble actions with simplicity, and without suspecting how much they would cost any other but himself.

In the course of July, 1792, the conduct and disposition of the court indicating hostile designs, every one talked of the means of preventing or frustrating their execution. On this subject Chabot said, with that ardour which proceeds from a heated imagination, and not from strength of mind, that it was to be wished that the court might attempt the lives of some of the patriotic members, as it would infallibly cause an insurrection of the people, the only mean of setting the multitude in motion, and producing a salutary crisis. He grew warm on this head, on which he made a copious comment. Grangeneuve, who had listened to him without saying a word, in the little society where the discourse took place, embraced the first opportunity of speaking with Chabot in private. 'I have been struck with your reasons,' said he: 'they are excellent: but the court is too cunning ever to afford us such an expedient. We must make it for ourselves. Find you but men to strike the blow; and I will devote myself as the victim.'—'What! you will * * * * ?'—' Certainly. What is there so wonderful in that ? My life is of no great utility: my person of little account: I shall feel the greatest pleasure in offering myself up as a sacrifice for my country's good.'——' Ah, my friend, you shall not fall alone:' exclaimed Chabot, with a look of enthufiafm: 'I am determined to fhare the glory with you.'—'As you pleafe: *one* is enough: *two* may be better. But there will be no glory in the bufinefs; for it is neceffary that it remain a fecret to all the world. Let us then devife the means of execution.'

Chabot undertook to provide them; and a few days after informed Grangeneuve, that he had found fit inftruments for the purpofe, and that every thing was prepared. —'Very well: let us appoint the time. We will repair to the committee to-morrow evening: I will leave it at half after ten: we muft go through fome unfrequented ftreet, in which you will take care to have your people pofted. But let them mind what they are about. It is their bufinefs to fhoot us properly, and not to make us cripples for life.' —The hour was fixed, and every thing was agreed upon. Grangeneuve went to make his will, and arrange fome domeftic concerns, without any buftle; and was punctual to the appointment. Chabot did not make his appearance. The hour elapfed, and no Chabot came; whence Grangeneuve concluded he had given up his defign of participation; but fuppofing that the project held good as to himfelf, he fet off, took the road agreed on, walked with meafured fteps, met nobody on his way, walked back again, for fear of any miftake, and was obliged to return home fafe and found, much difpleafed at having made all his preparations in vain. Chabot faved himfelf from reproach by fome paltry excufe, taking good care not to depart from the ufual poltroonery of a prieft, or the hypocrify of a capuchin friar.

BARBAROUX,

Whose features no painter would difdain to copy for the head of an Antinous, active, laborious, ingenuous, and brave, with the fiery fpirit of a youthful Marfeillois, was deftined to become a man of merit, and a citizen, equally ufeful and enlightened. Enamoured of independence, proud of the revolution, rich in acquired talents, capable of affiduous attention, habituated to application, and thirfting after fame; he is one of thofe men, whom a great politician would feek to attach to himfelf, and who was made to flourifh and diftinguifh himfelf in a happy republic. But who can venture to fay to what a degree injuftice, profcription, and misfortune, may reprefs the generous efforts of fuch a mind, and how far it may tarnifh its good qualities? Moderate fuccefs would have encouraged Barbaroux in his career, becaufe he is fond of fame, and poffeffes every qualification neceffary to procure him reputation: but the love of pleafure is at hand; and if once it take the place of glory, in confequence of difappointment or difguft, it will debafe an excellent temper, and turn him afide from his noble deftination.

During Roland's firft adminiftration, I had an opportunity of feeing feveral letters from Barbaroux, addreffed rather to the man than to the minifter, and intended to enable him to judge of the means it would be proper to employ, in order to keep ardent and irritable minds, like thofe of the department of the mouths of the Rhone, in the paths of duty. Roland, a ftrict obferver of the law, and like the law fevere and inflexible, was incapable of

fpeaking

speaking more than one language, when charged with its execution. The administrators had gone a little astray: the minister had chidden them with severity; and their minds were irritated. It was then that Barbaroux wrote to Roland, to vindicate the purity of his countrymen's intentions, excuse their errors, and to make Roland understand, that gentler methods would bring them back to subordination with greater speed and effect. These letters were dictated by the best intentions, and by such consummate prudence, that when I saw their author, I was astonished at his youth. They had the effect they could not fail to have upon an equitable man, who sought only to do good: Roland laid aside a little of his austerity, assumed a tone rather brotherly than ministerial, brought the Marseillois back to their duty, and gave Barbaroux his esteem.

After Roland quitted the ministry, we saw him more frequently. His open disposition and ardent patriotism inspired us with confidence. It was then, that, reasoning on the bad state of affairs, and on the danger of seeing despotism revive in the north, we formed the conditional project of a republic in the south.—' That will be our last stake,' said Barbaroux with a smile: ' but the Marseillois who are here will prevent our recurring to such an expedient.'—From that speech, and some others of a like tendency, we conjectured, an insurrection was in agitation; but as his confidence did not lead him to be more communicative, we asked him no questions about the matter. Towards the latter end of July, he almost entirely discontinued his visits; telling us, the last time he called, it would be wrong to judge of his sentiments in regard to us from any presumption furnished by his absence,

absence, as it was merely meant to keep us out of harm's way. After the tenth of August he returned to Marseilles, and came back a member of the national convention, where he did his duty like a man of courage. Many of his printed speeches display excellent argumentation, and considerable knowledge of the administrative department of commerce: that on the supply of provisions, excepting the work of Creuze-la-Touche, is the best thing of the kind. But it would be necessary for him to labour if he would become an orator.

The lively and affectionate Barbaroux is attached to the delicate and susceptible Buzot: I used to call them Nysus and Euryalus. May they meet with a better fate than those two friends! Louvet, more acute than Barbaroux, more gay than Buzot, and in goodness of heart equal to either, is intimate with both; but more particularly with the latter, who serves as a link to connect him with Barbaroux, of whom Buzot's natural gravity makes him in some sort the Mentor.

LOUVET,

WITH whom I became acquainted during Roland's first administration, and whose agreeable society I shall ever covet, may sometimes chance, like Philopœmen, to pay forfeit for his mean appearance. Little, slender, short-sighted, and negligent in dress, he seems of no consequence to the vulgar, who remark not the nobleness of his forehead, nor the fire which animates his eyes;

and

and features upon the utterance of an important truth, a generous sentiment, a witty saying, or a refined piece of raillery. His pleasing novels, where the graces of imagination are combined with fluency of style, philosophical remarks, and attic salt, are known to all men of letters, and to all persons of taste. Politics are indebted to him for more serious works, the matter and manner of which bear witness alike to the goodness of his head and of his heart. He has shewn, that his able hand can alternately jingle the bells of folly, hold the *burin* of history, and launch the thunders of eloquence. It is impossible to unite more wit with less pretension and greater good-nature. Bold as a lion, simple as a child, a man of feeling, a good citizen, and a vigorous writer; he can make Cataline tremble in the senate, dine with the graces, and sup with Bachaumont *.

His Philippic, or *Robespierride*, deserved to be pronounced in a senate possessed of energy to do justice. His *Conspiracy of the* 10*th of March* is another piece of value to the history of the times. His *Sentinel* is a pattern for that kind of bills, and daily instructions intended for a populace, whom it is meant to inform as to facts, without ever influencing them unless by the force of reason, moving them unless for the good of all, or inspiring them with any affections but such as do honour to human nature. It is an excellent contrast to those atrocious and disgusting papers, whose coarse style and filthy expressions are well suited to the sanguinary

---

* A famous French wit, who, in concert with la Chapelle, wrote a celebrated account, in prose and verse, of an excursion they made together.—*Transl.*

doctrine and impure falsehood for which they serve as a common-sewer; the impudent works of calumny, of which intrigue pays the hire to imposture, in order to complete the ruin of public morals, and by means of which the gentlest people in Europe has had its disposition perverted to such a degree, that the peaceable Parisians, whose kindness of heart was proverbial, are become the rivals of those ferocious pretorian guards, who sold their votes, their lives, and the empire, to the best bidder. Let us dismiss these sad images, and turn our attention to the *Observations on St. Just's Report against the confined Deputies, by a Society of Girondines*, printed at Caen the 13th of July. In it I recognized the style, the acumen, and the gaiety, of Louvet: it is Reason in dishabille, sporting with Ridicule, without laying aside her strength or dignity.

Lazowski,

A Polander by birth, came to France no one knows how, destitute of all fortune; but being rich in the interest of the duke of Liancourt, either because related to some person in his service, or because connected with him in some other way, Lazowski obtained the appointment of inspector of manufactures.

It was one of those very inferior offices of administration which conferred no authority; of which the salary was moderate, and the duties such as to require nothing but

but honefty, and a certain fhare of merit; which confequently feemed to fuit every body, or for which every one at leaft thought himfelf fit. Thofe places were in the gift of the king's council, on the prefentation of the minifter of the finances, and were fubordinate to the fuperintendants of trade, petty magiftrates of mighty pretenfions, who gave themfelves great airs of importance; who like many others obtained credit from the public on their own report; and who in reality, from the multitude of affairs that came before them, had extenfive connections, and gave audiences, at which, fometimes, men of the firft rank did not difdain to attend.

Lively, enterprifing, and paffing himfelf off for a man of underftanding, Lazowfki had perfuaded his patron, that it was not fitting for fuch a man to remain a fimple infpector of manufactures. It is true, that, in order to find him employment, an infpectorfhip had been created at Soiffons, where there was fcarcely any manufacture but of priefts, and fcarcely any objects of infpection except nuns; for it was a town as full of convents as deficient in induftry, and deftitute of all commerce but that of the abfolute neceffaries of life. Mr. de Liancourt, who was led to defire the promotion of his dependant by the vanity common among courtiers, was further impelled by the native excellence of his heart. He was preffing with the minifter, and ftill more fo with the fuperintendants of commerce; for the fecondary agents are always the really effective men. Calonne was comptroller-general: he had an inventive mind, and was ready at taking up ingenious ideas. The creation of a travelling infpectorfhip was devifed. That was no effort of genius,

genius, since such a place had already existed, and its inutility had been acknowledged: but it will readily be admitted, that the second creation was not without a motive, since it afforded the means of obliging a man of consequence, while the number of places, which amounted to four, gave the operation something of the appearance of an affair of state, to say nothing of the advantage of three places remaining for favour and intrigue. They were soon filled. Salaries of 8000 livres (333l. 6s. 8d.) a year were given them; a residence in Paris for four months out of the twelve; excursions through the provinces during the remaining eight; the right of succeeding the inspectors-general on their decease, and permission to solicit gratifications in proportion to the length of their journies and the importance of their services. It is true, that this sapped the foundation of an institution, the spirit of which was excellent. It deprived the inspectors of the generalities of the hope of arriving at the inspector-generalship by merit or seniority: it discouraged them, by sending into their respective departments men for the most part strangers to the business: and it deprived the minister of the possibility of being well-informed of the state of arts, manufactures, and commerce; and in short of all the objects of industry; of which it was natural to expect a much better account from men settled in the several generalities for that purpose, than from these birds of passage, employed in running over them all. But the views of the old government did not extend so far: and who knows whether the individuals who compose the new, are of a more capacious mind, or more disinterested spirit.

This happened in the spring of 1784, when I was brought

to

to Paris by family affairs. I heard mention made of a change in the infpections; and I learnt, that the infpectorfhip of Lyons, given up by the ambitious Briffon for a travelling one, was conferred upon a very young man. I reflected, that Roland was always looking forward to his retirement, and intended to afk for it, as foon as he fhould finifh his labours in the Encyclopedia, that he might go into his own country, forget Paris, and the meanneffes to which a man muft ftoop for the preferment that was refufed to merit. I thought it would be better for him to go home with a place, than without one; and it occurred to me, to folicit the exchange of that of Amiens, where we then were, for that of Lyons, which would fix him in his own country. This trifling favour I fuppofed would be readily granted to an old fervant, whofe knowledge, and whofe difpofition efpecially, the fuperintendants of commerce dreaded enough to be pleafed with his removal. The commiffions were already made out. I ftated my reafons with all the advantage a woman had in thofe days in dealing with people who piqued themfelves on their politenefs: on the other hand were ftated the objections, which I frankly rated at their due value; and I obtained the place, almoft as foon as my hufband was informed of the requeft I had thought fit to make.

 In the public offices who fhould I meet with but Lazowfki, then a fine gentleman, his hair well powdered, his clothes well put on, affecting a little ftoop in his fhoulders, walking upon his heels, fporting deep ruffles, giving himfelf, in fhort, thofe little airs of confequence, which were then taken for claims to confideration by fools, and laughed at by men of fenfe.

The conſtituent aſſembly, by overthrowing the nobility and ſuppreſſing the inſpectorſhips, deprived Lazowſki at once of his place and of his patron. Not daring to hope for a penſion, which muſt have been reduced to nothing*, conſidering the ſhort time he had been employed, and finding himſelf without a ſhilling, he became a patriot, combed the powder out of his greaſy locks, made ſpeeches at one of the ſections, and turned ſans-culotte in good time, ſince he was really in danger of wanting breeches.

Poſſeſſed of vigour, conſiderable remains of youth, a thundering voice, and an excellent turn for intrigue, he ſoon diſtinguiſhed himſelf, and was appointed a *capitaine de quartier* in the national guard. In that quality he ſerved on the 10th of Auguſt, and boaſted much of the dangers of the day, like many others who mixed in the tumult to reap ſome profit, and afterward ſtood boldly forward as the ſaviours of their country. But his exploits date from the 2d of September, and from the activity he contrived to keep up in the ſection of Finiſtere, to which he belonged, at the maſſacre of the prieſts at St. Firmin. He was of equal utility in diſpatching the priſoners from Orleans.

He had occaſion to come, as deputy of his ſection, to the hotel of the miniſter of the home department, where I ſaw him, and had an opportunity to obſerve his aſtoniſhing metamorphoſis. The pretty gentleman, with his affected

---

* In ſettling the amount of penſions for diſcarded placemen, the conſtituent aſſembly eſtabliſhed a maximum and minimum, with intermediate degrees, according to their length of ſervice; but gave nothing to thoſe who had not been employed a certain number of years. *Tranſ.*

ſmiles,

smiles, had assumed the savage aspect of a furious patriot; the purple face of a drunkard; and the haggard eye of an assassin.

Dear to the jacobins, who well knew his worth, and meant to make him a great man, he was fixed upon to direct the conspiracy of the 10th of March; but he died suddenly, at Vaugirard, of an inflammatory fever, the fruit of debauchery, brandy, and bad hours.

Who has not heard of the grief of the whole horde at this unexpected loss; of the funeral oration delivered by the high-priest Robespierre, his affecting lamentations, and his pompous eulogium of the *great man unknown*; of the splendid funeral celebrated by the venerable commune, and the holy societies; of the adoption of his child, whom papa Pache kissed in the town-hall; and, lastly, of Lazowski's interment near the tree of liberty, in the square of the Carrouzel, where his humble grave, covered with turf, is still to be seen?

Let those who are astonished at his posthumous importance, recollect, that it emanated from the focus of the jacobins, when they were become as formidable to the timid Parisians as they were atrocious; at the time that Marat was in all his glory, and Danton in the plenitude of his power.

Assuredly the people who took the former for their prophet, and the latter for their lord, might well honour Lazowski as a *saint* or a *hero*, which in the religion of the Septembrizers are the same thing.

ROBERT.

Robert.

'What have you done to Robert?' said a person to me lately: 'his wife and he revile you more virulently than any of your enemies.'—'I have seen but little of them; I have done them some service; but I have not concurred in flattering their ambition, as you are about to hear.'

When I was setting off from Lyons for Paris, in 1791, Champagneux asked me, if I was acquainted with madame Robert, a woman of wit, an author, and a patriot.—Not at all. I have heard indeed that mademoiselle *Keralio*, whose father is a literary man, was lately married to M. Robert, and that between them they compose the *Mercure national*, of which I have seen a few numbers. This is all I know about her.'—'Do you wish to see her? If you do, I will give you a letter to her; for as fellow journalists we correspond.'—'A woman of wit, an author, and a republican, must be well worth seeing. Give me a letter.'

I arrived at Paris, and had been there six weeks, when one of our friends, happening to mention madam Robert, whom he had occasion to visit, I recollected that I had a letter for her. I told him so: he offered to accompany me to the house: and thither we went.

I found a lively little woman of genteel address, and high spirit, who gave me a very pleasing reception: and there I found also her clumsy husband with a face as broad as a well-stalled priest's, beaming health and self-complacency, and with cheeks whose ruddy tinge no profound cogitation had ever impaired. They returned my visit; and there I suffered our acquaintance to rest. The 17th of July, on my return from the Jacobins, where I had been witness to the agitation produced by the mournful events of the Champ-de-Mars, whom should I find at home, at eleven at night, but M. and madam Robert.—' We are come,' said the wife to me, with all the confidence of an old friend, ' to ask you for an asylum. It is not necessary to be often in your company, to form a favourable opinion of your patriotism, and of the goodness of your heart: my husband was drawing up the petition on the national altar, and I was by his side: we have escaped the slaughter, and dare not take refuge in our own house, nor in that of any known friend, where search may be made for us.'—' I am much obliged to you,' replied I, ' for having thought of me on so lamentable an occasion, and am proud of affording a shelter to the persecuted: but you will be badly concealed here;' (I was then at the *Hotel Brittannique, Rue Guenegaud*) ' this house is much frequented, and the landlord is a great partisan of Lafayette.'—' It is only for to-night: to-morrow we will think of a retreat.'

I sent to inform the mistress of the hotel, that a kinswoman of mine having arrived at Paris at the very moment of tumult, had left her baggage at the coach-office, and would pass the night with me; and that I therefore requested her to make up a couple of field-beds in my apartment. They were accordingly spread in a parlour, and there our husbands lay, while madame Robert slept in my husband's bed, by the side of mine, in my own room. The next morning, I rose early, and hastened to write

write letters, to my distant friends, to inform them of the events of the preceding evening. M. and madame Robert, whom I supposed to be very active, and as journalists, to have a much more extensive correspondence than myself, dressed themselves very cooly, sat chatting, after the breakfast I had ordered for them, and placed themselves in the balcony facing the street. They even went so far as to call up a person of their acquaintance who was passing.

This conduct appeared to me very inconsistent in people who were hiding themselves. The person, whom they had called up, entered into earnest conversation with them, concerning the events of the day before; boasted that he had run his sword through the body of a national guard; and talked very loudly, though in a room adjoining to a large anti-chamber common to my apartment and to another.

I called madam Robert.—' I received you, madam, with that interest, which justice and compassion for worthy people in danger naturally inspire; but I cannot give an asylum to all your acquaintance. You expose yourself by conversing as you do, in a house like this, with a person of so little discretion. I am in the habit of receiving members of the assembly, who might stand a chance of being brought into trouble, if seen to enter this hotel while it contains a person who boasts of having yesterday committed acts of violence. I beg you will desire him to withdraw.'—Madam Robert called her husband; I repeated my observations, in rather a higher tone, because it seemed to me that the duller personage stood in need of a stronger impression; and the man was dismissed. I learnt that his

name

name was Vachard; that he was prefident of a fociety, called the indigent club; and much praife was beftowed upon his excellent qualities, and ardent patriotifm. I could not help lamenting inwardly its being neceffary to fet a value upon the patriotifm of a perfon who had every appearance of what is termed a wrong-headed man, and whofe heart I fhould not have imagined to be in the right place. I have fince been informed that he was one of the hawkers of Marat's paper, that he had never learnt to read, and that he is now an adminiftrator of the department of Paris, where he makes a very good figure among his fellows.

It was noon; and M. and madam Robert talked of going home, where every thing muft needs be in confufion. I told them, that fuch being the cafe, if they would take a dinner with me before they went, I would order it at an early hour. They replied, they would rather return, and engaged themfelves accordingly as they were going out of the room. Before three o'clock they made their appearance again in full drefs: the wife had long plumes upon her head and plenty of rouge upon her cheeks: the hufband had put on a fuit of fky-blue filk, with which his black hair, hanging down his fhoulders in large curls, formed a fingular contraft: a long toledo by his fide, added every thing to his drefs, that could ferve to make him remarkable.— 'Why, my god!' faid I to myfelf: 'are thefe people mad?' and I liftened to their difcourfe, to fatisfy myfelf, that their brains were not really turned. The fat and portly Robert ate wonderfully well; and his wife prattled to her heart's content. At length they took leave, nor did I ever fee them, or fpeak of them afterwards to any body.

On our return to Paris the following winter, Robert, meeting Roland at the Jacobins, made him some civil reproaches, or polite complaints, on account of our having broken off all intercourse with them; and his wife came several times to call upon me, inviting me in the most pressing manner to go to her house, where she received company twice a week, and where I should be sure to meet with meritorious members of the legislature. I went once, and there I found Antoine, with whose mediocrity I was well acquainted, a little man, well enough to put upon a toilette, and a pretty poetaster, writing agreeably upon trifling subjects, but destitute of every thing like spirit or consistency. There I found also several other members, sworn patriots, and several women of *ardent* civism, who with some honourable members of the fraternal society, completed a circle which suited me little, and to which I never returned.

A few months afterwards Roland was called to the administration of public affairs. Four-and-twenty hours had scarcely passed, when I saw madam Robert walk into my apartment.—' So, your husband is in place: well, as patriots ought to serve one another, I hope you will not forget mine.'—' I should be very happy, madam, to render you any service; but I do not know how far it may be in my power: M. Roland, however, will no doubt attend to the interest of the public by employing persons of capacity. In four days time, madam Robert returned to pay me a morning visit; and, in a few days after, another, always insisting upon the necessity of giving her husband an appointment, and upon his being entitled to one by virtue of his patriotism. I informed madam Robert,

Robert, that the minister of the home-department had no kind of places in his gift, except those in his own office, which were all filled: that, notwithstanding the advantages which might accrue from changing some of his agents, it behoved a prudent man to study things and persons, previous to alterations, lest the progress of the public business should be impeded; and that, from what she had said herself, it did not seem likely her husband would accept a clerk's place.——'Certainly Robert is qualified for something better.'—'In that case, the minister of the home-department can do nothing to serve you.'—'But he can speak to the minister of foreign affairs, and get some mission for Robert.'—'I believe that it is contrary to the strictness of M. Roland's principles to solicit any thing, or to interfere in the departments of his colleagues: but as you probably mean nothing more than the bearing witness to your husband's civism, I will mention it to mine.'

Madame Robert laid close siege to Dumouriez and Brissot: and three weeks after, returned to tell me, that the former had given her a promise, which she begged me to remind him of, whenever he might chance to come in my way.

In the course of that week he came to dine with me, Brissot and several other persons being present.—'Have you not promised a certain very pressing lady,' said I to Dumouriez, 'to give her husband a place? She has requested me to remind you of it; and so great is her solicitude, that I shall not be sorry to be able to quiet her with respect to myself, by telling her, that I have done what she desired.'—'Is it not Robert you mean?' asked Briffot immediately. —' It is.'—' Aye!' resumed he, addressing himself to Dumouriez, with his usual simplicity: ' you ought to give that man an appointment. He is a sincere friend of the revolution, a strenuous patriot, and not very easy in his circumstances: the reign of liberty ought to be beneficial to its friends.'—' What?' said Dumouriez, interrupting him, with great good-humour and vivacity, ' are you speaking of that little black-headed man, as broad as he is long? I have no inclination, faith, to disgrace myself; and should be sorry to send such a blockhead any where.'——' But,' replied Briffot, ' in the number of agents you have occasion to employ, all do not require equal capacity.'—' Pray, are you well acquainted with this Robert?' said Dumouriez.—' I am very well acquainted with Keralio, his wife's father, a man of infinite respectability, and at his house I have seen Robert. I know he is accused of a few follies; but I believe him to be an honest man, possessed of an excellent heart, actuated by the true spirit of patriotism, and standing in need of employment.'—' I employ no such madmen.'—' But you promised his wife?'—' Certainly: an inferior place, with a salary of a thousand crowns; which he refused. Do you know what she asks? the embassy to Constantinople.'—' The embassy to Constantinope!' exclaimed Briffot, with a laugh: ' impossible!'—' It is fact, however.'—' I have nothing more to say.'—' Nor I,' added Dumouriez: ' except, that I will order that hogshead to be rolled into the street, the next time he comes, and shut my door in his wife's face.'

Madame Robert returned once more to the charge.
I wished

I wished much to get rid of her without coming to a quarrel, and could find but one way that was consistent with my natural frankness. As she complained bitterly of Dumouriez, on account of his tardiness, I told her I had spoken to him; and that I thought it incumbent on me to let her know she had enemies, who propagated ill reports concerning her; that I would advise her to trace them to their source, and destroy them, in order that a man in a public capacity might not expose himself to the detraction of the malevolent, by employing a person who was the object of unfavourable prejudices; and that for the above purpose nothing was wanting but an explanation, which I exhorted her to give. Madame Robert repaired to Brissot, who ingenuously told her, that she had been guilty of great folly in asking for an embassy, and that people with such ill-founded pretensions might expect, in the end, to get nothing at all.

We saw her no more: but her husband wrote a pamphlet against Brissot, to denounce him as a distributor of places, and a deceiver, who had promised him the embassy to Constantinople, and then forfeited his word. He entered into the club of Cordeliers, courted an acquaintance with Danton, submitted to be his clerk when the latter became minister on the 10th of August, was pushed by him into the electoral body, and into the deputation from Paris to the convention, paid his debts, lived expensively, gave entertainments to d'Orleans, and a thousand others, is now rich, calumniates Roland, and slanders his wife. All this is easily conceivable: he follows his trade, and earns his salary.

CHAMPFORT, a man of letters, living in the fashionable world, familiar with the great people of the old government, and connected with men of talents who have made a figure in the revolution, is acquainted with the court and the city, with characters and intrigues, with politics and mankind, still better than with the age in which he lives.

Champfort partook of that extreme confidence, with which I have always reproached the philosophers who have acted a part in the new order of things. He could not believe in the ascendancy of a few wrong-headed fellows, nor in the confusion they would find means to create.—' You carry things to an extreme,' he would say to me sometimes: ' because, placed in the centre of movement, you suppose its sphere of action extensive. It appears to you to be violent; and you therefore consider it as formidable. These fellows will ruin themselves by their own intemperance: they will never be able to extinguish the light of eighteen centuries.'— *These fellows* rule however; and Champfort is now a prisoner, with all those who will not idolize their power.

A great stock of wit, a tolerable portion of morality, the graces of good breeding, the acquirements of literature, and the philosophy of a sound and cultivated understanding, rendered Champfort's conversation equally solid and entertaining. At first I thought he talked too much; and I accused him of that exuberance of speech, and that sort of preponderance, which our men of letters very commonly assume. I liked him better in a select
society

society of five or six persons, than in a mixed company of fifteen or twenty, of which I had to do the honours. But after all, I could not help forgiving him for speaking more than any body else, because he afforded me more amusement: he abounds in those happy sallies, which produce the rare effect of making you laugh and think at the same time.—' Do you believe Champfort to be a thoroughly sincere patriot?' said, one day, a man of more than Spartan austerity.—' Let us not misunderstand one another,' replied I. ' Champfort's views are good, and his judgment excellent: he has a sound understanding, and is never wrong as to principles: he acknowledges and reveres those of public freedom, and human happiness, nor will he betray them. But would he sacrifice to them his peace, his enjoyments, and his life? That, indeed, is quite a different question; on which, I believe, he would take time to deliberate.'—' It is plain then that he is not a virtuous man.'—' Why he is virtuous, as Ninna was chaste: and amidst the corruption which preys on our vitals, it would be lucky for us if we had many such virtuous men.'—Our hypocrites and enthusiasts could never be brought to understand that men should be employed according to the compound ratio of their talents and civism, so that they should be interested in employing the former to the advantage of the latter. I have seen Servan in a rage on finding excellent engineers, whom he had employed in the camp near Paris, dismissed, under pretence of their not being ardent republicans, while sturdy patriots, so completely ignorant as not to know how to draw a line, were put in their place.—' I would not send for them,' said he very justly, ' to give their opinions on a form of government: but I am convinced they will ferve *him* well who knows how to employ them. We are in want of *redoubts,* and not of *motions.'*—That was being too rational: it was talking like the *faction of ſtateſmen*; and thus it was, men of intellect acquired the title of *conſpirators.*

When Roland was recalled to the miniſtry on the 10th of Auguſt, it was neceſſary to change the director of the national library. That place was held by one *d'Ormeſſon,* whoſe name gave umbrage to the new government, and whoſe mediocrity left no room for regret. The miniſter of the home department thought of dividing the duties of librarian between two perſons; of reducing the ſalary from twelve thouſand livres [£.500] a year to eight [333l. 6s. 8d.]; and of making it a rule to have the library open every day; ſo that the public would be a gainer, on the ſcore of inſtruction; the nation, on that of œconomy; and the government, by the employment of two uſeful men. In the choice of perſons, he fixed on Champfort, who, as a man of letters and a philoſopher, had openly declared for the revolution; and on Carra, already employed in the library, whoſe extreme zeal, if not his talents, ſeemed to entitle him to that reward. He had never ſeen either of them, and was determined ſolely by thoſe conſiderations, to which was ſuperadded, the neceſſity of making a choice agreeable to the public. I received the viſits of both of them, in conſequence of their appointment, and their neceſſary intercourſe with the miniſter of the home department; and I ſhould have continued to ſee Champfort with pleaſure, if circumſtances had not kept us at a diſtance from each other.

Carra,

Carra, when he became a deputy, appeared to me a very good kind of man, with a very indifferent head. It is impossible to be more enthusiastic in favour of the revolution, liberty, and a commonwealth; or a worse judge of men and things. Giving way entirely to his imagination; making his calculations accordingly, instead of grounding them upon facts; arranging in his mind the interests of foreign powers in the way that best suited our success; and seeing every thing in the most flattering point of view, he talked of his country's happiness, and the emancipation of all Europe, with inexpressible complacency. It cannot be denied, that he contributed greatly to our political commotions, and to the insurrections of which the object was the overthrow of tyranny. His *Annals* succeeded wonderfully with the populace, by means of a certain prophetic style, which always has weight with the vulgar. When we behold such a man brought to trial, as a traitor to the republic, we are tempted to ask, whether Robespierre be not doing the work of Austria. But it is evident, that he is labouring for himself; and that, in his insatiate ambition to pass for the sole deliverer of France, he would wish to annihilate all those who have gained any thing like fame or reputation in the service of their country.

DORAT-CUBIÈRES

Is a name I had so often seen in the *Almanac of the Muses*, and other compilations of equal importance, that I could

I could not help laughing, when I found it connected with the title of secretary-register of the municipality. It seemed an absurdity; and so indeed it was. Cubières, faithful to that double character of insolence and baseness, which his forbidding countenance wears in a supreme degree, preaches sans-culotism as he hailed the graces, writes verses upon Marat as he did upon Iris, and sanguinary, as he was before apparently amorous, without feeling any impulse of the passions, he prostrates himself humbly before the idol of the day, be it Venus or be it Tantalus. Provided he creep through life, and get bread, what can it signify how; yesterday it was by writing " a sonnet to his mistress's eye-brow," to-day it is by copying a report, or signing an order of police.

Getting, somehow or other, admission into my house, when my husband was minister, I knew him only as a wit, and had an opportunity of shewing him some little civility. He dined with me twice: the first time I thought him odd; the second, insupportable: an insipid sycophant, a fulsome flatterer, stupidly conceited, and meanly polite; he is more at variance with good sense and reason than any other being I ever saw. I soon felt the necessity of giving to my open manner that air of solemnity which lets a person, of whom we wish to get rid, know what he has to do. Cubières took the hint; but some time after he wrote to me notwithstanding, to beg permission to introduce a prince, who was desirous of being admitted to my acquaintance. He dwelt on the title of prince in a manner truly laughable; and added the most disgusting praises of my person. I answered as I usually do when I wish to call people to order without putting them in a passion, and to make a

jest

jest of them without giving them a right to complain. As to the prince, and his introduction, I contented myself with observing, that, in the retired life I led, a stranger to every thing that might be termed a circle, and avoiding company as much as possible, I made it a rule to receive only such persons as business, or long habits of friendship, made my husband wish to see now and then at his table. Cubières sent me in return excuses as tedious as his eulogium, and requested a single moment to explain himself at my feet. I made him no answer, nor did I ever throw away a thought upon him, till the day I was apprehended, when I perceived his signature to the order of the commune; for there were two: one from the committee of insurrection of the 31st of May, the other from the commune. Both were shewn to me, lest I should object to that of the committee: and yet the latter was the only one exhibited by my guards to the keeper of the Abbey, whither I was conveyed.

The request of Cubières had led me to suspect some hidden views of interest, and I diverted my husband at the time by a recital of what had passed. I learned afterwards, that the prince of Salm-Kirbourg, the person in question, was then importuning the ministers, in order to obtain from the council an indemnification of some sort or other for his possessions in Alsace. Hence I concluded that I had guessed aright, and that the desire of seeing me had arisen solely from an idea that the new system might resemble the old, when women were prevailed upon to ask favours of their husbands. I gave myself credit for my conduct, and found in this anecdote a fresh trait of the character of Cubières. It would be

serving

serving him properly to publish his servile letters, as contrasts to his affectation of frankness and a love of liberty. I should have possessed curious pieces of that sort, if I had preserved all the trash I have received. How many relations and admirers, of whom I had never heard before, sprang up all at once, when I became the wife of a minister!—As I admitted no company, they wrote to me; and I had quite enough to do to read their letters; which I answered briefly and politely, but with great frankness, in order to leave them no room to suppose that I either could or would interfere in any thing, and to convince them of the perfect inutility of paying me compliments, or calling themselves my relations.

The most curious circumstance is, that some of these people were angry, and made me very ungracious replies. I remember one M. David, who had planned some establishment, in favour of which he solicited my interest. It availed me nothing to answer, that he would accomplish his purpose by applying directly to the minister; that my interference could be of no use; and that I never employed it, as it would be setting myself up for a judge of matters quite out of my way: he considered my principles as abominable, and wrote to me in a very angry stile.

Thus in private was I persecuted for my perseverance in confining myself to my own sphere; and in public I was assailed by envy, as if I had been governing the state. And yet people think it very pleasing and desirable to fill places of eminence! No doubt the wife of a good man devoted to the service of the public, who is proud of his virtues, and feels herself capable of supporting his courage, has her gratifications, and derives enjoyment

from

from his glory; but thefe pleafures are not obtained gratuitoufly, and few are the people who could pay the price they coft, without regretting the purchafe.

ANECDOTES.

When I was brought to the Abbey, the family of Defilles was ftill there; but was foon after removed to the Conciergerie, whence feveral of the perfons concerned in the confpiracy in Brittany were conducted to the fcaffold. Angelica Defilles, the wife of Roland de la Fouchais, the fimilarity of whofe name to mine led one of my friends into fome curious blunders in an attempt to carry me off, was one of the victims. Her fifters were acquitted, and ought confequently to have enjoyed their liberty; but, as a meafure of general fafety, they were again taken into cuftody, and conveyed to St. Pélagie. I found them there, and converfed with them feveral times. They were young, amiable, and polite women, the elder of whom, a widow of twenty-feven, was neither deftitute of perfonal charms nor energy of mind; the younger was in a very precarious ftate of health. At firft, overwhelmed with grief, they appeared likely to fink under it: but being both mothers of helplefs children, to whom their exiftence was neceffary, they called up all their courage.

They mentioned to me repeatedly the bafe treachery of Cheftel, a man of wit, well known at Paris, where he
practifes

practises physic, a Breton by birth, who had infinuated himself into the moſt intimate confidence of their father, was acquainted with his wiſhes, and appeared to favour his ſchemes; but, connected at the ſame time with Danton, he received through his means a commiſſion from the executive power, repaired to Brittany, to pay court to his friend, took up his abode at his country houſe, received entertainments from his relations, encouraged his deſigns, and gave them freſh activity by his aſſiſtance. At the moment that appeared moſt convenient, he ſecretly informed againſt him, and ſent for perſons who were in waiting to take him into cuſtody.

Deſilles eſcaped. But all his family were apprehended; his effects were ſealed up, and a ſtrict ſearch was made in all the places which might ſerve to conceal his correſpondence, and which Cheftel had pointed out. The young women, who ſtill thought him a friend to the family, begged his advice, and implicitly followed his directions. Not knowing what to do with a purſe of two hundred louis intended for their father, they put it into his hands, ordered the beſt horſe in the ſtable to be ſaddled, and preſſed Cheftel to make his eſcape. He made a ſhew of being determined to ſhare their fate; accompanied them accordingly, but not as a priſoner; and endeavoured to perſuade the commander of the armed force, that had charge of the priſoners, to bring them by day into the great towns. 'Surely you are not in earneſt,' ſaid the officer; 'it would endanger their lives.'

They arrived at Paris. The trial commenced. The name of Cheftel was eraſed from the correſpondence, becauſe he had diſcloſed the plot; and the poor victims then

then discovered the serpent they had fostered in their bosom. Tried, acquitted, detained notwithstanding, and destitute of money, the two young women recollected the purse of gold. They confided the circumstance to a man of courage and probity, who went to Cheftel, and demanded the two hundred louis. Cheftel, taken by surprise, at first denied the fact; but, terrified at the firmness of the demander, who threatened to expose him to the eyes of all the world, he stammered out a confession of the receipt of half that sum, and repaid it in assignats, but not till after repeated interviews.

Cheftel, formerly physician to madam Elizabeth*, assiduous in pursuit of fortune, had in like manner gained the confidence of a wealthy individual, whose name I believe to be Paganel, or something like it, and who, among other possessions, has immense estates in Limousin. Paganel, desirous of emigrating, to shelter himself from the storms of the revolution, made a fictitious sale of his property to Cheftel. He set off, and depended upon the income, which was to be remitted to him by his faithful friend; but Cheftel kept it for himself, and enjoys with Danton the pleasures of an opulence, which both have acquired by similar means.

At length repeated solicitations, assisted, perhaps, by more prevailing arguments, procured the two sisters their liberty. I saw them depart: but I did not know their secret on that head. I have just seen Castellane, however, purchase his enlargement, at the price of thirty thousand livres [£.1250], paid to Chabot. Dillon got out of the Magdelonettes in the same manner. Both

---

* The king's sister. *Transf.*

were involved in the charge of a counter-revolutionary plot. This very moment, August 22, I have before my eyes a certain Mademoiselle Briant, a kept girl, who lives at N⁰· 207, *Cloitre Saint-Benoit*, and whose keeper is a forger of assignats. Having been informed against, apparent endeavours were made to apprehend him; but a shower of gold poured into the hands of the administrators. The man who sends out the armed force employed to seek and take him into custody, knows where he is concealed; his mistress is apprehended for form's sake; the administrators, who appear to come in order to examine her, bring her accounts of her keeper; and very soon they will both enjoy their liberty, since they have wherewithal to pay for it.

Fouqier-Tainville, public accuser to the revolutionary tribunal, notorious for his dissolute life and impudence in drawing up articles of impeachment without cause, is in the habit of receiving money from the persons accused. Madam Rochechouart paid him eighty thousand livres [£.3333] for Mony the emigrant. Fouqier-Tainville pocketed the sum; Mony was executed; and madam Rochechouart was given to understand that, if she said a word about the matter, she would be instantly immured, never more to behold the face of day. Is it possible? the reader will exclaim.—Well! hear more. In the hands of a late president of the department of the Eure two letters exist, from Lacroix the deputy, formerly judge-fiscal of Anet. One contains an engagement for five hundred thousand livres [£.20833], to be applied to the purchase of national domains: the other is to withdraw the engagement, and stop the purchase, in consequence of the decree which obliges members of the convention

vention to account for any increase of their fortune since the revolution. But this decree has been laid asleep since the troublesome twenty-two were expelled; and Lacroix possesses estates as well as Danton, after having pillaged in the same manner.

A Dutchman went lately to the commune of Paris, for a passport to enable him to return to his own country. It was refused. The Dutchman made no complaint; but, seeing which way the wind blew, took out his pocket-book, and laid an assignat of a hundred crowns upon the desk. The language was well understood, and he received his passport.

Here Marat will be quoted to me, in whose house, at his decease, according to the public papers, no more than a single assignat of twenty-five sols [1s. od.$\frac{1}{2}$] was found. What edifying poverty! Let us, however, cast an eye upon his lodgings: it is a lady, who is going to describe them. Her husband, a member of the revolutionary tribunal, is confined in the prison of la Force, for differing in opinion from the ruling powers; and she has been sent to St. Pélagie, as a measure of safety, it is said; but probably because the active solicitations of this little woman from the south were dreaded. She is a native of Toulouse, and possesses all the vivacity of the ardent climate under which she first drew breath. Being strongly attached to a handsome cousin, she was rendered quite disconsolate by his apprehension, which took place a few months ago. She had given herself much pains to no purpose, and knew not to whom to apply, when she thought of trying the effect of a visit to Marat. She asked to speak with him, and was told he was not at home: but he heard a female voice, and came out of his own accord.

accord. He had boots on, without stockings, an old pair of leather breeches, and a white silk waistcoat. His dirty shirt, open at the bosom, exhibited his skin of yellow hue; while his long and dirty nails displayed themselves at his fingers ends, and his horrid face accorded perfectly with his sordid dress. He took the lady by the hand; led her into a parlour newly fitted up, furnished with blue and white damask, and decorated with silk curtains elegantly drawn up in festoons, with a splendid chandelier, and with handsome porcelain jars filled with natural flowers, then scarce, and of high price; sat down by her side on a voluptuous sopha; listened to her tale; expressed his concern; kissed her hand; squeezed her knees a little; and promised her, that her cousin should be enlarged.—' I would have let him go any length he liked,' said the little woman, gaily, in her southern accent, ' upon condition of his restoring me my cousin—I should only have been obliged to bathe myself afterwards.' That very evening Marat went to the committee, and her cousin left the Abbey on the following day. But ere four and twenty hours had passed, the *friend of the people* wrote to the husband, sending him a person who stood in need of a certain favour, which it would not have been safe to refuse.

M. Dumas, a natural philosopher by profession, or rather a pedant by trade, waited upon the famous committee of public safety, some time in the month of June, in order to make some very important proposals. He offered to reconnoitre the army of the rebels in la Vendée, and to give an exact account of its situation and numbers; circumstances concerning which we have remained in the utmost ignorance, even since the commencement

mencement of the war. M. Dumas undertook to inspect the whole most accurately, by taking a bird's eye view of it from a balloon.—' Why, indeed, it is an ingenious thought,' said some of the profound politicians of the committee.—' Yes,' replied citizen Dumas: ' and it may be put into immediate execution. I know of a balloon, which is lying, with all its appendages, in the hotel of an emigrant; so that the *nation* need not be at the expence of the purchase.'—Bravo! He then proceeded to give the necessary information, which was received with transport, and officially forwarded to the minister of the home department, that he might send for the balloon without delay. The minister's people took the field, and made a forced march to the emigrant's hotel. It was an inn, and the apartment he had occupied one little room, where not a rag remained. A report was made in consequence; the committee was distressed beyond measure; Dumas was clamorous; and a fresh injunction was laid upon the minister, requiring him to make stricter search after the balloon. On this the minister held a consultation with his principal clerk, and decisive measures were resolved upon. A letter was written to the department; the department turned the business over to the municipality; and the municipality referred it to the administrators of police. Here the matter ended with the public functionaries; and I laughed heartily at the Abbey with Champagneux, who wrote the ministerial letter, at the charlatanry of the brazen-faced Dumas, the stupidity of the committee, the complaisance of the minister, and the whole of this long litany of follies; but I met with the sequel of the story at St. Pélagie.

Citizen Jubert, one of the administrators of the police,

and one also of those who signed the contradictory orders for apprehending and setting me at liberty, a true section orator, of great corpulence, thundering voice, awkward gait, and forbidding countenance, found out a certain mademoiselle Lallement, a fine tall girl of fifteen, kept by St. Croix, an emigrant officer, who was a dependent, if I recollect aright, of Philip d'Orleans. She was taken up, and sent to St. Pélagie, and in her apartment were found the cover of a balloon, the net, and every thing else belonging to it. This was the very prize described by Dumas; but the committee had forgotten the expedient; the philosopher had lost all hopes of making himself of consequence; the minister cared little about the result of the orders he had given; and the administrators had no objection to take possession of a thing that was now become valuable.

The youthful Lallement's charms made an impression on the heart of Jubert, who had laid his hands upon several of her effects, seized Sainte-Croix's portrait, and thought her a fool for pretending to be faithful to her keeper. At length imagining, that kindness would render her more tractable, he procured an order for her enlargement, came to fetch her in a carriage, conducted her to her lodgings, ordered a dinner, restored, with great reluctance, the portrait of Sainte-Croix, of which he had put out the eyes, and then laid claim to his reward. The young girl laughed at his pretensions, as well as at his way of making love, shewed him the door, and repaired to the police-office, to upbraid him publicly with his attempts, and claim the other effects that had been taken away. The adventure made some noise; but Jubert's colleagues are not likely to condemn it; and it

passed

passed along with a multitude of others, still more disgusting or atrocious, of which the legislators of the 2d of June daily set the example to all the constituted authorities.

August 22.

To-day a misunderstanding has broken out between the tyrants. Hebert, dissatisfied at not being appointed minister, sets his father Duchesne* upon the ringleaders of the faction, falls foul upon the fortune-making patriots, names Lacroix, and is paving the way for an attack upon Danton. Danton, more villainous than any of them, but more circumspect, endeavouring to keep some measure in the conduct of public affairs, is already styled a *moderé*: the committee of public safety abhors his society; the jealous Robespierre holds forth against him; and the *cordeliers* and *jacobins* are on the point of coming to a rupture. What a noble spectacle is preparing for us miserable victims: the tygers are about to worry one another; and perhaps will forget us, unless agonizing rage impel them to exterminate us all before their own defeat.

Chabot is desirous of transporting all suspected persons: of course the wives of *Pétion* and *Roland*, confined under that appellation, are threatened with a voyage to Cayenne. What a charming destination!

* The title of a daily paper replete with oath and vulgarity, of which Hebert was the author. *Transf.*

September 23.

Do not my ears deceive me?—What! that wretched woman who lived unknown in the very heart of the country, and who came to Paris for the sole purpose of soliciting her daughter's enlargement, is condemned to die?—How villanous is such a condemnation!

Pétion's proscription as a royalist, was one of the wonders of the last revolution. His wife, whom the shafts of calumny had never reached, had retired to Fécamp, among her own relations, there to wait in silence and retirement for happier days; she was going to set off for the sea-side, that her son, a fine boy of ten years of age, and the sole fruit of her marriage, might have the benefit of a salt-water bath. She was taken up, and imprisoned with her child; and both have since been brought to Paris, and confined at St. Pélagie. Daily examples teach the wives of the proscribed to expect persecution; and Pétion's has sufficient strength of mind to support her own misfortunes without murmuring; but the situation of her son afflicts her, as equally detrimental to his health and education. She was desirous of trying the effect of solicitations; but how could she render them interesting? How was audience to be obtained?—She wrote to her mother, who lived at Chartres, requesting her to urge her prayer in such a way as became the feelings of the maternal mind. Her mother came; repaired to the bar of the convention; presented her petition with a flood of tears; was referred to the committee; and waited upon all the members who composed it. Some of them seemed to give her hope, but from the greater number she experienced a very unfavourable reception. The inutility of her solicitations becoming evident, she resolved

resolved to depart, and repaired to her section, to get her passport signed. There she was denounced and taken into custody. She was then carried before the mayor: a man who resided in the hotel where she had taken up her abode, swore to her having said that the French stood in need of a king: two hired witnesses, natives of Liege, and deserters, gave the like testimony; she was condemned to lose her head, and is now on her way to the scaffold.

I saw the unfortunate woman several times, when she came to keep her daughter company. Madam Lefevre was in her fifty-seventh year: she had been handsome, and her features still retained some traces of their former regularity: she had also preserved an easy shape, and a beautiful head of hair. As the desire of pleasing had occupied the greater part of her life, but had not led her to acquire any accomplishment, there was nothing about her, but the remains of her former pretensions, and no small share of self-love, which was perceptible on every occasion. She had no political opinion: indeed she was incapable of forming one, for she could not reason two minutes together on any subject whatever. It is possible, that, in a conversation excited by ill-designing people, she may have said, that she did not care whether there were a king or not, provided there were but peace; or words of a like kind may have been laid hold of, in order to bring her to trial. But who does not perceive in this false and atrocious application of the law, an intention to mislead the people, by making them suppose the family of Pétion royalists, and the persecution it suffers consequently just?

Dreadful days of the reign of Tiberius, we not only see your horrors revived, but multiplied in proportion to the number of our tyrants and their favourites! This wretched people, whose morals are destroyed and whose instinct is perverted, thirsts after blood; and every thing except justice, is employed to satisfy its demand. I have seen in the prisons, during the four months that I have been their inhabitant, malefactors purposely forgotten; and yet what haste is made to inflict the penalty of death on madam Lefevre, not because she has committed any crime, but because she is guilty of having for her son-in-law, the worthy Pétion, whom the tyrants detest!

I can conceive nothing more ridiculous than the knavish impudence with which the advantages of a constitution decreed with equal zeal and rapidity are extolled. But did not the very people, who produced it, decree immediately after, that France was, and remained, in a state of revolution? and may not the constitution be considered as abortive, since no part of it is put in force? What benefit then do we derive from it? It is a dead letter, which serves only to attest the impudence of those, who wish to make a merit of it, without caring whether we taste the sweets of it or no.

The multitude who accepted it without examination, merely through weakness and indolence, from the hope of seeing peace, which they would not take the pains to deserve, are well rewarded for their apathy. Unfortunately it is with nations and their affairs, as with individuals and their undertakings: the folly and fears of the many lead to the triumph of villany, and to

the

the ruin of good men. Posterity will put every one in his place; but it is in the temple of memory. Themistocles died nevertheless in exile, Socrates in prison, and Sylla in his bed.

September 26.

THE decree, that orders the act of impeachment against Brissot to be presented to-morrow, was passed in the same sitting, in which it was proposed to shorten the forms of trial before the revolutionary court, and in which the four sections of that tribunal were organised: so that the means of proceeding to judgment are multiplied, sentence is enjoined to be passed more speedily, and the defence of the accused is circumscribed, at the very moment, when it is resolved to destroy Brissot, and the rest of the imprisoned deputies, that is to say, those men of talents, who might otherwise have confounded their accusers.

Four months have passed, without its having been possible to fabricate that act of accusation, the drawing up of which has been decreed several times over in vain. An increase of power, and the universal sway of terror, were necessary, to enable our tyrants to sacrifice the founders of liberty. But after the arbitrary imprisonment of a fourth part of France, under the appellation of *suspected* persons, has been resolved upon; after a silly people has been inspired with such a furious fanaticism that it demolishes Lyons, as if the second city in the republic belonged to the emperor, and as if those whom it thinks proper to call *muscadines* were wild beasts; after an iron sceptre, held over all France,

France, has established the reign of guilt and fear; after a law has been enacted, by virtue of which those who are accused, are bound to answer simply *yes*, or *no*, without making any speech in their defence; then indeed they may venture to send to execution those guiltless victims, whose eloquence was still dreaded, so formidable does the voice of Truth appear even to those, who are powerful enough, to refuse it a hearing.

What care is taken to stifle it! But history stands there, and holds a graver in her hand, preparing in silence to take a tardy vengeance for the fate of the imitators of Barnevelt and Sidney.

October 4.

I am reading a daily paper, and there I see that Robespierre accuses *Roland* and *Brissot* of having spoken ill of *d'Aubigny*, who stole 100,000 livres [£4167] at the Tuileries on the tenth of August, against whom a prosecution was meant to be set on foot, and whose wife in his absence brought the 100,000l. to the commune. I see that Robespierre asserts that Roland appointed Restout to the superintendance of the jewel-office, in order to pave the way for its being robbed; while in fact it was Pache, who, upon refusing the place when offered to him by Roland, recommended Restout as a proper person to fill it. It is a fact also, that the hall of the convention resounded with Roland's complaints against the commander of the national guard, for neglecting to post sentries at the jewel-office, notwithstanding the repeated injunctions of the minister of the home department.

That Robespierre, whom once I thought an honest man, is a very atrocious being. How he lies to his own conscience! How he delights in blood!

Infirmary of St. Pèlagie. October 23.

WITHIN these solitary walls, where oppressed innocence has now dwelt near five months with silent resignation, a stranger appears.—It is a physician, brought by my keepers for their own tranquillity; for to the ills of nature, as to the injustice of man, I neither can nor will oppose aught but calmness and fortitude. When he heard my name, he said he was the friend of a man, whom perhaps I did not like.—'How can you know that, and who is the person you mean?'—'Robespierre.'—'Robespierre! I once knew him well, and esteemed him much: I thought him a sincere and zealous friend of freedom.'—'Why, is he not so?'—'I am afraid that he loves power: perhaps from an idea, that he knows how to do good as well as any man, and desires it no less. I am afraid that he is very fond of revenge, and inclined to exercise it particularly upon those whom he considers as blind to his merit. I believe that he is very susceptible of prejudices; that his resentment is easily excited; and that he is too ready to think every one guilty, who does not subscribe to all his opinions.—You never saw him above once or twice in your life!—I have seen him much oftener!—Ask him: let him lay his hand upon his heart; and you will see whether he have it in his power to say any thing to my disadvantage.'

Robespierre, if I deceive myself, I put it in your
power

power to convince me of my error. It is to yourself that I repeat what I have said of you, and it is to your friend that I mean to deliver this letter, which my keepers will perhaps suffer to pass, for the sake of the person to whom it is addressed.

I write not to entreat you, as you may well suppose. I never yet entreated any one: and most assuredly I shall not begin to do so from a prison, while writing to a man who has me in his power. Prayers become the guilty, or the slave: innocence vindicates herself, which is quite sufficient; or complains, as she has a right to do, when the object of persecution. But even complaints accord not with my disposition; I can suffer, and dare look any shape of misfortune in the face. Besides I know that, at the birth of republics, revolutions, which are almost inevitable, and which give too great scope to the passions of mankind, frequently expose those who serve their country best to become the victims of their own zeal, and of the delusion of their countrymen. They will have a good conscience for their consolation, and history for their avenger.

But by what strange chance is a woman like me, incapable of any thing but wishes, exposed to those storms, which generally burst upon the heads of none but efficient individuals? And what is the fate that I have to expect? These are two questions, which I beg you to resolve.

I deem them of small importance either in themselves, or as far as my individual person is concerned; for what is a single emmet more or less, crushed by the foot of the elephant, in the general system of the world?

But

But they are of infinite interest in regard to the present liberty and future happiness of my country. For if its declared enemies, and its acknowledged friends and defenders be indiscriminately confounded; if the faithful citizen and generous patriot be treated in the same manner as the man of a corrupt and selfish soul, or the perfidious aristocrate; if the woman of virtue and sensibility, who is proud of the freedom of her country, and, who in her humble retirement, or in any other situation, makes every possible sacrifice to its welfare, find herself associated in punishment with the vain or haughty female, who curses equality; surely justice and freedom do not yet reign, and future happiness is doubtful.

I speak not here of my venerable husband. A report ought to have been made of his accounts, when he first gave them in: instead of refusing him justice at first, in order to retain the power of accusing him when calumny should have deprived him of the public esteem. Robespierre, I defy you not to believe, that Roland is an honest man. You may be of opinion, that he does not think justly, with respect to this or that measure: but your conscience must secretly do justice to his integrity and civism: he needs to be seen little, to be thoroughly known: his book is always open, and is intelligible to every one. He has the ruggedness of virtue, as Cato had its asperity; and has made by the harshness of his manner as many enemies as by his inflexible equity: but these inequalities of surface disappear at a distance, and the great qualities of the public man will remain for ever. It has been reported, that he fanned the flames of civil war at Lyons: and this

pretext

pretext has been brought forward as a reason for my apprehension! The supposition was not more just than the consequence. Disgusted with public affairs, irritated by persecution, tired of the world, fatigued by his toils, and bending beneath the weight of years, what could he do but conceal his sorrows in an obscure retirement, and save the unworthy age in which he lives from the commission of a crime?

—He has corrupted the public mind, and I am his accomplice!—This is the most curious of all reproaches, of all imputations the most absurd. You cannot wish me, Robespierre, to take the trouble of refuting them here: the task would be too easy, especially as you cannot be one of the well meaning people, who believe a story because it is in print, or because they have heard it related. My pretended implication in the guilt would be truly laughable, were not the whole rendered atrocious by the misty medium through which it is presented to the people, who, being able to perceive nothing distinctly, figure to their imagination a thousand monstrous forms. Great must be the inclination to injure me of those, who include me in this malicious and premeditated manner, in an accusation strongly resembling the charge of high treason, so often brought forward under the reign of Tiberius, against every one who was destined to destruction, though guilty of no crime. Whence, then, does this animosity arise? It is what I cannot conceive: I, who never injured any one, and who am even incapable of wishing evil in return for the injuries I receive.

Brought up in retirement; devoted from my youth to
those

those serious studies, which have given some degree of energy to my mind; blest with a taste for simple pleasures which no change of circumstances has been able to pervert; an enthusiastic admirer of the revolution, and giving way to the energy of the generous sentiments it inspires; kept a stranger to public affairs by principle as well as by my sex, but conversing about them with warmth, because the public weal takes the lead of all other concerns as soon as it exists; I regarded the first calumnies invented against me as contemptible follies; I deemed them the necessary tribute levied by envy upon a situation, which the vulgar had still the imbecility to consider as exalted, and to which I would have preferred the peaceful state, in which I had spent so many happy days.

These calumnies, however, have increased with effrontery proportionate to my calmness and security: I have been dragged to prison, and have remained there near five months; torn from the embraces of my helpless daughter, who can no longer recline her head on that bosom whence she drew her first nourishment; far removed from every thing dear to me; cut off from all communication with the world; the but of all the rancorous abuse of a deluded populace, who believe that my death would be conducive to their happiness; hearing the guards, who watch under my grated window, diverting themselves with the idea of my punishment; and reading the offensive reproaches cast upon me by writers, who never saw my face, any more than the other persons of whose hatred I am the object.

I have wearied no one with my remonstrances; I have

have hoped for juftice, and an end to prejudice, from the hand of time; wanting many things, I have afked for nothing : I have made up my mind to misfortune, proud of trying my ftrength with her, and with trampling her under my feet. My neceffities becoming urgent, and afraid of bringing trouble upon thofe to whom I might have addreffed myfelf, I wifhed to fell the empty bottles in my cellar, which had not been fealed up, becaufe it contained nothing of greater value. Immediately the whole town was in an uproar! The houfe was furrounded; the proprietor was taken into cuftody; the guards were doubled; and perhaps I have reafon to fear for the liberty of a poor fervant, who is guilty of no crime but that of having ferved me for the laft thirteen years with affection, becaufe I took care to render her life comfortable. So much does the people, mifled with regard to me, and deluded by harangues againft confpirators, think me deferving of that name.

It is not, Robefpierre, to excite your compaffion, which I am above afking, and which I fhould perhaps deem an infult, that I prefent you with a picture far lefs melancholy than the truth : it is for your inftruction.

Fortune is fickle; and popular favour is not lefs liable to change. Contemplate the fate of thofe, who have agitated, pleafed, or governed the people, from Vifcellinus to Cæfar, and from Hippo, the haranguemaker of Syracufe, to our Parifian orators. Juftice and truth alone remain, and are a confolation in every misfortune, even in the hour of death itfelf; while nothing can afford a fhelter from ftrokes of confcience

and

and remorse. Marius and Sylla proscribed thousands of knights, a great number of senators, and a multitude of wretched men. But could they stifle the voice of history, which has devoted their memories to execration? or was content an inmate of their minds?

Whatever be the fate reserved for me, I will find courage to undergo it in a manner worthy of myself; or to anticipate the stroke, as may suit me best. After the honours of persecution, do those of martyrdom await me? am I destined to languish in protracted captivity, exposed to the first catastrophe, that it may be judged requisite to bring about? or am I to be sentenced to transportation as it is called, in order to experience, when a few leagues out at sea, that trifling negligence on the part of the captain, which rids him of the trouble of his living cargo, and enriches the waves? Speak! it is something to know our fate, and a soul like mine is capable of looking it in the face.

If you wish to be just, and attend to what I write, my letter will not be useless to you, and in that case it may possibly be of service to my country. But be it as it may, Robespierre, I know, and you cannot help feeling, that a person, who has known me, cannot persecute me without remorse.

ROLAND, formerly *Phlipon*.

Note. The idea of this letter, the care of composing, and the intention of sending it, held their place in my my mind for four-and-twenty hours: but what effect can my reflections have on a man, who sacrifices colleagues, of whose integrity he is well assured?

If my letter were to do no service, it would be ill-timed. It would only embroil me to no purpose with a tyrant, who may sacrifice, but cannot debase me. It shall not go.

END OF THE FIRST PART.

AN APPEAL TO IMPARTIAL POSTERITY.

PART II.

ROLAND'S
FIRST ADMINISTRATION.

How came Louis XVI. to select for the administration of public affairs a man like Roland, to whom, as an austere philosopher, and a laborious student, retirement was doubly dear? This will be a question with many people, and it would be one with me, were I any other than what I am. I am going to answer it by facts.

Resident at Lyons, during the winter, and belonging to the scientific and literary academies of that city, Roland was employed by the agricultural society to draw up its memoirs for the information of the States General. His principles, and his turn of mind, made him naturally look forward with pleasure to a revolution which promised the reform of so many abuses. The publicity of these sentiments and his well known talents procured him his admission into the electoral body upon the first formation of the commune, and his subsequent investment with the administration of the finances of the city, which was deeply involved in debt. Being sent as a deputy extraordinary to the constituent assembly, he connected himself at Paris with several of its members, and with some of the persons who devoted themselves to the study of public affairs. He returned home, however, when the suppression of his place of inspector, by changing his destiny, obliged him to reflect on the course it would become him in future to pursue. The question was, whether he should retire altogether to his estate in the country, and employ himself in its cultivation; or whether, continuing his literary labours, he should make a journey to Paris, with the double view of collecting materials for that purpose, and of enforcing his claims to a pension, as a reward for thirty years service in his administrative employ. The latter measure was adopted, because it would not prevent his recurring to the other, whenever he should deem it advisable so to do. We returned, then, to Paris on the 15th of December, 1791; but the affairs of the nation at large did not permit us to hope, that the legislative assembly, which had just met, would be soon at leisure to attend to the concerns of a private individual. Roland, intimate with Brissot, became acquainted with several of his colleagues in the legislative body; and not unfrequently went to the society of Jacobins, with old friends settled at Paris, who like him were delighted with a revolution which they esteemed friendly to liberty, who thought that the society had already been useful, and might still help to support a good cause.

Roland, content with being a peaceful auditor, never ascended the tribune to speak. He was known however, not indeed to the illiterate, who had as yet gained no ascendance, but to many others; and was appointed one of the committee of correspondence. This committee, of which the functions are indicated by the name,

was

was composed of a considerable number of members, but only a few were actively employed. Roland often came home with a considerable packet of letters to answer: for though the business was divided into departments, and particular ones assigned to particular members, it became nevertheless a matter of necessity for the more diligent to take upon themselves the duty of the rest, that no part of the correspondence might remain in arrears.—I read those letters, and often undertook to answer them, epistolary writing having ever appeared to me singularly easy and agreeable, because it adapts itself to every subject, and to every style alike, giving to discussion the most pleasing form, and to reason all the scope it can desire.—I remarked in most of the letters from the departments, a style exalted and emphatical, sentiments tinctured with bombast, and consequently with affectation, and in general a desire of the public good, or the ambition of appearing an ardent patriot. I considered that the parent society might exert its influence in disseminating good principles, taking care always to confine itself to the instruction of the people, and to the communication of sentiments calculated to strengthen the social tye, and consequently to inspire the true love of our country, which ought to be only that of human kind, carried to the highest pitch in regard to those who live under the same laws with ourselves, and exalted by a disregard of self-interest in the unfrequent, but sometimes urgent, cases, which require the greatest sacrifices. Persuaded that a revolution is no better than a terrible, and destructive storm, if the improvement of the public mind do not keep pace with the progression of events; and sensible of the good that might be done by taking hold of men's imaginations, and giving them an impulsion towards virtue, I employed myself with pleasure in the correspondence. The committee gave Roland credit for his industry; nor indeed was he idle; but the work of two expeditious persons must necessarily have been great in the eyes of those, to whom the labours of either would have appeared considerable.

A few members of the assembly used to meet frequently in private, at a house in the Place Vendôme, where one of them lodged, and where a worthy and opulent woman had it in her power, without putting herself to inconvenience, to lend them an apartment, of which they were to make use, even in her absence. Roland, who was esteemed for his good sense and integrity, was invited to join them; but he seldom went, on account of the distance. As to me, I lived at home according to custom; I was not in health, and kept little company.

The situation of affairs, and the discontent of the public mind, alarmed the court. The ministers soon became the objects of public animadversion, and indeed their whole proceeding only tended to undermine a constitution which the king had sworn to contrary to his inclination, and which he did not mean to maintain. The court, uneasy and perplexed, in the midst of the frequent changes and agitation of the ministry, knew not on whom to fix its choice. But there were people who declared openly, that if Louis XVI. were sincere, he would take men of undoubted patriotism for his agents. At length, impelled by weakness or by fear, the court came to a decision, but it was with the hope of corrupting,

rupting, or if that hope failed, with the intention of dismissing, the ministers it should appoint. The court then shewed itself inclined to make choice among those called patriots; and at that time the term had not been abused. How was this brought about? I never knew, nor did I ever enquire, because it appeared to me, that in that, as in all other cases, the idea was first started by some few individuals, propagated by others, and at last taken up and acted upon by people in power. By reflecting minds it was considered as important, to direct the attention of the court towards men of abilities, and of respectable character; for it was possible that it might take a malicious pleasure in selecting hot headed Jacobins, whose extravagance might justify complaint, and serve to bring patriotism into contempt. I know not who first mentioned Roland, in the committee at the *Place Vendôme*, as one of those who ought not to be overlooked. The name of Roland was necessarily associated with the idea of a well informed man, who had written upon the subject of administration, who was not destitute of experience in that line, who was besides in possession of a fair reputation, and whose age, manners, and decided character, joined to the principles he had openly professed, even before the revolution, bespoke him a worthy partizan of liberty, in every point of view.—The king himself was no stranger to the above considerations, or at least to the facts upon which they were founded, as I shall hereafter have occasion to shew. Those ideas arose so naturally out of the circumstances of the moment, that they were communicated to us only three days before the formation of the new ministry.—Brissot called upon me one evening when I was alone, and informed me of the probability of Roland's elevation. I smiled, and asked him the meaning of his pleasantry. But he assured me it was no joke, related to me the particulars I have just mentioned, and added, that he was come to know whether Roland would consent to take upon him such a task. I promised to consult him, and make known his resolution on the following day. Roland was as much astonished at the event as myself: but his natural activity rendered him by no means averse to a multiplicity of business, and he said to me with a smile, he had always seen people in power so miserably deficient, that he had never ceased to wonder how the public concerns could go forward at all; and that consequently the thing in itself gave him no alarm. The circumstances of the times were indeed critical, on account of the interests of the court, and the uncertainty of the king's intentions; but to a man attached to his duty, and caring little for the loss of his place while fulfilling its duties, the risk of acceptance was not great. Besides, a zealous man who had a right to some confidence in his talents, could not be insensible to the hope of serving his country. Roland then decided in the affirmative, and made known his intentions to Brissot. The following day, the latter accompanied Dumouriez, who came to Roland's house at eleven o'clock at night, after the breaking up of the council, to inform him, in consequence of orders, of which he was the bearer, that the king had just chosen him minister for the home department. Dumouriez, a minister of recent date, spoke of the king's sincere determination to support the constitution, and of his hope of seeing the machine set to work

as

as soon as the same spirit should pervade the whole council, testifying at the same time to Roland his particular satisfaction at seeing a virtuous and enlightened patriot like him, called upon to take a share in the government.

 Brissot observed, that in the present situation of affairs, the business of the home department was the most delicate, and the most laborious; and that the minds of the friends of liberty would be at ease on seeing it entrusted to hands so steady and so pure. The conversation passed lightly over these matters, and an hour of the next day was appointed for Roland to be presented to the king, and to take his oath and his seat in the council. I found in Dumouriez the deliberate air of a soldier, the address of a skilful courtier, and the conversation of a man of wit, but not the smallest trace of sincerity or truth.—On comparing this man with his new colleague, whose frankness and austerity sometimes bordered upon rudeness, I asked myself if it were possible for beings so dissimilar to act long in concert?——' There goes a man,' said Roland, on their taking leave, ' who discovers a great deal of patriotism, and appears to possess abilities.'—' Yes,' said I, ' and against whom you will do well to be on your guard; for I believe him capable of worming you out of place as soon as any man, if you do not steer a course to please him.'—' We shall see,' said Roland.

 The first time that Roland appeared at court with his usual philosophic dress, adopted long since for the sake of convenience, a few scattered hairs combed over his venerable forehead, a round hat, and strings in his shoes, all the court lackeys, who attached the utmost importance to that etiquette on which their existence depended,

pended, were scandalized, and in a manner terrified at the sight.—One of them stepping up to Dumouriez with horror pictured in his countenance, whispered with a look that indicated consternation, *Monsieur**, *point de boucles a ses souliers*. Dumouriez, ready at repartee, and assuming a tragi-comic tone, cried out, *Monsieur †! tout est perdu!* The saying was soon put in circulation, and provoked a laugh from those who were least inclined to be merry.

Louis XVI. behaved to his new ministers with the greatest appearance of simplicity and good nature. This man was not precisely what he was represented to be by those who took a pleasure in vilifying him: he was neither the brutish blockhead, who was held up to the contempt of the people; nor was he the worthy and kind creature, whom his friends extolled to the skies. Nature had endowed him with ordinary faculties, which would have served him well in an obscure station, but he was depraved by his princely education, and ruined by his mediocrity in difficult times, when his salvation could only be effected by the union of genius and virtue. A common understanding, educated for the throne, and taught dissimulation from the earliest infancy, has a great advantage in its commerce with mankind. The art of shewing to each person only what it is proper for him to see, is *in him* no more than a habit, the practice of which gives him the appearance of ability; but a man must be born an idiot indeed to appear a fool in such a situation. Louis XVI. pos-

---

* Sir! there are no buckles in his shoes!
† Sir! we are all ruined!

sessed

sessed besides an excellent memory, and an active turn of mind; was never idle, and read a great deal. He had also a ready recollection of the various treaties existing between France and the neighbouring nations, was well read in history, and was the best geographer in the kingdom. His knowledge of the names, and his application of them to the faces, of all the persons about the court to whom they belonged, as well as his acquaintance with the anecdotes peculiar to each, had been extended to all the individuals who had distinguished themselves in any manner during the revolution; so that it was impossible to present to him a candidate for any place, concerning whom he had not formed an opinion, founded on particular facts. But Louis XVI. without elevation of soul, energy of mind, or firmness of temper, had suffered his views to be still further contracted, and his sentiments to be twisted, if I may use the expression, by religious prejudices, and jesuitical principles. Elevated ideas of religion, a belief in God, and the hope of immortality, accord well with philosophy, and fix it upon a broader basis, at the same time that they compose the best ornaments of the superstructure. Woe to the legislators who despise these powerful means of inspiring political virtue, and of preserving the morals of the people! Even if they were illusions yet unborn, it would be necessary to create and foster them for the consolation of mankind. But the religion of our priests presents nothing but objects of puerile fear, and miserable mummeries, to supply the place of good actions; and sanctifies besides all the maxims of despotism which the authority of the church calls in to its aid. Louis XVI.

was

was afraid of hell, and of excommunication: with such weakness as this it was impossible not to make a miserable king. Had he been born two centuries before, and had his wife been a rational woman, he would have made no more noise in the world, than many other princes of the Capetian line, who have "fretted their hour upon the stage," without doing much good or much harm.—But raised to the throne when the profligacy of Louis XV's court was at the highest, and the disorder of the finances extreme, he was led away by a giddy woman, who joined to Austrian insolence the presumption of youth and high birth, an inordinate love of pleasure, and all the thoughtlessness of a light mind; and who was herself seduced by the vices of an Asiatic court, for which she had been but too well prepared by the example of her mother.—Louis XVI, too weak to hold the reins of a government that was running to destruction, hastened their common ruin by innumerable faults. Necker, who always mixed up pathos in his politics as he did in his style, was a man of moderate abilities, of whom the public entertained a good opinion, because he had a very high opinion of himself, and proclaimed it without reserve; but void of all political foresight, a kind of outrageous financier, who could calculate nothing but the contents of a purse, and who spoke for ever of his character without rhime or reason, as women of gallantry do of their virtue; Necker was a bad pilot for France, when such a storm was gathering round the horizon. France was in a manner destitute of *men*; their scarcity has been truly surprising in this revolution, in which hardly any thing but pigmies have appeared. I do not mean

that

that there was any want of wit, of knowledge, of learning, of accomplishments, or of philosophy. These ingredients, on the contrary, were never so common: it was like the last glimmering of an expiring taper; but as to that energy of soul which J. J. Rousseau has so well defined by calling it the first attribute of a hero, supported by that solidity of judgment which knows how to set a true value upon every thing, and by those extensive views which look into futurity, constituting together the character of a great man, they were sought for every where, and were scarcely any where to be found.

Louis XVI. constantly fluctuating between the fear of irritating his subjects, and the inclination of keeping them in awe, while incapable of governing them, convened the states general instead of retrenching his expences, and introducing order into his court. After having himself sowed the seeds, and provided the means of innovation, he attempted to prevent it by the affectation of a power, against which he had established a principle of counteraction, and by so doing only taught his people to resist. Nothing remained for him but to sacrifice one portion of his authority with a good grace, in order to preserve in the other the means of recovering the whole; but for want of knowing how to go about it, he turned his attention to petty intrigues, the only kind familiar to the persons chosen by himself, or favoured by the queen. He had however reserved in the constitution sufficient means of power and of happiness, had he known how to be content; so that, wanting as he was in abilities to prevent its establishment, he might still have been saved by the rectitude of his conduct,

conduct, if after having accepted it, he had sincerely endeavoured to promote its execution. But always protesting, on one hand, his intention to support what he was undermining on the other, the obliquity of his proceedings, and the fallacy of his conduct, began by awakening distrust, and ended by exciting indignation.

As soon as he had appointed patriotic ministers, he made it his sole study to inspire them with confidence; and so well did he succeed, that during the first three weeks, Roland and Claviere were enchanted with the good intentions of the king. They dreamt of nothing but a better order of things, and flattered themselves that the revolution was at an end. 'Good heaven!' I used to say, 'I never see you set off for the council with that wonderful confidence, but it seems to me that you are about to commit some egregious act of folly.' 'I assure you,' would Claviere answer, 'the king is perfectly sensible, that his interest is connected with the observance of the new laws: he reasons too pertinently on the subject not to be convinced of it.' '*Ma foi,*' added Roland, 'if he be not an honest man, he is the most arrant knave in the kingdom: it is impossible for dissimulation to be carried to so great a length.' As to me, I always replied, I had no faith in that love for the constitution professed by a man who had been brought up in the prejudices of despotism, and in the habits of enjoying it, and whose recent conduct proved him wanting both in genius and virtue.—My great argument was the flight to Varennes.

The sittings of the council were held in a manner that might pass for decent, in comparison of what they afterwards became; but with puerility, if regard be had
to

to the important matters which called for difcuffion. Each of the minifters who had *bons* * to be figned, or bufinefs of a fimilar nature, regulated by the law, peculiar to his department, and concerning which there was no occafion to deliberate, waited upon the king, on the day appointed, previoufly to the meeting of the council, to tranfact thofe particular and fubordinate affairs. They all repaired afterwards to the council chamber; and there the proclamations that related to the fubjects of difcuffion were taken out of the port-folio. The minifter of juftice next prefented the decrees for the royal affent; and then the council proceeded, or ought to have proceeded, to deliberate upon the operations of government, the ftate of affairs at home and abroad, the queftion of peace and war, &c. As to proclamations adapted to exifting circumftances, it was only neceffary to examine the decree, and the propriety of its application, which was readily done. All this time the king fuffered his minifters to confer, while he read the gazette, or the Englifh newfpapers in the original language, or elfe wrote a few letters. The fanctioning of decrees obtained more of his attention: he feldom gave his confent eafily; and never without a refufal, always declining to accede to the firft requeft, and poftponing the matter to the next meeting, when he came with his opinion ready formed, though appearing to ground it upon the arguments brought forward in the debate. As to great political affairs, he often eluded their inveftigation, by fhifting the converfation to general topics, or to fubjects fuited to each particular perfon. If war were the queftion, he would talk of tra-

---

* Orders on the Treafury.

velling; if diplomatic concerns were upon the carpet, he would advert to the manners, or inquire into the local peculiarities of the country; or if the state of affairs at home were in difcuffion, he would dwell upon fome trifling detail of economy or agriculture. Roland he would queftion about his works, Dumouriez concerning anecdotes, and fo on: the council-chamber was converted into a coffee-room, where the governors of the empire amufed themfelves with idle chat: no minutes were taken of the proceedings; there was no fecretary to keep them; nor was any thing done in a fitting of three hours except figning a few papers. Such was the farce that was acted three times a week. ——' Why it is pitiable!' cried I out of all patience, when on Roland's return, I inquired what had paffed— ' You are all in good humour, becaufe you experience no contradiction, and are treated with civility. You feem indeed to do whatever you pleafe in your feveral departments; but I am fadly afraid that you are duped —' the public bufinefs however is not at a ftand'— ' no, but much time is loft; for in the torrent of affairs that overwhelms you, I would rather fee you employ three hours in folitary meditation on the great interefts of the ftate, than fpend them in idle converfation.' In the mean time the enemy were making preparations, and it had become abfolutely neceffary to declare war; a meafure which was the fubject of an animated difcuffion, and which the king did not feem to take without extreme repugnance. He had long delayed the decifion; and appeared only to yield to the well-known opinion of the majority of the affembly, and to the unanimous voice of the council. Soon after, the con-

tinuation

tinuation or the multiplicity of religious troubles rendered those coercive measures indispensable, which the minister of the interior had long solicited in vain; while the threatening, and formidable attitude of the foreign armies inspired the minister of war with the idea of a regulation, which the convention adopted with enthusiasm, and decreed without delay.

It is true that these two decrees, one for the formation of a camp of twenty thousand men near Paris, the other concerning the priests, were altogether decisive. The court perceived that they would overturn its secret treachery, the partial revolts fomented by fanaticism, and the progress of the enemy, which it favoured. The king was too firmly resolved to refuse his assent, to be in any haste to confess his determination, and devised various pretences by means of which he eluded the question for more than a fortnight. The discussion of this matter was several times renewed. Roland and Servan were urgent in their representations, because each of them felt the importance and necessity of the law that regarded his particular department; the general advantage was evident to all, and the six ministers in this respect were all of the same opinion. In the mean time Dumouriez, whose loose conversation the king encouraged, and whose manners did not render him unfit for the meridian of a court, was sent for several times to the queen. He had a little affront to revenge, and wished to get rid of colleagues, whose austerity accorded ill with his gay turn of mind: hence he was induced to enter into agreements of which the effect was soon perceived.

As to me, I felt a kind of agitation difficult to describe;

scribe: delighted with the revolution; perfuaded that, with all its faults, it was neceffary to enforce the conftitution; and ardently defiring to fee my country profper, the lowering afpect of public affairs gave me a moral fever, which raged without intermiffion. The king's delays demonftrated his duplicity; and Roland had no longer any doubt upon the fubject: there remained then but one refolution for an honeft minifter to take, and that was to go out of office, in cafe Louis XVI. fhould obftinately refufe to take the meafures neceffary for the falvation of the ftate.

That ftep, unattended by any other, might perhaps have fatisfied the confcience of a timid man; but for a zealous citizen, it is not enough to renounce a poft in which good is no longer to be done; it behoves him to fay fo with energy, that he may throw light upon the public calamities, and render his refignation beneficial to his country.—Roland and I had long lamented the weaknefs of his colleagues. The tardinefs of the king had fuggefted the idea, that it might be of great ufe to addrefs a letter to him from the minifters collectively, fetting forth the reafons which had already been given in the council, but which, when expreffed upon paper, and figned by them all, with the offer of their refignation in cafe his majefty fhould not think proper to liften to their reprefentations, might either force him to compliance, or expofe him to the eyes of all France. I drew up the letter, after having agreed upon the fundamental points with Roland, and Roland made the propofal to his colleagues.—All approved of the idea, but moft of them differed as to the execution. Claviere objected to fome phrafe or other; Duranthon was inclined to temporize; and Lacofte was

in

in no haste to subscribe his name. As such a measure should be the effect of a first glance and of a lively sense of its propriety, the failure of our attempt was a hint not to repeat it. It became then necessary to act in an insulated character, and since the council had not spirit enough to stand forth together, it behoved the man who set events at a defiance to take upon himself a task which the whole body should have fulfilled: the question was no longer to resign, but to deserve to be dismissed—to say, do thus or we will retire; but to assert that all was lost unless a proper line of conduct were pursued.

I composed the famous letter. Here I must digress for a moment to clear up the doubts, and to fix the opinion of a number of persons, of whom the greater part only allow me a little merit, that they may deny it to my husband, while many others suppose me to have had a kind of influence in public affairs entirely discordant with my turn of mind. Studious habits and a taste for literature made me participate in his labours, as long as he remained a private individual—I wrote with him as I ate with him, because one was almost as natural to me as the other, and because my existence being devoted to his happiness, I applied myself to those things which gave him the greatest pleasure. Roland wrote treatises on the arts; I did the same, although the subject was tedious to me. He was fond of erudition; I helped him to pursue his critical researches. Did he wish, by way of recreation, to compose an essay for some academy? we sat down to write in concert, or else separately, that we might afterwards compare our productions, choose the best, or compress them into one.

If he had written homilies, I should have written homilies also. When he became minister I did not interfere with his administration; but if a circular letter, a set of instructions, or an important state paper, were wanting, we talked the matter over with our usual freedom, and impressed with his ideas, and pregnant with my own, I took up the pen, which I had more leisure to conduct than he had.

Our principles and our turn of mind being the same, we came to a final agreement as to the form, and my husband ran no risk in passing through my hands. I could advance nothing warranted by justice or reason, which he was not capable of realizing, or supporting by his energy and conduct; but my language expressed more strongly than his words, what he had done or what he promised to do. Roland *without me* would not have been a worse minister; his activity, and his knowledge, as well as his probity, were all his own; but *with me* he attracted more attention, because I infused into his writings that mixture of spirit and of softness, of authoritative reason, and of seducing sentiment, which are perhaps only to be found in a woman endowed with a clear head and a feeling heart. I composed with delight such pieces as I deemed likely to be of use, and felt greater pleasure in so doing than if I had been known as the author. I am avaricious of happiness: with me it consists in the good I do: I do not even stand in need of glory; nor can I find any part in this world that suits me, but that of Providence. I allow the malicious to look upon this confession as a piece of impertinence which it must somewhat resemble;

those who know me however will see nothing in it but what is sincere, like myself.

I return to the letter, which was sketched with a stroke of the pen, as was nearly the case with every thing I did of the kind; for to feel the necessity and propriety of a thing, to conceive its good effect, to desire to produce it, and to cast into the mould the object from which that effect was to result, were to me but one and the same operation. While we were reading over this letter together, who should be present in my husband's closet, but that very *Pache*, who, before the expiration of the year, calumniated Roland, and now persecutes us, as the enemies of liberty.—' 'Tis a very bold step,' said the hypocrite, whom I took for a sage.—' Very bold! without doubt, but just and necessary; what signifies any thing else?'— Roland repaired to the council, on the 10th of June, with the letter in his pocket, and with the design of first reading it aloud to his colleagues, and then putting it into the king's hands. The debate concerning the sanctioning of the two decrees began; but was suspended by the king, who told his ministers to have each his written opinion ready to deliver to him at the next meeting of the council. Roland could have delivered *his* without delay: he thought however, after what had just been said, that it was incumbent on him to wait out of a sort of regard to his colleagues; but on his return home we were of opinion, that he could not do better than dispatch his letter, to which he added three or four missive lines.

The next day, at eight o'clock in the evening, I saw Servan walk into my apartment with a joyful countenance,

nance. 'Congratulate me,' said he, 'I am turned out.' 'I am much mortified,' answered I, 'at your being the first to have that honour; but I hope that, ere long, it will be awarded to my husband.'—Servan related to me that having been on business with the king in the morning, he had endeavoured to speak to him about the camp; that the king, with evident marks of ill humour, had by turning his back upon him put an end to the conversation; and that at the very instant Dumouriez came up, in his majesty's name, to demand his *port folio*, of which he was going to take charge himself.—'Dumouriez? His conduct surprises me little, but it is infamous, and the other ministers in that case ought not to wait for their dismission. It would become them better to write to the king, that they can no longer fit at the council board with Dumouriez: we must send for them to consult about it.' Nobody but Claviere and Duranthon came, and they were people who never knew how to take a decisive measure. It was agreed upon that they should return the next morning, after due deliberation, and that Roland should have a letter prepared for them all to sign. At the same time he communicated to them the one which he had sent in the morning, and from which he expected the same treatment as Servan had met with before.—I do not know whether, for that very reason, these gentlemen, who were fond of their places, might not imagine, that the two ministers the most urgent for the decrees, would be the only ones sacrificed, and that they ought not to expose themselves rashly to the same fate. The next morning they did not think proper to write, but deemed it most adviseable to go and speak

to

to the king in perſon; a meaſure contrary to common ſenſe; for when it is neceſſary to ſpeak plain truths to a perſon entitled by his ſituation to a great deal of reſpect, it is much more advantageous to do it by letter. Roland, who had fulfilled his taſk, could do no more than join them upon this occaſion; and they all repaired to Lacoſte's, with the intention of aſking him to be of the party. Lacoſte was doubtful, and appeared to heſitate, when a meſſenger from the king brought Duranthon an order to go immediately, and alone, to the palace.— 'We will go and wait for you at your own houſe,' ſaid Claviere and Roland.—Scarcely had they reached the palace of juſtice, when Duranthon returned with a long face, and a hypocritical look; and drew ſlowly out of his pocket what was called a *lettre de cachet*, containing the diſcharge of his two colleagues. 'You make us wait a long while for our liberty,' ſaid Roland, taking the paper with a ſmile. 'Ay, our liberty is here indeed.'—He returned home, and brought me the intelligence, for which I was well prepared.—' One thing remains to be done,' ſaid I, with animation; 'and that is, to be the firſt to acquaint the aſſembly with your diſmiſſion, ſending them at the ſame time a copy of your letter to the king, by which it has certainly been occaſioned.' This idea pleaſed him much, and we put it immediately into execution.—I foreſaw that it would have a great effect; nor was I deceived: it anſwered a double purpoſe; *utility* and *glory* were the conſequences of my huſband's retreat. I had not been proud of his elevation to the miniſtry, but I was proud of his diſgrace.

I have ſaid that Dumouriez had a little affront to revenge by entering into a league with the court againſt his colleagues. The circumstance that gave rise to it was as follows.

Bonne-Carrere, a handsome man, who had the reputation and manners of an intriguer, and who owed the cross of St. Lewis which decorated his person to the interest of Dumouriez, was chosen by the latter for his principal agent, and appointed director general of the department of foreign affairs.

I saw him once only, when Dumouriez brought him to dine with me; and was as little imposed upon by his agreeable outside as by that of Herault de Sechelles. 'All these handsome fellows,' said I to a friend, 'seem to me to be but poor patriots; they appear too fond of themselves not to prefer their own pretty persons to the public good; nor can I ever help being tempted to lower their conceit, by affecting to be blind to the advantage on which they pride themselves the most.'

I more than once heard grave men, members of the legislature, some of those noble originals who kept honour and probity alive, and who are now declared infamous on that account; I heard them lament the choice that Dumouriez had made, and contend that patriotic ministers, to give strength to the cause of liberty, should be particularly careful to commit every part of the administration to the purest hands. I know that Dumouriez was mildly remonstrated with, and that he urged in excuse the understanding and talents of Bonne-Carrere, to whom wit, versatility, and a mind fertile in resources, could not be denied; but a rumour got abroad of an affair managed by Bonne-Carrere, on account of which a hundred thousand livres had been deposited in a notary's hands. A part of it was intended for madam de Beauvart.

Beauvart. This lady was Dumouriez' miſtreſs, a woman of eaſy virtue, and ſiſter to Rivarol, living in the midſt of people of diſſolute manners, and diſguſting ariſtocracy. I have forgot the nature of the affair, and the parties; but the names, the dates, and the particulars, were known, and the fact was undoubted. It was agreed that Dumouriez ſhould be ſeriouſly requeſted to diſmiſs Bonne-Carrere, and to preſerve, or to put on a decency of demeanor, without which it was impoſſible for him to remain in the miniſtry, and to avoid injury to the good cauſe. Genſonné, who was intimately acquainted with Dumouriez; and Briſſot, to whom all Bonne-Carrere's tricks had been denounced, determined to ſpeak to him at Roland's, in his preſence, and in that of three or four other perſons, either his colleagues, or members of the legiſlative body. Accordingly, after dining at my table, and retiring into the room which I generally inhabited, the grievance was ſet forth, and the obſervations it warranted, were made to Dumouriez. Roland, with all the gravity of his age and character, took the liberty of inſiſting upon the matter, as intereſting to the whole miniſtry. Nothing being leſs agreeable to Dumouriez than this preciſion, and the tone of remonſtrance, he endeavoured at firſt to give the ſubject a light turn; but finding himſelf hard preſſed by ſober argument, he grew angry, and took leave with an air of diſcontent. From that day he ceaſed to viſit the members of the aſſembly, and did not ſeem ſatisfied when he met them at my houſe, whither he came much leſs frequently than before. Reflecting upon this conduct, I told Roland, 'that, without pretending to be verſed in intrigue, I believed, according to the practice of the world, the hour of ruining Dumouriez was at hand, if he did not wish to be overturned himself. 'I know very well,' added I, ' that you will not defcend to fuch manoeuvres; but it is not the lefs true, that Dumouriez will certainly endeavour to get rid of thofe by whofe cenfure he has been offended. When a man once begins to read lectures, and does it to no purpofe, he muft punifh, or expect to be molefted.' Dumouriez, who was partial to Bonne-Carrere, made him his confidant as far as he was perfonally concerned; and Bonne-Carrere, who had accefs to the queen by means of feveral women with whom he was connected, found means to hufh up the difgraceful ftory. Intrigues were fet on foot; the famous decrees followed; and although Dumouriez was for giving them the royal affent, he contrived to keep in favour at court, and was of ufe, after the departure of his colleagues, either by propofing fucceffors, or by accepting the war department; though, by the way, he did not keep it long; for the court, which at firft had been glad to retain him, that they might not appear to difmifs all the minifters denominated patriots at once, got rid of him foon after. But he was too dexterous not to avoid a total difgrace, and obtained employment in the army conformable to his rank.

Even the patriots imagined it was advifable to turn his talents to account, and were in hopes that he would make a good ufe of them in his military career. —One of the principal difficulties that embarraffed government, after the 10th of Auguft, was to find perfons fit to fill public employs, particularly in that line. The old government had conferred the rank of officer upon
none

none but nobles; and knowledge and experience were concentrated in their order; but the people were uneasy at seeing them intrusted with the conduct of the forces intended to support a constitution adverse to their interest. Struck with this contrast, they could not, like the enlightened part of mankind, judge of the reasons of confidence, founded on one man's disposition, on the passions of another, and on the principles of a third. Their flatterers, on the contrary, aggravated their fears, and excited their distrust: everlasting denunciators, they set themselves up as enemies to every man in place, that they might establish themselves in those places which best suited their ambition: such is the system of all agitators, from Hippo, the orator of Syracuse, to Robespierre, the *speechifier* of Paris.

Roland, recalled to the ministry, thought that the public good, and the circumstances of the times, made it his duty to do away all idea of opposition between Dumouriez and himself, since each was serving the republic in his way. " The chances in politics," said he in his letter, " are as uncertain as in war; *I* am again in
" the executive council; *you* are at the head of an
" army: you have the errors of your administration to
" efface from the public mind, and laurels to gather in
" the field of Mars! You were led into an intrigue
" which made you do an ill office to your colleagues,
" and were duped, in your turn, by the very court
" whose favour you were striving to preserve. But
" you are not unlike those valorous knights, who were
" every now and then guilty of little roguish tricks,
" at which they were the first to laugh themselves; but
" who fought nevertheless like furies, when their ho-
                                                          " nour

"nour was at ſtake. It muſt be confeſſed that this character does not very well accord with republican auſterity: it is the conſequence of thoſe manners, which we have not yet been able to throw off, and for which you will be ſure of a pardon, if you beat the enemy. You will find me in the council ever ready to ſecond your enterpriſes as long as they have the public welfare in view. Where that is concerned I am a ſtranger to all favour and affection; and ſhall look up to you as to one of the ſaviours of my country, provided you devote yourſelf ſincerely to its defence."—Dumouriez's anſwer was ſpirited, and his conduct no leſs ſo—he repulſed the Pruſſians.

I remember at this period, ſome hopes were entertained of detaching them from the league, and ſome overtures made in conſequence; but they led to nothing. He came to Paris after the enemy had evacuated our territory, to concert the plan of his Belgic campaign. Roland ſaw him at the council chamber, and once he came to dine at our houſe, with ſeveral other gueſts. When he entered the room, he appeared a little embarraſſed, and offered me a beautiful bouquet which he had in his hand, with ſomewhat of an awkward air for a man of ſo much aſſurance. I ſmiled, and told him, that the tricks of fortune were whimſical enough; and that doubtleſs he never expected ſhe would enable me to receive him again in that hotel; but flowers did not the leſs become the conqueror of the Pruſſians, and that I received them with pleaſure from his hand. After dinner he propoſed going to the opera. That, again, was a remnant of the old folly of our generals, whoſe cuſtom it was to ſhew themſelves felves at the playhoufe, and feek theatrical crowns whenever they had obtained an advantage over the enemy. Somebody afked me if I did not intend to be there; but I declined giving an anfwer, becaufe it was neither confiftent with my character nor my manners to appear in public with Dumouriez. When the company was gone, however, I propofed to Vergniaux to take a feat in my box, in company with my daughter and myfelf. We went thither, and were told by the aftonifhed box-keeper that the minifter's box was full. 'That is impoffible,' faid I; for nobody could go into it without a ticket figned by him, and I had not given a fingle one away.—'But it is the minifter himfelf, and he infifted upon admiffion.'—'No, that cannot be: open the door, and I fhall foon fee who it is.' Two or three *fans-culottes*, in the fhape of bullies, were ftanding in the lobby. 'Don't open the door,' cried they, 'the minifter is there.'—'I cannot help it,' anfwered the woman, who inftantly obeyed me; and there I difcovered Danton's broad face, that of Fabre, and two or three women of fufpicious appearance. The opera was begun; their eyes were turned upon the ftage; and Danton was leaning over towards the next box to fpeak to Dumouriez, whom I recognized immediately. All this I faw at a fingle glance, without being perceived by any body in the box, and pufhing the door to, made a hafty retreat. 'Why, indeed,' faid I to the box-keeper, 'a certain *ci-devant* minifter of juftice is there, whom I would rather leave to enjoy the fruits of his impertinence, than enter into any altercation with him: I have nothing to do here.' On faying this, I retired, well pleafed upon the whole that Danton's folly had faved me

from

from the incongruity I wished to avoid of appearing in public with Dumouriez, whose seat would have been so very near to mine. I afterwards heard that Danton and Fabre constantly attended him to all the other theatres, where he was weak enough to shew himself. As to me, I have never seen him since. This, then, is the whole of our connection with a man, whose accomplices people were pleased to suppose us at the time of his treachery. Dumouriez is active, vigilant, witty, and brave; calculated alike for war and for intrigue. Possessed of great military talents, he was the only man in France, in the opinion even of his jealous competitors, able to command a large army properly; but he was better fitted by his versatile disposition, and by his dissolute morals, to serve under the old court, than under the new government. His extensive views, and the spirit with which he pursues them, render him capable of forming vast projects; nor does he want abilities to carry them into execution; but his temper is not equal to his understanding, and his impatience and impetuosity hurry him into measures precipitate or indiscreet. He is excellent at devising a stratagem; but incapable of concealing his purpose for any length of time. Dumouriez, in short, to become the leader of a party, wanted a cooler head.

I am persuaded he did not go to the Belgic provinces with treacherous intentions: he would have served the republic as he had served the king, provided it had tended to his glory and advantage; but the injudicious decrees passed by the convention, the infamous conduct of its commissaries, and the blunders of the executive power, ruining our cause in that country, and the aspect of affairs threatening a general convulsion, he conceived the idea of giving them a turn, and for want of temper and prudence bewildered himself in his combinations. Dumouriez must be very amiable in orgies of his own sex, and agreeable to women of diffolute manners: he appears to have still all the sprightliness of youth, and all the gaiety of a lively and free imagination; but with women of a reserved disposition there is something formal in his politeness. He used to divert the king in council by the most extravagant stories, at which his grave colleagues could not help laughing; and not unfrequently he seasoned them with truths equally bold and well applied. What a difference between this man, vicious as he is, and Lukner, who at one time was the only hope of France! Never did I meet with any thing so contemptible. He was an old soldier, half *brutified*, wanting in common sense, and destitute of all energy of mind; a mere phantom of a man, who, by means of his broken French, his fondness for wine, a few oaths, and a kind of intrepidity, had acquired great popularity in the army, among mercenary machines, ever the dupes of any one who taps them on the shoulder, speaks to them with familiarity, and punishes them from time to time. 'O my poor country!' said I next day to Guadet, who asked me what I thought of Lukner, 'you are undone indeed, if you are obliged to send abroad for such a being, and to confide your destiny to such hands!'

I am perfectly ignorant of tactics, and Lukner, for aught I know, might understand the routine of his profession; but I am well assured that no man can be a great general without good sense and rationality.

The thing which surprised me the most, after my husband's elevation had given me an opportunity of being acquainted with a great number of persons, particularly of those employed in important affairs, was the universal meanness of their minds: it surpasses every thing that can be imagined, and extends to every rank, from the clerk, who stands in need of nothing but sense to comprehend a plain question, method to treat it, and a decent style to draw up a letter, to the minister charged with the government, the general at the head of armies, and the ambassador employed to protect the interests of the state. But for that experience, never should I have thought so poorly of my species; nor was it till that period that I assumed any confidence in myself: till then I was as bashful as a boarder in a convent, and thought people who had more assurance than myself, had more abilities also.—I no longer wonder, indeed, that I was a favourite: my friends perceived I was not without my share of merit, and yet I sincerely did homage to other people's vanity.— In this scarcity of men of abilities, the revolution having successively driven away those whose birth, fortune, education, and circumstances, had rendered them superior to the mass of the people by a somewhat higher degree of cultivation, it is no wonder if we fell gradually into the hands of the grossest ignorance, and most shameful incapacity. There are a great many degrees between de Grave and Bouchotte. The former was a little man, whom nature had made gentle, whose prejudices inspired him with pride, and whose heart persuaded him to be amiable; but who, for want of knowing how to reconcile those various affections, at last became nothing at all. I think I see him now, walking upon his heels, with his elbows turned out, and his head erect, very often shewing nothing but the whites of his great blue eyes, which he could not keep open after dinner without the assistance of two or three cups of coffee; speaking little, as if out of discretion, but in reality for fear of exposing himself; and truly anxious about his official concerns, but distracted by their multiplicity. The consequence was, that at last he abandoned a place for which he felt himself unfit. I will say nothing of Bouchotte; an idiot is described in three syllables; but his faults were innumerable. Of Servan I have spoken elsewhere; a brave soldier, an excellent citizen, and a man of information, he possessed a degree of merit seldom to be met with: the world would be too happy if there were many men of that character. Claviere, a man of understanding, but of that disagreeable disposition so common among people, who passing much of their time in their closets, form opinions there, which they afterwards maintain with obstinacy, was neither deficient in knowledge nor philosophy; but financial habits had in some measure narrowed his mind. Pecuniary calculations indeed always spoil the happiest dispositions; for it is impossible for a man not to set a high value upon that which constitutes his daily occupation. A banker may be an able and well-informed man; but he will never number the disinterestedness of Aristides among his virtues. Claviere is very laborious, easy to be led by those who know his weak side, but insupportable in his commerce with any body who partakes of his own obstinacy in dispute; a bad judge of mankind, of whom he never studied but one part, their understandings, without

attending

attending to their difpofitions, their interefts, and their paffions; timid in council, although fometimes carried away by the warmth of his temper; in a word, he is rather a good adminiftrator than an able minifter.

I never yet could underftand what it was that promoted Duranthon to a place in the adminiftration, unlefs indeed it were the idea of the little ability neceffary to fill that of minifter of juftice. Heavy, flothful, vain, and talkative, timid and confined in his notions, he was in truth no better than an old woman. His reputation for integrity, the fober manners of a decent advocate, a few teftimonies of attachment to the revolution, and the age of experience, probably ferved him as a recommendation; but he had not even fenfe enough to make a feafonable retreat, the only meafure by which he could have acquired a portion of glory. When I recollect what kind of men he has had for his fucceffors, I am lefs angry with thofe who thought him worthy of his place; but I cannot help afking myfelf where we are to feek for men qualified to hold the reins of government.

Lacofte had the official knowledge, the laborious habits, and the infignificance of a clerk. Having been long employed in the admiralty-office *(Bureaux de la marine)*, he was thought fit to be put at the head of that department, in which he committed no blunders. But he was deftitute of the capacity and activity which ought to characterize the adminiftrator of fo confiderable a branch of the public bufinefs, and his want of them was expofed by the exigencies of the times. Nothing fhort of the inability of Monge, could have afforded an advantageous object of comparifon for Lacofte.—Beneath the mafk of a countenance almoft indicating timidity, the

latter

latter concealed an irritable difpofition, which, in cafe of contradiction, degenerated into the moſt ridiculous violence.

Such was the compofition of the miniſtry the firſt time that Roland belonged to it. There prevailed, in the beginning, a great union between the members of the council; and I verily believe they were all fincerely attached to the conſtitution, with more or lefs of regard to their own intereſt on the part of feveral. As they aſſembled at each other's houfes on the days the council met, I had them to dine with me once a week. Some of the members of the legiflative body were alfo invited; and the converfation ufed to turn on the affairs of the nation, with a common defire of promoting the public good. This was a happy time in comparifon of that which followed!

ROLAND's SECOND ADMINISTRATION.

At the time of the recal of Roland, Claviere, and Servan, the compofition of the miniftry was completed by the appointment of Danton, whom I have fufficiently depicted elfewhere, and by that of Monge and le Brun; the former to the marine department, the latter to that of foreign affairs. Nothing is fo diftreffing as the difficulty of making a choice in circumftances like thofe of the times in queftion. Every man who had belonged to the court, directly or indirectly, was profcribed by public opinion; nor could any thing fhort of the brilliant proofs of patriotifm given by Servan, efface that original fin, even fmall as it was in regard to him. The perfons employed to make a choice were ill calculated to do fo. New themfelves to public affairs, our legiflators could not boaft of thofe extenfive connections which lead to an acquaintance with a great number of individuals, and enable a man to felect from them the perfons beft fitted for important employments. The committee was puzzled to make a choice, when the idea of Monge, who was known to Condorcet as a fellow academician, and of whofe patriotifm feveral others had heard favourable mention, prefented itfelf. Monge, a mathematician, fometimes fent to examine officers at the out-ports, an honeft citizen, the father of a refpectable family, and a zealous member of the club of the Luxemburg, was for a moment weighed in the fcale againft Meunier, his colleague at the academy, and an officer of engineers; but as the latter was known to have paid his court to the great, Monge was preferred.

Good-

Good-humoured, thick-witted, and inclined to buffoonery, Monge was a stone-cutter at Mezieres, where the Abbe Boffut, perceiving him to have a turn for the mathematics, initiated him in that science, and encouraged him by a donation of six livres a week: but when by application he had got forward in the world, he ceased to visit his benefactor, considering himself as his equal. Accustomed to calculate immutable elements, Monge was destitute of all knowledge of the world, or of public affairs: heavy and awkward in his pleasantry, he recalled to my recollection, in his clumsy attempts at wit, the bears kept in the ditches of the city of Berne, whose playful tricks, corresponding with their uncouth forms, amuse the passengers.

The new minister filled his office with men as little capable of acting as he was of judging: he took great pains without doing any good, and suffered the marine to be disorganized at a time when it was most important to keep up, and even to increase the establishment. Praise, however, is due to the goodness of his intentions: he was frightened at the burthen, and wished to lay it down; but the difficulty of finding a better man, procured him an invitation to remain at his post. By degrees his duty came to sit easy on him, and he fancied that he did it as well as it could have been done by any body else. But though a bad administrator, he was still worse as a counsellor, and served only to fill a chair during the debates of the executive power, concurring constantly in sentiment with the most timid, because having none of his own, he naturally followed that which was most conformable to the views of a narrow mind.

When Pache was promoted to the miniſtry, he became the oracle of his friend and admirer Monge, who was no longer of any opinion but his, and received it as if it had been the inſpiration of the divinity. Thus was he *Maratized*; and thus did this man, who was deſtined by nature to play a better part, become the abettor of the moſt atrocious and ſanguinary doctrines.

Le Brun, employed in the office of foreign affairs, paſſed for a man of ſound underſtanding, becauſe he never had any flights of fancy, and for a man of abilities, becauſe he had been a tolerable clerk. He was tolerably acquainted with the diplomatic chart, and could draw up a ſenſible letter or report. In ordinary times, he would have done very well for the department which is the leaſt laborious, and where the buſineſs is of the moſt agreeable kind. But he had none of that activity of mind and diſpoſition, which it was neceſſary to diſplay at the moment he was called to the miniſtry. Ill-informed of what was going on among our neighbours, and ſending miniſters to foreign courts, who, although not deſtitute of merit, had none of thoſe qualities which ſerve to recommend a man, and who could hardly penetrate further than the anti-chambers of the great; he neither made uſe of that kind of intrigue, by which employment might have been found at home for thoſe who wiſhed to attack us, nor of that kind of dignity with which a powerful ſtate ought to inveſt its acknowledged agents in order to procure itſelf reſpect—
‘ What are you about ?’ Roland ſometimes uſed to ſay.
‘ In your place, I would have put all Europe in motion, and have inſured peace to France, without the aid of arms; I would take care to know what is going on
in

in every cabinet, and exert my influence there.' Le Brun was never in a hurry; and now, in Auguft 1793, Semonville, who ought to have been at Conftantinople eight months ago, has juft been intercepted in his way through Switzerland. The laft choice of Le Brun will ferve to characterize him completely, without my adding another trait. He has appointed Grouvelle, the fecretary to the council, of whom in that quality I ought already to have fpoken, minifter plenipotentiary at the court of Denmark.

Grouvelle, a pupil of Cerutti, of whom he learned nothing but to conftruct affected phrafes, which contain the whole of his philofophy; narrow-minded, frigid, and vain, the laft editor of the *Feuille Villageoife*, become as flat as himfelf; Grouvelle had been candidate for fome place or other in the miniftry, and was appointed fecretary to the council on the tenth of Auguft, according to a conftitutional law, againft the difregard of which Roland had remonftrated with fo much warmth, that the king had at laft determined to attend to it. Roland was in hopes that the keeping of a regular regifter, in which an entry might be made of the debates, would give to the proceedings of the council a more ferious, as well as a more ufeful turn: he perceived befides, that it would afford to men poffeffed of a firm temper of mind an opportunity of authenticating their opinions, and of fecuring a teftimony fometimes ufeful to hiftory, and always neceffary to their own juftification. But the beft inftitutions are only advantageous when in the hands of people incapable of perverting them. Grouvelle did not know how to take minutes of the proceedings, and the minifters, for the moft most part, cared little whether any traces of their opinion remained. The secretary was never able to do more than draw up a summary of the resolutions taken, without the assignment of any reasons, or the mention of any opposition; nor could Roland ever find means to get his objections inserted, even when he formally resisted the resolution of the council. Grouvelle constantly interfered in the discussion, and by his captious manner contributed not a little to render it perplexing, till Roland, out of all patience, observed to him one day that he did not recollect his business there.—'What, am I nothing but an ink-horn!' exclaimed the important secretary in an angry tone. - - - 'You ought to be nothing else here,' replied the severe Roland; 'every time you interfere in the debate you forget your duty, which is to take it down; and this is the reason why you have only time to make a little insignificant statement upon a loose sheet of paper, which, when entered in the register, gives not the smallest idea of the operations of government; whereas the register of the council ought to serve as archives to the executive power.' - - - Grouvelle was much incensed, but he neither improved nor altered his method, which, as my reader will easily perceive, was quite good enough for such men as I have described above. The salary of his place was twenty thousand livres (£833), to which he thought it would be convenient to add an apartment in the Louvre, spacious enough to lodge himself and his clerks, and made his representation to the minister of the home department accordingly. It requires but little knowledge of Roland's character to conceive the indignation with which he received this proposal, and

the

the vigour with which he repelled it. 'Clerks! said he, for bufinefs that I could tranfact myfelf in a few hours, and better than you if I were in your place.—I defire that you will take a copyift to fave you the trouble of delivering fuch copies or extracts of the proceedings as you may be called upon to furnifh; but twenty thoufand livres are quite fufficient to pay his falary, and to find a lodging for him as well as for yourfelf: the fum is even extravagant, in a free government, for the place you occupy.'

Grouvelle certainly has a right not to be fond of Roland, and I believe that he exercifes it to its full extent.

As to me, I felt, in the moft lively manner, that his ridiculous pretenfions were intolerable.—Thefe men, made up of vanity, whofe wit is a mere jargon, whofe philofophy is pitiable oftentation, and whofe fentiments are recollections, appear to me a kind of eunuchs, in a moral fenfe, whom I defpife and deteft more cordially than fome women hate and difdain thofe creatures. Such, however, is the minifter of a great nation at a foreign court, of which it is important to preferve the efteem, and fecure the neutrality. I am unacquainted with the fecret of his appointment; but I would wager that Grouvelle, half-dead with fear, on feeing the difaftrous pofition of public affairs, requefted le Brun to get him fent out of France in any way whatever; and that le Brun, in quality of minifter, made him ambaffador, as he would have made him a travelling-clerk, if he himfelf had been a merchant. It is an arrangement between individual and individual, in which the republic is no otherwife concerned than in conferring the title, and advantages attached to it, and in receiving the injury that may arife from being fo badly reprefented.

The choice of an envoy to the United States was conducted with more wifdom; and affords a new argument in favour of Briffot, againft whom the fhare he had in it is brought forward as a crime. Bonne-Carrere having been fixed upon, I know not at what period, Briffot obferved to feveral members of the council, that it was of confequence to the maintenance of our good underftanding with the United States, as well as to the glory of our infant republic, to fend to America a man whofe difpofition and manners might be agreeable to the Americans. In that refpect Bonne-Carrere was not a fuitable perfon: an amiable libertine of the fafhionable world, and a gamefter, whatever might be his talents and abilities, was very unfit to play the grave and decent part becoming a minifter refident with that tranfatlantic nation.

Briffot was actuated by no perfonal intereft; he was the laft man in the world to be fo influenced: he mentioned Geneft, who was juft returned from a refidence of five years in Ruffia, and who, befides his being already converfant with diplomatic affairs, poffeffed all the moral virtues, and all the information, that could render him agreeable to a ferious people.

That propofal was wife; it was fupported by every poffible confideration; and Geneft was preferred. If this be an intrigue, let us pray that all intriguers may refemble Briffot. I faw Geneft, I defired to fee him again, and fhould always be delighted with his company. His judgment is folid, and his mind enlightened: he has as much amenity as decency of manners;

ners; his converfation is inftructive and agreeable, and equally free from pedantry and from affectation: gentlenefs, propriety, grace, and reafon, are his characteriftics; and with all this merit he unites the advantage of fpeaking Englifh with fluency. Let the ignorant Robefpierre, and the extravagant Chabot, declaim againft fuch a man, by calling him the friend of Briffot; let them procure by their clamours, the recall of the one, and the trial of the other: they will only add to the proofs of their own villany and ftupidity, without hurting the fame of thofe whom they may find means to deprive of exiftence.

During Roland's fecond adminiftration, as well as the firft, I determined to receive no female, and that was a rule to which I fcrupuloufly adhered. My circle was never very extenfive, and never did the greater part of it confift of my own fex. Befides my neareft relations, I faw nobody but the perfons whofe congenial tafte and ftudies gave them claims to my hufband's attention. I was fenfible that while he was in the miniftry, I fhould expofe myfelf to very troublefome company;—to company that might even be attended with danger. It appeared to me that madame Pétion's conduct at the *Mairie** was highly prudent; and I deemed it as laudable to follow, as to fet, a good example. Accordingly I had neither circle nor vifits: that, in the firft place, was a great economy of time, an ineftimable advantage to thofe who have the means of turning it to any account. Twice a week only I gave a dinner: once to my hufband's colleagues, with a few members of the Affembly; and once to a mixed company, compofed

---

* The refidence of the mayor.

either

either of national reprefentatives, of firft clerks in the public offices, or of fuch other perfons as took a part in politics, or were concerned in the bufinefs of the ftate. Tafte and neatnefs prefided at my table, but profufion and the luxury of ornaments were equally unknown: every one was there at his eafe, without devoting much time to conviviality, becaufe I gave only a fingle courfe, and relinquifhed to nobody the care of doing the honours of the table. The ufual number of guefts was fifteen; it feldom exceeded eighteen; and once only amounted to twenty. Such were the repafts which popular orators in the roftrum of the Jacobins, converted into fumptuous entertainments, where, like another Circe, I corrupted all thofe who had the misfortune to partake of the banquet. After dinner, we converfed for fome time in the drawing-room, and then every one took leave. We fat down to table about five; at nine not a creature remained; and yet that was the court, of which they made me the queen, and there, with the doors wide open, did we carry on our dark and dangerous confpiracies.

The other days, confined to our family, my hufband and myfelf generally fat down to table alone; for the tranfaction of the public bufinefs delaying our dinner to a very late hour, my daughter dined with her governefs in her own room. Thofe, who faw me at that time, will bear witnefs in my favour, whenever the voice of truth can make itfelf heard: I fhall then perhaps be no more; but I fhall go out of this world with the perfuafion, that the memory of my perfecutors will be loft in maledictions, while my name will fometimes be recollected with a figh.

Among

Among the persons whom I was in the habit of receiving, and of whom I have already described the most remarkable, *Paine* deserves to be mentioned. Declared a French citizen, as one of those celebrated foreigners, whom the nation was naturally desirous of adopting, he was known by writings which had been useful in the American revolution, and which might have contributed to produce one in England. I shall not, however, take upon me to pronounce an absolute judgment upon his character, because he understood French without speaking it, and because that being nearly my case in regard to the English language, I was less able to converse with him than to listen to his conversation with those whose political skill was greater than my own.

The boldness of his conceptions," the originality of his style, and the striking truths which he throws with defiance into the midst of those whom they offend, have necessarily attracted great attention; but I think him better fitted to sow the seeds of popular commotion, than to lay the foundation or prepare the form of a government. Paine throws light upon a revolution better than he concurs in the making of a constitution. He takes up, and establishes those great principles, of which the exposition strikes every eye, gains the applause of a club, or excites the enthusiasm of a tavern; but for cool discussion in a committee, or the regular labours of a legislator, I conceive *David Williams* infinitely more proper than Paine. Williams, made a French citizen also, was not chosen a member of the convention, in which he would have been of more use; but was invited by the government to repair to Paris, where he passed several months, and frequently conferred with the most

active

active representatives of the nation. A profound thinker, and a real friend to mankind, he appeared to me to combine their means of happiness, as well as Paine feels and describes the abuses which constitute their misery. I saw him, from the very first time he was present at the sittings of the assembly, uneasy at the disorder of the debates, afflicted at the influence exercised by the galleries, and in doubt whether it were possible for such men, in such circumstances, ever to decree a rational constitution. I cannot help thinking that the knowledge which he then acquired of what we were, attached him more strongly to his country, to which he was impatient to return. How is it possible, said he to me, for men to debate a question, who are incapable of listening to each other? Your nation does not even take pains to preserve that external decency, which is of so much consequence in public assemblies: a giddy manner, carelessness, and a slovenly person, are no recommendations of a legislator; nor is any thing indifferent which passes in public, and of which the effect is repeated every day.— Good heaven! what would he say at this time, if he were to see our senators drest, since the 31st of May, like watermen, in long trowsers, a jacket and a cap, with the bosom of their shirts open, and swearing and gesticulating like drunken *sans-cullottes*? He would think it perfectly natural for the people to treat them like their lackeys, and for the whole nation, debased by its excesses, to crouch beneath the rod of the first despot who shall find means to reduce it to subjection.—Williams is equally competent to fill a place in the parliament, or the senate, and will carry with him true dignity wherever he goes.

By what sally of imagination is Vandermonde present

sent to mine? Never did I see eyes so false, more truly express the turn of mind of the person to whom they belong. One would suppose the man to have had his understanding cut into two equal parts: with one he is capable of beginning any kind of reasoning; but it is impossible for him with the other to carry on an argument, or to draw from the whole a reasonable conclusion. What a poor figure does science make in a head so badly organized! Accordingly Vandermonde, an *academician* by the way, and the friend of Pache and of Monge, boasted of serving the latter as a counsellor, and of being called his wife. Speaking to me one day of the *cordeliers* (to which sect he confessed himself to belong), in opposition to the persons who considered them as *madmen*, ' We,' said he, ' desire order by reason, and you are of the party that desires it by force.' After such a definition I have nothing further to say of this man's crazy brain. But since I have been speaking of an academician, I must say a word or two of *Condorcet*, whose mind is capable of soaring to the sublimest truths, but whose spirit will ever be on a level with the base sentiment of fear. It may be said of his understanding, in relation to his person, that it is an exquisite liquor imbibed by cotton. Never will the saying of, a stout heart in a feeble body, be applied to him: he is as defective in fortitude as in constitution. The timidity which characterizes him, and which he carries into company in his face and attitude, is not only a defect in his temperament, but seems to be a vice inherent in his soul, which all his philosophy cannot overcome.—Hence it was, that after having ably established a principle, or demonstrated a truth, he voted in the Assembly contrary

contrary to his own opinion, when obliged to stand up before the thundering galleries, armed with injurious words, and prodigal of menaces. He was very well in his place of Secretary to the academy: men like him may write, but ought never to be actively employed. It is even a fortunate circumstance when they can be made of any use of at all, for most timid men are absolutely good for nothing. Look at those poltroons of the Assembly, pouring forth their lamentations: if they had possessed fortitude enough to procure their own arrestation, by protesting against that of the *twenty-two*, nobody would have dared to hurt a hair of the heads of two or three hundred representatives of the people, the republic would have been saved, and the departments would not have relapsed into submission. The people acquiesced in the loss of twenty men, but an assembly, of which one half should have retired, would never have been considered as the national convention.

PUBLIC

PUBLIC SPIRIT.

WHAT was the *Office for Public Spirit*, which has been objected to Roland as so great a crime?—I am tempted to repeat this question to the very persons who ask it; for I can conceive nothing so chimerical as that phrase.

Roland, restored to the ministry after the 10th of August, thought that nothing was more urgent than to diffuse the same spirit through all the departments of the state, so that every thing proceeding in an uniform course, the success of the revolution might be insured: he therefore addressed a circular letter of that tendency to all the administrative bodies, nor did it fail to produce a favourable effect. The Legislative Assembly felt the necessity of supporting it; and for want of a body of Public Instruction, which was not yet drawn up, determined that an hundred thousand livres (£.4167) should be left at the disposal of the minister of the interior, for the purpose of dispersing such useful writings as he might think fit.

Roland, rigid in his economy, made it his business to lay out this money to the best advantage: availing himself of the public papers, then in the highest estimation, he ordered them to be forwarded *gratis* to the popular societies, to the parish priests, and to such zealous individuals as appeared desirous of contributing to the welfare of the state. Some of those societies, and several of those individuals, seeing that the government interested itself in their instruction, took courage, and now and then wrote to the minifter, to requeft works which the Convention had ordered to be printed, and which they had not received. The minifter, defirous of fatiffying them, affigned to one of his offices the care of anfwering thofe letters, and of forwarding the publications defired. In thefe things alone confift all the mighty machinations which have made fo much noife, and which were nothing more than the mere execution of duties impofed by a decree. Roland was fo careful of expence, that at the end of fix months he had only difburfed thirty-four thoufand livres, out of the hundred thoufand of which he was at liberty to difpofe; and of thofe he delivered an exact account, together with a lift of the works purchafed and given away. But as in confequence of the nature of his place, and of the circumftances in which he found himfelf, he fometimes drew up inftructions, which he difperfed in the fame manner; and as his writings in general breathed nothing but philofophy and a love of his fellow-creatures, fears were entertained left the perfonal confideration that might thence refult fhould render him too powerful.

It could only be inferred that he infpired great confidence, which, by facilitating adminiftrative operations, was productive of confiderable advantage; but fuppofing it neceffary to prevent his acquiring too much efteem, and too great an afcendancy, nothing was neceffary but to repeal the decree, and to forbid his forwarding any thing which did not neceffarily belong to his correfpondence with the adminiftrative bodies. It was not however any regard to the public weal, but jealoufy of the individual, which raifed fuch a fermentation in men's minds; and accordingly they occafioned a clamour,

and

and accused and denounced him in a vague manner, without pointing out the object of their complaint; for if he could have imagined its nature, he would have been the first to apply a remedy to the evil apprehended. Instead of employing himself in that manner, he thought only of defending himself, at first by continuing to do his duty, and afterwards by explaining his conduct, and refuting his calumniators. His triumphant answers exasperated envy; he was no longer mentioned but as a public enemy; and a real struggle took place between the courageous functionary, who remained at the helm in spite of the tempest, and the jealous deceivers or deceived, who endeavoured to bury him beneath the waves. He stood firm, as long as he hoped it could answer any purpose; but the weakness and insufficiency of the sober party having been demonstrated on an important occasion, he retired.

His enemies dreaded his accounts; and prevented not only their examination, but the report of them from being made to the Assembly. The calumniators, when once embarked, thought only of justifying their false aspersions by the ruin of the man who had been the object of them; hence their redoubled efforts, their open persecution directed even against me; and for want of well-founded reasons, the accusation so often repeated of *corrupting the public spirit*, and of an office established for that purpose, with my pretended share in the delinquency; and all without citing a *fact*, a *writing*, or even a reprehensible *phrase*.—And yet Roland's glory, in future times, will be in part attached to the able and instructive productions of his pen!

MY SECOND ARRESTATION.

Sainte-Pelagie, August 20.

THE twenty-fourth day of my confinement in the Abbey was beginning to pafs away: the period of that confinement had been employed in ftudy and literary labours, principally in writing *memoirs,* of which the compofition muft have borne marks of the excellent difpofition of mind I was in. The infurrection of the 31ft of May, and the outrages of the fecond of June, had filled me with indignation; but I was perfuaded that the departments would not look on them with an eye of fatisfaction, and that their reclamations, fupported by the requifite meafures, would make the good caufe triumphant. Little did I care, while indulging this hope, whether in fome critical moment, or in the ftruggle of expiring tyranny, I fell a victim to private hatred, or to the rage of fome furious madman. The fuccefs of my friends, and the triumph of true republicans, confoled me for every thing beforehand: I could have undergone the execution of an unjuft fentence, or have funk under the ftroke of fome unforefeen atrocity, with the calmnefs, the pride, and even the joy of innocence, which defpifes death, and knows that its wrongs will be avenged.—Here I cannot help once more expreffing my regret for the lofs of thofe *Memoirs,* which defcribed fo well the facts that had come to my knowledge, the perfons by whom I had been furrounded, and the fentiments I had experienced in the varying fucceffion of events. I am informed that fome of them have efcaped deftruction;

but

but they only contain the particulars of my firſt arreſtation. The day will come perhaps when the union of thoſe fragments will afford to ſome friendly hand the means of exhibiting the truth in more glowing colours.

The publication of a groſs falſehood, and the loud bawling of the hawkers under my window, while announcing one of the numbers of the *Pere Duchesne*, a filthy print with which Hebert, ſubſtitute of the commons of Paris, every morning poiſons the ignorant populace, who ſwallow calumny like water, perſuaded me that ſome new atrocity was in agitation. That paper pretended that its author had paid me a viſit in the Abbey, and that having obtained my confidence by aſſuming the appearance of one of the Vendean banditti, he had brought me to confeſs the connexions of Roland and the Briſſotines with the rebels of that department and with the Engliſh government. In this ridiculous ſtory, interlarded with the uſual ornaments of ſtyle of *Pere Duchesne*, phyſical and moral probabilities were diſregarded alike. I was not only transformed into the abettor of a counter-revolution, but into an old toothleſs hag, and was exhorted to weep for my ſins till the time ſhould come for expiating them on the ſcaffold. The hawkers, in purſuance no doubt of their inſtructions, did not leave the vicinity of my reſidence for a moment, but accompanied their proclamation of *Pere Duchesne's Great Viſit* with the moſt ſanguinary advice to the people of the market. I took up my pen, and wrote a few lines to that cowardly Garat, who thinks himſelf a ſage, becauſe he is actuated by no paſſion but fear, which makes him pay his court to whatever party chances to be uppermoſt, without the leaſt regard to juſtice. I pointed out to him the infamy of an administration which exposes innocence, already oppressed, to the last outrages of a blind and furious populace. I certainly had no hope of converting him; but I sent him my farewell to prey like a vulture upon his heart. About the same time a young woman, who has no great talents to boast of, but who combines the graces of her sex with that sensibility which is its principal merit, and its greatest charm, found means to make her way into my prison. How was I astonished to see her sweet countenance, and to feel myself pressed to her bosom, and bathed in her tears! I took her for an angel; and an angel she was, for she is good and handsome, and had done all she could to bring me news of my friends: she furnished me also with the means of informing them of my situation. This alleviation of my captivity had contributed to make me forget it, when at noon on the 24th of June, the gaoler's wife came and begged me to step into her apartment, where an administrator was waiting to see me.—I was in pain, and in bed—I rose and followed her into her room, where a man was walking up and down, and another writing, without either of them appearing to perceive my arrival.—' Am I the person, gentlemen, whom you asked for?'—' You are the wife of citizen Roland?'—' Yes, Roland is my name.'—' Be so good as to sit down.'—The one continued to write, and the other to walk about.—I was endeavouring in vain to divine what this comedy might mean, when the *writer* deigned to address me—' I am come,' said he, ' to set you at liberty.'—I know not how it was, but I felt myself very little affected by the information.—' Why, indeed,' answered I, ' it is very right to remove me from this place;

place; but that is not all; I wish to return home, and the door of my apartment is sealed up.'—' The administration will have it opened in the course of the day; I am writing for an order, because I am the only administrator here, and two signatures are necessary for the gaoler's discharge.'—He rose, delivered his message, and returned to speak to me, with the air of a man desirous of inspiring confidence.—' Do you know,' said he all on a sudden, and as if without design, ' where M. Roland is at present ?'—I smiled at the question, observed that it was not candid enough to deserve an answer; and as the conversation grew tiresome, retired to my own room to prepare for my departure. My first idea was to dine quietly, and not to remove till towards the evening; but, upon further reflection, I thought it a folly to remain in a prison when I was free to go away. Besides the gaoler came to know if I was getting ready, and I plainly saw that he was impatient to turn me out of my lodgings. It was a little closet, rendered very uncomfortable by the dirtiness of the walls, the closeness of the grates, and the neighbourhood of a pile of wood, where all the animals belonging to the house deposited their ordure; but as it could contain only one bed, and as the prisoner consequently had the advantage of being alone, the honour of inhabiting it was generally conferred upon a new comer, or upon an individual desirous of solitude. Lavacquerie (the gaoler), who had never seen it occupied by any body so contented as I was, and who used to admire the pleasure I took in arranging my books and my flowers, told me, that in future he should call it the pavilion of Flora. I was ignorant that at the very moment he was speaking he intended it for Briſſot, whom I did not even ſuppoſe to be my neighbour; and that ſoon after, it would be inhabited by a heroine, worthy of a better age, the celebrated Charlotte Corday. My poor maid, who was juſt come to ſee me, wept for joy while packing up my things; the order for ſetting me at liberty, founded upon the want of evidence, was ſhewn to me; I ſettled my accounts, and diſtributed my little favours to the poor, and to the ſervants belonging to the priſon; and in my way out met the prince of Linanges, one of the hoſtages, who congratulated me in obliging terms upon my enlargement. I anſwered, that 'I ſhould be happy to pay him the ſame compliment, as it would be a pledge of the releaſe of our commiſſioners, and of the return of peace:'—then ſending for a hackney-coach, I walked down ſtairs, much ſurpriſed at finding that the adminiſtrator had not yet left the priſon, and at his coming to the door to ſee me into the carriage.

Driving home with the intention of leaving a few things there, and of proceeding immediately after to the houſe of the worthy people, who have adopted my daughter, I quitted the hackney-coach with that activity which never allowed me to get out of a carriage without jumping, paſſed under the gate-way as if upon wings, and ſaid cheerfully to the porter as I went by, 'Good-morrow, Lamarre.' Scarcely, however, had I got up four or five ſtairs, when two men, who ſome how or other had kept cloſe at my heels, called out ' *Citoyenne* Roland!'——' What do you want?' ſaid I, turning about. —' In the name of the law, we arreſt you.' Thoſe who know what it is to feel, will eaſily conceive all that I experienced at that moment. I deſired the order to be

read

read to me; and coming to a resolution immediately, stepped down stairs, and walked hastily across the yard. —' Whither are you going?' – ' To my landlord's, where I have business; follow me thither.'—The mistress of the house opened the door with a smile.—' Let me sit down and breathe,' said I, ' but do not rejoice at my being set at liberty: it is nothing but a cruel artifice: I am no sooner released from the Abbey, than I am ordered to be confined at Sainte-Pelagie. As I am not ignorant of the resolutions lately entered into by my section, I am determined to put myself under its protection, and will beg you to send thither accordingly.'—Her son immediately offered to go with all the warmth and indignation of a kind-hearted young man *. Two commissioners from the section came; desired to see the order; and made a formal opposition; but they afterwards begged me to accompany them to the residence of the mayor, where they were going to give notice of it, and to assign their reasons. With this request I could not refuse to comply. After employing the intermediate time in writing notes to my friends to inform them of my new destination, I took leave of a family which this scene had affected with terror and surprise, and was conducted to the mayor's. There I was put into a little anti-chamber with the inspectors charged to take care of my person, while the commissioners proceeded to the office of the administrators of the police. The debate began, continued for some time, and grew warm. Ill at my ease, and dissatisfied with the

---

* He was dragged to the scaffold on this account, and his father died of grief.

place I was in, I asked myself by what fatality innocence was obliged to play the part of a criminal, expecting judgment, and to remain in the mean time exposed to the inquisitive eyes of every body who came into the anti-chamber. At length, out of all patience, I rose, and opened the door of the office.—' There can certainly, gentlemen, be no harm in my being present at a discussion of which I am the subject.'—' Get you gone,' cried a little man, whom I recognized for the very Louvet that had examined me so awkwardly at the Abbey—' But, gentlemen, I have no intention to commit any act of violence, I am not prepared for it; I do not even ask to be heard; I only desire to be present.'— ' Get you gone; get you gone.—*Gendarmes*, come hither!'—Any one would have supposed that the office was besieged, because a woman of common sense wished to hear what they were saying of her. It was however necessary to withdraw, that I might not be carried away by force. Soon after I perceived them making signs, running backwards and forwards, and sending for a coach; and at last an inspector of the police came and begged me to follow him. I turned round to the door of the office, and set it wide open.—' Commissioners of the section of Beaurepaire, I give you notice that they are taking me away.'—' We cannot help it; but the section will not forget you; it will take care that you be examined.'—' After having been set at liberty at one o'clock, because *there was no evidence against me*, I should be glad to know how I could become a *suspected person*, in my way home from the Abbey, and thus give cause for a new detention.'—Joubert, another administrator, as violent as Louvet, and still more awkward and stupid

than

than he, addressing me in a magisterial tone, confessed that my first arrest was illegal, and that it had been necessary to enlarge me, that I might afterwards be taken into custody according to the terms of the law. This opened to me a fine field; and I was going to avail myself of it; but tyrants, even when they suffer the truth to escape them, cannot bear to hear it from the lips of others; noise and anger left no room for reason; I quitted the company, and was conveyed to *Sainte-Pelagie*.

The name of this house, which under the old government, was inhabited by nuns, keepers of those female victims of *lettres-de-cachet*, whose conduct was supposed to be immoral, added to its lonely situation in a remote quarter of the town, inhabited by what may truly be called populace, and but too well known on account of the ferocious spirit which it manifested in the month of September, by the massacre of so many priests: all this did not present my new asylum to my eyes in a consolatory point of view.

While a note was taking of my entry, a man of a sinister countenance opened my bundle, and began to examine it with particuliar curiosity. I perceived it at the moment when he laid upon the gaoler's desk some newspapers which it contained. Surprised and offended at a behaviour only authorized in cases of secret confinement, I observed that it by no means became a man to examine a woman's night clothes in so indecent a manner. He was accordingly ordered to let them alone; but he was the turnkey of the corridor in which I lodged; and twice a day I was doomed to see his horrible countenance. I was asked if I chose a room with one or two beds—' I am alone, and want no company.'—' But the

room

room will be too small.'—' It is all the same to me.'—Upon inquiry, it was found that they were all full, and I was conducted to a double-bedded room, six feet wide by twelve feet long, so that with the two *little tables*, and the two *chairs*, there was hardly any space to spare. I was then informed that I must pay the first month's lodging in advance; fifteen livres for one bed; twice as much for the two. As I wanted only one, and should have taken it in a room which contained no more, I paid only fifteen livres. 'But there is no water-bottle, nor other vessel?'—'You must buy them,' said the same officious personage, very ready to make a tender of services, of which it was easy to perceive the interested motive. To these acquisitions I added an ink-stand, paper and pens, and established myself in my new apartment.

The mistress of the house coming to visit me, I made inquiry concerning my rights and the customs of the place, and was told that the state allowed nothing to the prisoners.—' How then do they live?'—'They receive a plate of kidney-beans only, and a pound and a half of bread per day; but you would not be able to eat either of them.'—' I can easily believe that they are not like what I have been accustomed to; but I wish to know what belongs to every situation, and will make a trial.'— I made a trial accordingly; but, either the state of my stomach, or want of exercise, made me reject the prison diet; and I was obliged to have recourse to Madame Bouchaud's kitchen. She had made an offer of boarding me, which I accepted; and found her fare both good and economical, in comparison of what I might have sent for from the cook's shop, at a great dis-

tance,

tance, and in a desolate quarter of the town. A mutton chop, and a few spoonfuls of vegetables, for dinner, a sallad for supper, never any desert, and nothing but bread and water for breakfast; such were the dishes I ordered, and such was the fare I had been accustomed to at the Abbey. I mention it here, by way of opposing this manner of living, to the complaints soon after made by the section of the obfervatory, of my expences at Sainte Palagie, where it was said that I was endeavouring to corrupt the gaoler by giving treats to his family: hence great indignation among the *Sans-culottes*, and a proposal from some of them to dispatch me to the other world. This accords well with the clamorous nonsense of those women, who pretend that by dressing themselves up in fine clothes, they got admission into the circle of old countesses, at which I presided, in the Hotel of the Interior, and with the articles of the journal of the Mountain, which inserts letters written to me by refractory priests.

O Danton! thus it is that you direct the knife of the assassin against your victims. Strike! one more will add little to the catalogue of your crimes; but the multiplicity of them cannot cover your wickedness, nor save you from infamy. As cruel as Marius, and more terrible than Catiline, you surpass their misdeeds, without possessing their great qualities; and history will vomit forth your name with horror, when relating the carnage of the first days of September, and the dissolution of the social body in consequence of the events that took place on the second of June.

My courage did not sink under the new misfortunes I experienced; but the refinement of cruelty with which

they

they had given me a foretaste of liberty, only to load me with fresh chains, and the barbarous care with which they took advantage of a decree, by applying to me a false designation, as the mode of legalizing an arbitrary arrest, fired me with indignation. Feeling myself in that disposition of mind when every impression becomes stronger, and its effect more prejudicial to health, I went to bed; but as I could not sleep, it was impossible to avoid thinking. This violent state, however, never lasts long with me. Being accustomed to govern my mind, I felt the want of self-possession, and thought myself a fool for affording a triumph to my persecutors, by suffering their injustice to break my spirit. They were only bringing fresh odium on themselves, without making much alteration in the situation I had already found means so well to support: had I not books and leisure here as well as at the Abbey? I began indeed to be quite angry with myself for having allowed my peace of mind to be disturbed, and no longer thought of any thing, but of enjoying existence, and of employing my faculties with that independence of spirit which a strong mind preserves in the midst of fetters, and which thus disappoints its most determined enemies. As I felt that it was necessary to vary my occupations, I bought crayons, and had recourse to drawing, which I had laid aside some time. Fortitude does not consist solely in rising superior to circumstances by an effort of the mind, but in maintaining that elevation by suitable conduct and care. Whenever unfortunate or irritating events take me by surprise, I am not content with calling up the maxims of philosophy to support my courage; but I provide agreeable amusements for my

mind,

mind, and do not neglect the art of preserving health to keep myself in a just equilibrium. I laid out my days then with a certain sort of regularity. In the morning I studied the English language in Shaftsbury's Essay on Virtue, and in the poetry of Thomson. The sound metaphysics of the one, and the enchanting descriptions of the other, transported me by turns to the intellectual regions, and to the most touching scenes of nature. Shaftsbury's reason gave new strength to mine, and his thoughts invited meditation; while Thomson's sensibility, and his delightful and sublime pictures, went to my heart, and charmed my imagination. I afterwards sat down to my drawing till dinner time. Having been so long without handling the pencil, I could not expect to acquit myself with much skill; but we always preserve the power of repeating with pleasure, and of attempting with facility, whatever in our youth we have practised with success. Accordingly, the study of the fine arts, considered as a part of the education of young women, ought, in my opinion, to be less directed towards the acquisition of distinguished talents, than to inspiring them with the love of employment, making them contract a habit of application, and multiplying their means of amusement; for it is thus we escape from that *ennui* which is the most cruel disease of man in society; and thus we avoid the quicksands of vice, and seductions still more to be feared than vice itself.

I will not then make my daughter a professor *(une virtuose)*: I shall ever remember that my mother was afraid of my becoming too great a musician, or of my devoting

devoting myself entirely to painting, because she desired, above all things, that I should be fond of the duties of my sex, and learn to be a good housewife, in case of my becoming the mother of a family. My Eudora then shall learn to accompany herself in a pleasing manner on the harp, or to play with ease on the *forte piano*; and shall know enough of drawing, to enable her to contemplate the masterpieces of art with pleasure, to trace or imitate a flower which delights her, and to shew taste and elegant simplicity in the choice of her ornaments. It is my wish that the mediocrity of her talents may excite neither admiration in others, nor vanity in herself. It is my wish that she may please rather by her collective merit, than astonish at the first glance, and that she may rather gain affection by her good qualities, than applause by her brilliant accomplishments. But, good heavens! I am a prisoner, and a great distance divides us! I dare not even send for her to receive my embraces; for hatred pursues the very children of those whom tyranny persecutes; and no sooner does my girl in her eleventh year appear in the streets with her virgin bashfulness, and her beautiful fair hair, than wretches, hired or seduced by falsehood, point her out as the offspring of a conspirator. Cruel wretches! they well know how to break a mother's heart!

Could not I have brought her with me? - - - - I have not yet said what is the situation of a prisoner at Sainte Pelagie.

The wing appropriated to females, is divided into long and very narrow corridors, on one side of which are little cells like that which I have described as my lodging. There, under the same roof, upon the same line, and

and only separated by a thin plastered partition, I dwell in the midst of murderers and women of the town. By the side of me is one of those creatures who make a trade of seduction, and set up innocence to sale; and above me is a woman who forged assignats, and with a band of monsters to which she belongs, tore an individual of her own sex to pieces upon the highway. The door of each cell is secured by an enormous bolt, and opened every morning by a man who stares in impudently to see whether you be up or in bed: their inhabitants then assemble in the corridors, upon the staircases, or in a damp or noisome room, a worthy receptacle for this scum of the earth.

It will be readily believed that I confine myself constantly to my cell; but the distance is not great enough to save the ear from the expressions which such women may be supposed to utter, but which without hearing them it is impossible for any one to conceive.

This is not all: the wing where the men are confined, having windows in front of, and very near the building inhabited by the women, the individuals of the two sexes of analagous character, enter into conversation, which is the more dissolute, as those who hold it are unsusceptible of fear: gestures supply the place of actions, and the windows serve as the occasions of the most shameful scenes of infamous debauchery.

Such is the dwelling reserved for the worthy wife of an honest man!—If this be the reward of virtue on earth, who will be astonished at my contempt of life, and at the resolution with which I shall be able to look death in the face? It never appeared to me in a formidable shape; but at present it is not without its charms; and I
could

could embrace it with pleasure, if my daughter did not invite me to stay a little longer with her, and if my voluntary *exit* would not furnish calumny with weapons against my husband, whose glory I should support, if they should dare to carry me before a tribunal.

In the latter part of Roland's administration, conspiracies and threats succeeded each other so fast, that our friends often pressed us to leave the hotel during the night. Two or three times we yielded to their entreaties; but soon growing tired of this daily removal, I observed that malevolence would hardly go so far as to violate the abode of a man in office, while it might waylay and immolate him out of doors; and that, after-all, if such a misfortune were to happen, it would be more conducive to public utility, and to his personal glory, for the minister to perish at his post.

Accordingly we no longer slept out; but I had my husband's bed brought into my own room, that we might run the same hazard, and under my pillow or upon my night-table I kept a pistol, which I meaned to use, not for a vain defence, but to save myself from the outrages of assassins, in case I should see them approach. In that situation I passed three weeks; and certain it is that the hotel was twice beset, and that another time the Marseillois, hearing that some villanous project or other was on foot, sent eighty of their people to guard us. It is certain also that the Jacobins and Cordeliers were for ever repeating in their tribune, that a 10th of August was as necessary against Roland as it had been against Louis XVI; but as they said so, it might be presumed that they were not ready to realize their threat. Death, which I cheerfully braved at that time, cannot but appear

pear defirable to me at Sainte-Pelagie, did not powerful confiderations chain me to the earth.

My keepers foon began to fuffer more than myfelf from my fituation, and were at great pains to render it lefs difagreeable. The exceffive heat of the month of July rendered my prifon uninhabitable. The paper with which I covered the grates, did not prevent the fun from ftriking upon the white walls of my narrow cell, and though my windows remained open all night, the burning and concentrated air of the day did not get cool.

The gaoler's wife invited me to pafs my days in her apartment; but I limited my acceptance of this offer to the afternoon. It was then I thought of fending for a *forte-piano*, which I put into her room, and with which I fometimes charmed away the heavy hours. But what a modification did my moral fituation fuffer during that period! The rifing of fome of the departments feemed to announce the indignation they had conceived at the violence offered to their reprefentatives, and their refolution of avenging it, by reftoring the convention to its former integrity.

I knew that Roland was in a fafe and peaceful retreat, receiving the confolation, and the attentions of friendfhip; my daughter, taken into the houfe of venerable patriarchs, continued her exercifes, and her education, under their immediate infpection, and with their own children; and my friends, the fugitives, welcomed at Caen, were there furrounded by a refpectable force. I thought I faw the falvation of the republic growing out of events; and refigned to my own fate, I was happy ftill; for our happinefs depends lefs on external objects,

jects, than on the dispositions and affections of the mind. I employed my time in an useful and agreeable manner; I sometimes saw the four persons who used to visit me at the Abbey; the worthy *Grandpré*, whose place authorised him to come, and who came accompanied by a charming woman; the faithful Bosc, who brought me flowers from the *Jardin des Plantes*, of which the beautiful forms, the brilliant colours, and the sweet fragrance, diminished the horrors of my melancholy abode; and the kind Champagneux, who persuaded me so earnestly to continue the historical memoirs I had begun, that at his desire I resumed my pen, and for a while laid by my Tacitus and my Plutarch, to whom I was accustomed to devote my afternoons.

Madame Bouchaud did not think it enough to have offered me the use of her apartment. Perceiving that I availed myself of it with great reserve, she determined to remove me altogether from my gloomy cell, and to lodge me in a comfortable room with a fire-place, situated on the ground floor, and underneath her own chamber. Thus am I delivered from the shocking company which for three weeks has been my greatest torment. It will no longer be necessary for me to pass twice a day through a throng of the women of my neighbourhood, for the purpose of getting out of their way for a little time at least. I shall no longer see the turnkey of sinister countenance open my door every morning, and shut me in every night with a monstrous bolt, like a criminal whom it is necessary to keep in close confinement. It is the good-natured face of Madame Bouchaud, which offers itself to my eyes; whose kind attentions I perceive every moment. There is nothing, even to

the

the very jeffamine carried up before my window and winding its flexible branches round the bars, that does not teftify her defire to oblige. I look upon myfelf as her boarder, and forget my captivity. All my articles of ftudy and amufement are united around me; my *forte-piano* is by my bedfide, and receffes in the walls afford me the means of arranging my little effects in fuch a way as to preferve in my afylum that neatnefs in which I delight ...... But gold, and falfehood, and intrigue, and arms, are employed againft the departments which the truth was beginning to enlighten: foldiers deluded, or bought over, betray the brave Normans; Evreux is evacuated; Caen abandons the members to which it had afforded a refuge; domineering banditti, in what is ftill called a convention, declare them traitors to their country; their perfons are outlawed; their property is confifcated; their wives and children are taken into cuftody; their houfes are demolifhed; the members who chofe to remain in confinement are impeached, without any reafon being affigned; and every thing announces the triumph of audacious guilt over unfortunate virtue. That cowardice which marks the felfifhnefs and corruption of a degenerate people, whom we thought it poffible to reclaim by the light of reafon, but who were too far debafed; that cowardice delivers over to terror the perfidious adminiftrators, and the ignorant multitude. Every where the idea of peace and the defire of repofe, always illufory when it is not deferved, counfel the acceptance of a monftrous conftitution, which, had it even been better, ought not to have been received from the unworthy hands that held it out. There, where any refiftance might have arifen, it is ftifled by corruption; and the money of the nation is lavished to infure the fuccefs of its oppreffors. In their filly ftupor, a majority, incapable of reafoning, confider the facrifice of a few individuals as a trifling misfortune; they think to eftablifh juftice, peace, and fecurity, for themfelves, by fuffering them to be violated in the perfons of their reprefentatives; and receive the pledge of their fervitude as the fign of falvation. In the mean time a rod of iron is held over the weak Parifians, the pufillanimous witneffes of horrors, which they lament, but dare not make known: famine threatens them; poverty preys upon their vitals; oppreffion overwhelms them; the reign of profcriptions begins; denunciations come fhowering down on every fide; and the prifons overflow. Every where an infamous recompenfe awaits him who has a victim to offer; the porters of private houfes, kept fecretly in pay, become the chief informers, and fervants are no longer any thing but fpies.

An aftonifhing woman taking counfel, from her courage alone, came to inflict death upon the apoftle of murder and pillage. She deferves the admiration of the univerfe. But not being well acquainted with the ftate of things, her time and her victim were ill chofen. There was a greater criminal, to whom her immolating hand fhould have given the preference. The death of Marat only ferved the purpofes of his abominable fectaries: they transformed into a martyr the man whom they had taken for a prophet; and fanaticifm and knavery, always in a league, derived from this event an advantage fimilar to that which the murder of le Pelletier had procured them. Certainly that murder had been too fatal in its confequences to permit us to think that the

fugitive

fugitive members, entire strangers to the action of Paris*, were not equally so to that of Charlotte Corday; but their adversaries laid hold of it as a new mean of ruining them in the minds of the people. The most determined republicans, the only men of the assembly who joined to the courage of strict probity the authority of talents and knowledge, were represented as the favourers of despotism, and vile conspirators. At one time they are supposed to be in a league with the rebels of La Vendée, and on the sabres of the warriors desirous of defending them, the words *Vive Louis XVII.* are said to be inscribed: at another time they are accused of endeavouring to divide France into little republics, and are reprobated as federalists. It is with equal consistency that Brissot is taken into English pay, and that his wife, in a report sent to all the departments, is gravely represented as having retired to the queen's apartments at Versailles, and as holding secret councils there.

Nothing can be more ridiculous than this story to those who are acquainted with Brissot's wife, devoted to the domestic virtues, wholly taken up with the cares of her houshold, ironing her husband's shirts herself, looking through the key-hole to see if she may safely open the door to those who knock, and hiring a little miserable room in the village of St. Cloud, in order to have it in her power to carry the child that she has just weaned into the open air. But she is taken into custody; is conducted to Paris; and a guard is placed over her. Petion's wife, who was going to retire among her friends

---

* The murderer of le Pelletier.

till the storm should blow over, is arrested with her son. Miranda, whom the revolutionary tribunal had acquitted, is remanded to prison as a suspected person, on the information of his valet, a spy of Pache; all the generals are put under arrest; and Custine, whom, as I have been told by the prince de Linanges, the Austrians dreaded more than any of the rest, is threatened with the loss of his head. Disorganization spreads itself over the whole face of France, and a civil war breaks out in a variety of places. The acceptance of the constitution cannot procure for Lyons an act of oblivion for the justice it dared to execute on two or three of Marat's banditti; it is called upon to deliver up the heads of its richest inhabitants, and to pay a considerable sum of money; the high spirited Marseilles sends succour to the Lyonnese; and troops are recalled from the frontiers, which are left exposed to the ravages of the enemy, in order to set brother against brother, and to spill the blood of Frenchmen by the hands of the French themselves. In the mean time the enemy advances in the north; Valenciennes no longer exists; Cambray is blocked up; and the Austrian light troops appear in the environs of Peronne. Paris, like another Babylon, sees its brutish populace run in crowds to ridiculous festivals, or feast their eyes upon the blood of a multitude of wretches sacrificed to their ferocious distrust; while the selfish and unfeeling fill the theatres, and the timid citizen stays trembling at home, where he is not sure of sleeping, if it please his neighbour to say that he has made use of *uncivic* expressions, blamed the carnage of the 2d of September, or lamented the fate of the victims of Orleans, put to death without proof of their being privy

to

to an affassination which was *not* committed on the person of the infamous Bourdon. O my country! into what hands art thou fallen. Chabot and his fellows announce that Roland is at Lyons, affirm that he is exciting an infurrection in that city, and call for his impeachment and for mine: and at the same time they search the cellars of the observatory, and invest the house of one of his friends, where they suppose him to lie concealed.

All my friends are proscribed, fugitives, or in confinement; my husband only escapes from the fury of his adversaries by keeping close in a retreat which may be compared to the severest imprisonment; and it is even decreed that the few persons who come to console me shall undergo persecution.—Grandpré, dining in company with a man whom he did not know to be a justice of peace, and a member of the tribunal of the district, lamented the negligence of the magistrates, who suffered so many persons to languish in the prisons. On this the unknown personage discovered himself; affected a great desire to be made acquainted with abuses, to the reform of which he might have it in his power to contribute; and begged Grandpré to let him have his name and address, that he might call, and take him with him in his next visit to the prisons. That was only a pretext,—the justice of peace hastened to the committee of general safety, and fabricated an atrocious denunciation against Grandpré, whom he accused of being an accomplice in the death of Marat.—It seems as if we were living in the time of Tiberius; for, like his, this is the reign of informers.—Grandpré was taken up by an officer and four musketeers, who repaired to his apartment at five o'clock in the morning; ransacked his papers, and sealed up his effects. He had then about him a letter addressed by me to the unfortunate Briffot. What a crime might be made of this, to *me* for having written it, and to *him* for being the bearer! Luckily he found means to conceal it from their search; but it was not till after a tedious debate that he could obtain permission to remain under a guard at his office, instead of going to sleep at the abbey; nor was it till after the expiration of several days, that means were found to demonstrate the falsity of the charge.

Champagneux was less fortunate: to the crime of owing his appointment to Roland, he joined that of occupying a desirable place.—Collot d'Herbois went drunk to the office of the home department, between four and five o'clock in the afternoon, at the moment that the clerks had just left their desks to go to dinner: his business was to demand carriages, of which the minister had not the disposal. In a rage at not finding Garat, he swore, stormed, broke the legs of the chairs and table [*], went to the apartment of Champagneux, the first clerk, abused him, ordered the packets that were made up for the post-office to be opened, and quarrelled about the inclosure they contained. It was a kind of circular letter, consisting of questions, and intended to procure information concerning the state of the country. In his heated brain he arranged a denunciation, which he brought forward the next day, at the Convention, and on the strength of which a decree of arrest was passed both against Garat and Champagneux.

Garat came to the bar, made no complaint of Collot,

---

[*] These facts may appear exaggerated; but they are strictly true. I had them from an eye-witness, whose veracity is undoubted. They are confirmed by a late publication of Garat's.

explained

explained his conduct in the gentlest terms, pronounced a fulsome panegyric on the august assembly, and was sent back to his duty. Champagneux at first hid himself in a fright, but afterwards appeared. He was referred by the Convention to the Committee, and by the Committee was sent a prisoner to the *Force*. Garat solicited by others, and having an interest himself in the enlargement of Champagneux, whose services he could not dispense with, repaired to the Committee to obtain it. There he made it appear, that, without the assistance of a man so conversant in business, it would be impossible for him to remain in office, and by his friends, such as Barrere, if men like Barrere can be called friends, was encouraged to hope, that by offering his conditional resignation, Champagneux would be restored to him, as an inducement to continue in administration; but the rest of the Committee spoke out in plainer terms. He was required to fill up the place of Champagneux: his liberty and his life depended on his compliance. He was required to fill it up by the appointment of a young man, twenty-six years of age, destitute of experience in business, of all kinds of knowledge, and of every recommendation but the favour of the Committee, of which he was a tool. Garat, who never refused his masters any thing, submitted and then retired from his office, abandoning a post it was impossible for him to maintain*.

---

* Paré, formerly head-clerk to Danton, who had got him appointed secretary to the Council on Grouveile's departure, succeeded Garat; and the ex-minister, happy to effect a change, which, by delivering him from a place of responsibility, conferred on him one of twenty thousand livres a year, became secretary of the Council. It is not altogether useless to remark, that *Desforgues*, minister of foreign affairs, was also one of Danton's clerks.

But

But Champagneux was not set at liberty, and the fourth week of his detention has already passed. At the moment he was threatened with an arrest (for Collot had announced it as an act that would necessary follow his volition), Champagneux was in possession of almost the whole of my *Historical Memoirs*, the existence of which he wished to insure by taking a copy. Uneasy, agitated, and not doubting but the principles by which they were dictated, and the freedom with which they were written, were a direct passport to the scaffold, he committed them to the flames.—Yet these are the governors of the empire!—Collot, a strolling player by profession, by whose side sits a judge of the southern departments, who not long since condemned him to a year's imprisonment for an offence which he committed while a vagrant from barn to barn, and for which several of the judges wished to send him to the galleys!—Great strength of lungs, the gestures of a jack-pudding, the manœuvres of a knave, the extravagance of a madman, and the effrontery of ignorance; such were his means of success at the clubs, particularly at the club of the Jacobins, who were not ashamed to mention him at the time of the formation of the patriotic ministry under Louis XVI.

Collot thinking himself ill used by the appointment of Roland to the home department, to which he had directed his views, deemed him the more worthy of his hatred, as being an enemy by whom he was overlooked. From that moment his Jacobinical influence was directed against him, and that conduct, added to his other relative qualities,

qualities, procured him a seat in the Convention, as one of the Parisian deputation.

Champagneux, in his confinement, regrets his liberty less than the pleasure of sometimes alleviating my captivity, while I am afflicted at *his*, which he owes to his connexion with Roland and myself. As to Bosc, who has already given up his place of administrator at the post-office, and whom I endeavour to persuade not to run the risk of a prison by visiting me in mine, I see him once a week, as it were by stealth. In the midst of all these sorrows, I can however offer my friends a seat in the pleasant room, where the kind-hearted Madame Bouchaud has sequestered me from all the appearances of a prison. I am there exposed, it is true, to the inconvenience of having a sentry planted directly opposite my window, on whose account I am always obliged to keep my curtains drawn, and who comes to listen to every thing that is said when I am not alone; and I am disturbed by the horrible barking of three great dogs, whose kennel is at less than ten paces distance. I am also close to a large room, pompously styled the council-chamber, where the administrators of the police do their business when they come to examine a prisoner. It is to this neighbourhood that I am indebted for the knowledge of some curious scenes, of which I am going to say a few words.

Two men, whose names I once knew, and have either forgotten, or do not choose to repeat, because the names of such wretches are not deserving of mention, had been sent to prison for their malversations in the clothing of the troops, in which department of the public service they were employed. They had for friends, or for
accomplices,

accomplices, some people of their own description, and those people were actually administrators of the police. Charged in that quality with the maintenance of order in the prisons, and the superintendance of the gaolers, they came to Sainte-Pelagie once or twice a week, with other friends like themselves, ten or twelve in number, and sometimes more, sent for the two darling prisoners to the council-chamber, and there making the gaoler give them capons, chickens, eggs, wine, cordials, coffee, &c. consumed them at his expence, and kept up their orgies three or four hours together. No one would ever imagine, and most assuredly I shall not undertake to relate the brutal joy, the fulsome conversation, and the infamy of these entertainments. The word patriotism, stupidly applied, and repeated emphatically on every mention of the scaffold, to which it was proper to send all *suspected persons*; that denomination bestowed upon every one who had received a good education, or was possessed of a fortune not recently stolen; the disgusting kisses from those mouths, reeking with wine, smacking upon the cheeks of the new comers, and repeated in concert at the moment of breaking up; the obscene jests of men destitute of all morality, and strangers to all shame; and the silly pride of atrocious blockheads, who dreamed of nothing but denunciations, and whose sole science consisted in imprisoning their betters. - - - - -

Plato might well compare democracy to an *auction* of government, a kind of *fair*, where all possible modes of administration are intermixed. But how would he characterize that state of society where men like these are arbiters of the liberty of their fellow-citizens? Whenever

ever this agreeable company came, Bouchaud or his wife never failed to withdraw my key from the door, and to give me notice of their arrival. At laſt I took my reſolution, and ſhut my ears againſt their noiſe; I even found an entertainment in continuing my *Hiſtorical Memoirs*, and in writing vigorous paſſages, before the eyes, as it were, of wretches who would have torn me to pieces if they had heard only a ſingle phraſe.

As the 10th of Auguſt was at hand, and fears were entertained of a rehearſal of the 2d of September, in the priſons, the adminiſtrators found means to get out the rogues of their acquaintance; and by ſo doing put an end to the civic feaſts at Sainte-Pelagie. If I could perſuade myſelf to meddle with ſuch diſguſting matters, I could give very aſtoniſhing, and very ſhocking accounts, of the abuſes that prevail in the priſons—the criminals would there be ſeen converting into accomplices almoſt all the ſervants, and other perſons concerned in the buſineſs of the place; women of the town, guilty of ſerious offences, obtaining their enlargement without a trial, by means of the adminiſtrator, who ſleeps with them the night after; aſſaſſins, rich enough to pay an advocate *(defenſeur officieux)* with the produce of their robberies, bribing him to deſtroy the vouchers, and procure the impunity, of their crimes; and profeſſed thieves keeping up their intrigues with one another, and with their accomplices without; thieving ſtill, though immured in a priſon; and dividing the ſpoils with the turnkey, or with the *gendarme*, who appears to guard them. Every thing gets tainted or completely ſpoiled in theſe infectious places under a vicious adminiſtration,

tion, defiring only to deftroy, carelefs of correcting, and actuated by paffion alone.—'Compaffionate and generous Howard, who wanderedft over all Europe to vifit thofe gloomy dungeons, in which the wifdom of an equitable government ought never to let innocence languifh, and where it fhould alfo take care to diftinguifh weaknefs from criminality, how would your feeling heart have been hurt if you had been perfectly acquainted with the management of the prifons belonging to the nation then efteemed the gentleft upon earth!' There no diftinction is made between giddy youth and hardened guilt. I have feen a botanical ftudent, who had fpoken ill of Marat, confined in the fame room with highway robbers. There no refpect is fhewn to morals. I have feen a girl of fourteen, who was claimed by her parents, detained in the fame cell with the infamous woman who had juft feduced her, and who had been taken up for that offence. There no regard is had to decency, or attention to falubrity, in the conftruction of the edifice, or in the laying out of the internal fpace. A building is now erecting at Sainte-Pelagie, on an immenfe piece of ground, by an architect of confined ideas, a man of no mind, who is taking meafures contrary to every principle of rationality, and yet no perfon in the fuperior branches of adminiftration is either able or willing to correct his plan.

Here I muft do juftice to the prefent keeper. He does what he can in matters of detail, but nothing can prevent the bad confequences refulting from an organization effentially vicious. There ought to be either diftinct houfes, fome appropriated to criminals, and others to fufpicious or fufpected perfons, or elfe wings entirely detached;

detached; nor should there be any communication between the two sexes. But as this is not the place for a treatise upon the subject, I can only lament the destiny of a people, in the establishment of whose liberty it is impossible for those to believe who have once been witnesses to its extreme corruption.

On my first coming to Sainte-Pelagie, I was waited upon by a woman, confined for some trifling offence. Her services were an assistance to my weakness, while I had the means of making them an alleviation of her distress. Not but that I was very well able to be my own servant: *Tout sien bien au généreux courage**,' was said of Favonius performing for Pompey in his misfortunes the offices which valets are accustomed to perform for their masters. This may be applied with equal truth to the unfortunate man, stripped of his fortune, and providing for all his wants, and to the austere philosopher, disdaining every superfluity. Quintius† was roasting his turnips when he received the ambassadors of the Samnites; and I could have made my bed at Sainte-Pelagie; but, as in fetching water, and things of the like kind, it was necessary to go through long passages, and to mix with their various inhabitants, I was not sorry to have a person whom I could oblige by sending her on such errands. She continued to assist me in the room I had been indulged with, and was coming in one morning at the very moment that an administrator was

---

* Every thing becomes a noble spirit.

† By *Quintius*, Madame Roland means *Lucius Quintius Cincinnatus*, but *Marcus Curius Dentatus* is the personage of whom this anecdote is related by the Roman historians: ' *Legatis Somnitum aurum offerentibus, quum ipse in foco rapa torreret,*' &c. *Plin. de viris illustribus.* Transl.

at the door of the council-chamber. He asked who lodged there; desired to inspect the room; came in; cast an angry eye around him; and then went out, and complained to the keeper's wife of the degree of comfort she allowed me to enjoy.—' Madame Roland was indisposed (that was true); and I put her more in the way of receiving such assistance as she might stand in need of; besides she sometimes amuses herself with a *forte piano*, for which there is not room in a cell.'—' She must do without it: send her this very day into a corridor: it is your business to maintain equality.'

Unfeeling wretch! is it to maintain equality that you wish to confound me with the most abandoned of women?—Madame Bouchard, more distressed than can well be imagined, soon came to communicate to me the order she had received. I consoled her by conforming to it with much calmness and resignation; and it was agreed that I should come down in the course of the day to change the air, and to return to my studies, the materials for which I left where they were. Thus am I once more destined to see the turnkeys, to hear the creaking of the bolts, to breathe the fetid air of a corridor, sadly illumined in the evening by a lamp, of which the thick smoke blackens all the walls, and suffocates the neighbourhood. These are the humane actions, the signs of liberty given by those men, who upon the ruins of the Bastille recall to our recollection the cruelty of the governor killing Lauzun's spider, and who, in the *Champ de Mars*, send up birds carrying streamers, to announce to the inhabitants of the upper regions the felicity of the earth. Insolent comedians! you are playing your last parts: the enemy is at hand.—By the enemy I mean the departments

partments endeavouring to infure the triumph of reafon and of true liberty, and preparing your ruin.

Mine is inevitable, no doubt; I have deferved the hatred of all tyrants; but I only regret that of my country, which your chaftifement will confole, but cannot fave.

As to the reft, the confequences of oppreffion have filled the corridor I inhabit with women in whofe company I can remain without fhame, and even with pleafure. I have found there the wife of a juftice of peace, whofe neighbour afcribes to her expreffions ftyled uncivic; I have found there the wife alfo of the prefident of the revolutionary tribunal; and there I have found Madame Pétion.—' I little thought,' faid I on accofting her, ' when I was fharing your uneafinefs at the *Mairie* *, on the 10th of Auguft, 1792, that we fhould keep our fad anniverfary at Sainte-Pelagie, and that the fall of the throne would lead to our difgrace.'

* The refidence of the mayor.

RAPID OBSERVATIONS

On the Indictment drawn up by AMAR *against the Members of the Convention.*

IF there have existed a *conspiracy against the unity and indivisibility of the republic, against the liberty and the safety of the French people,* it is evident that it can only have been formed by the abettors of despotism, by ambitious men, wishing to monopolize power and riches, or by the enemies of mankind.

Brissot, Gensonné, Vergniaux, Guadet, Gorsas, Petion, Buzot, &c. are accounted such. These men must then have shewn, on more occasions than one, their hatred of liberty, their thirst of gain, their eagerness to obtain places, all the vices and corruption, in short, that are natural to such characters. Supposing even that they had assumed the mask of hypocrisy, it was impossible for the end they had in view to remain concealed: their conduct must have betrayed it, and their interested motives must have evidently appeared. Let us enquire into what they were; let us see how they have acted; and we shall be able to judge of what is laid to their charge. After that it will be time to go in search of the *conspiracy* itself, which very possibly may resemble the story of the *golden tooth* *; or may amount to nothing more than the

---

* After some of the greatest natural historians and philosophers in Europe had been long employed in endeavouring to account for the existence of a golden tooth in a living subject, they found out with surprising sagacity that the tooth was a false one. *Transf.*

well-

well-known efforts of aristocrates and royalists, manifested as early as the infancy of the revolution, and connected with the enterprizes of foreign powers.—Let us look at a few of these men in private life before the year 1789, the æra when the busy scene of politics, then opening, first brought them forward to public view; and let us observe the course they afterwards pursued. Advocates for the most part, some had distinguished themselves at the bar, others had made themselves known in the republic of letters; several, remarkable only for the integrity they had displayed in their professions, were seated in the States General, by the esteem that integrity had procured them, while several others devoted themselves to the laborious, but honourable functions of journalists, and struggled courageously with despotism driven to despair.

Pétion, simple in his manners, moderate in his desires, and married to a woman of excellent sense, resided at Chartres. Esteemed by his fellow-citizens, who had witnessed his birth, and already noted for that philosophy which marks a good understanding, at an early period in life he was deemed worthy of a seat in the assembly of the states.

Buzot, distinguished at Evreux by his strict probity, and premature prudence, inspired confidence, and deserved consideration at an age when so many others think of nothing but pleasure. A taste for study, and the solitary habits of a meditative mind, filled up all those moments which he did not devote to the bar; while manners equally pure and gentle, rendered him dear to his friends. The warmth of his sentiments, the ease of his elocution, and the austerity of his principles, procured him the honourable office of carrying his country's complaints and demands to the States General.

Gorsas, the father of a numerous family, undertook, from the very beginning of the revolution, to conduct a periodical paper, in which he combated the still powerful court, and devoted himself to the defence of the people, always endeavouring to establish, and never neglecting to reclaim, their rights.

Briffot, a writer from his early youth, had preached liberty in the time of despotism, and humanity during the reign of tyranny: he had long prayed for the revolution, had helped to bring it forward by exposing the abuses of the times, and had undergone imprisonment as a punishment for the freedom of his writings. More taken up with moral truths in politics than with the care of his fortune, he had engaged in several speculations, the failure of which had increased his poverty without injury to his honour. The revolution was the signal of his political life: he began his career in the midst of storms, discussing principles, sparing no one who appeared to violate them, and labouring without intermission for the public weal.

I stop for a moment at these four personages: the two first made a figure in the constituent assembly; Briffot obtained a seat in the succeeding legislature; and all four became members of the Convention. Was there a single circumstance in which they acted unlike themselves? Did they assume any authority? Did they acquire any wealth? Or did they aim at the supreme power for themselves and their friends?

Petion

Petion and Buzot served the cause of liberty in the constituent assembly, with a zeal and constancy which procured them the hatred of aristocracy, and the favour of the people: but popular favour is inconstant, while persevering hatred gains fresh strength by the accession of all the jealous, whose attacks never fail to follow any brilliant success. Buzot, belonging to the criminal tribunal of Evreux, preferred doing his duty in his native country to the exercise of the same functions at Paris, which would have better suited an ambitious man; he supported his reputation in the presence of his fellow-citizens, and of the enemies he had made himself by his civism; and obtained by his merit a seat in the Convention, after having established a popular society in the town, as an indispensable barrier against the struggles of despotism in chains, but not subdued. It cannot be said that he had either his re-election, or any kind of employ in view on leaving the constituent assembly, any more than Petion; for they were the very men who procured the passing of the decree forbidding the members of that assembly to hold any place or to be re-elected for four years to come. They had even demanded an interval of six; but at the time of the revision that decree was repealed, in spite of their endeavours to maintain it. Buzot then entered the Convention as pure as he had left the constituent assembly; and there for a while we will leave him. We shall see hereafter how he conducted himself, and shall be able to judge whether a man who braved clamour and outrages in support of his opinions, even admitting some of them to be erroneous, could be an ambitious hypocrite, or a conspirator.

Petion was elevated to the mayoralty by popular favour, and preserved it till after the 10th of August, as well as the hatred of the court, which manifested itself on every occasion, even to the very last. It is only of late that any one has ventured to accuse him of going to the palace for the purpose of defending it, while it is well known that he was exposed to its fire. The calumniating assertion of his having given *Mandat* orders to fire upon the people, is also of recent date. I ask what could tempt Petion, detested by the court, and beloved by the people, to betray the latter, and serve the former, when it stood on the very brink of ruin? Could he who had acquired popularity by combating regal power, have any reason to forfeit it, when the people were beginning to obtain power? Let us put the philosopher and the zealous citizen out of the question: let us look only to the man; and we shall see that even in the estimation of ambition and self-interest, the conduct attributed to Petion would have been absurd; and that if he had not too much principle, he had at least too much good sense, to fall into such an error. He was prevented by his office from putting himself at the head of the insurrection; and to prevent his opposing it, he should have been rendered incapable of acting, or confined. This the heedless commune forgot to do, and I remember, that Lanthenas went twice from the *Mairie* to the town-house, to advise their putting a strong guard on his hotel. The reporter (Amar) did not say a syllable of the massacres of the second of September: he wisely avoided the danger of touching on a question, both sides of which had been supported by the Mountaineers. When Roland denounced those massacres, the Jacobins said they were the work of the people and of its vengeance:

geance: they even made it a crime not to applaud them; and when Petion, with the reft of the right fide, obtained a decree to profecute the murderers, Petion and the right fide were called the enemies of liberty and of the people. But when the decree had fallen into defuetude, when the Jacobins triumphed, and the twenty-two were profcribed, the Jacobins themfelves, and Hebert among the firft of them, impudently afferted that the maffacres were Petion's work.

Guadet, *Vergniaux*, and *Genfonné*, diftinguifhed by their talents, and well known at Bourdeaux as friends to the revolution, were elected members of the legiflative affembly. They were the firft men for talents in that body, a kind of ariftocracy which procured them more numerous and more dangerous enemies than any want of civifm could have done. They alternately filled the prefident's chair on the tenth of Auguft, at that critical moment when the weak would have trembled at fuch a painful pre-eminence; nor can any but knaves reproach them with the moderation and the temper they difplayed in their conduct at that interefting period. Briffot naturally became intimate with them, becaufe he approached nearer to their level than any other perfon, in like manner as a fimilarity of fentiments had made him connect himfelf with the defenders of principles in the conftituent affembly, to which he did not belong: the countryman and friend of Petion, he became acquainted with fuch of his colleagues as fupported that caufe in favour of which his journal was compofed.

He had laboured under the fame miftake as many other perfons, in regard to la Fayette; or rather it may be faid, that la Fayette, fwayed at firft by the principles he had adopted, had no longer the strength of mind necessary to support them when the struggle became difficult; or that, fearing the consequences of too great a power in the hands of the people, he deemed it prudent to establish some kind of counterpoise. The fact is, that as he professed republicanism in private, Brissot was a long while before he could believe him guilty, when he was become so in the eyes of more violent men. But he had blamed him without reserve, and publicly declared his rupture with him, before the affair of the *Champ-de-Mars*. Here the reporter piques himself so little upon accuracy, that he confounds dates; he makes Brissot come to the Jacobins in *March* 1791, to prepare the business of the *Champ-de-Mars*, which did not take place till *July*, and which was solely occasioned by the flight and return of the king in the month of June. It is well known besides, that Brissot did not go to the Jacobins to excite them to sign the petition, but merely because he was appointed one of the committee to draw it up. I remember to have heard him relate on the following day, that *Laclos*, who was also of the committee, complained of such a violent head-ach that he could not hold the pen, and that he begged of Brissot to take it; that the same Laclos proposed the insertion of an article which he mentioned with an air of indifference, but which would have been favourable to d'Orleans; and that he (Brissot) rejected it with indignation, and substituted the passage recommending a republic, for which that moment was peculiarly proper, and might have been turned to great account. It is also well known that the assembly having decided in favour of the king, the Jacobins, instead of sending their petition to the *Champ-de-Mars*, sent deputies

deputies there to say, that it was not a proper place for their purpose, after the decree. This took place on the Saturday. I saw the deputies come to the *Champ-de-Mars* at noon, with not more than two or three hundred persons, and where Verrieres, the little hump-backed cordelier, and some others, were declaiming upon the national altar. It was on the Sunday morning, that two men were hanged, when there were not thirty persons assembled, a fact which I have heard attributed with some probability to the contrivance of the Lameths and others, who wanted an opportunity of employing force, and inspiring terror. Certain it is, that Sunday having brought together a great number of people, who had been attracted by the vague report of a petition, while that of the hanging business had not as yet got abroad, *Robert* set about drawing one up, completed it, and was getting it signed, when the military were called out, in consequence of a denunciation made to the assembly, and of the violent letter written by Charles Lameth, the president, to the commune of Paris, setting forth the necessity of repressing the horrid disorders of which two men had been the victims. Thus did the morning murder, committed, as it were, by stealth, serve as a pretext for shooting the people assembled in the afternoon. The red flag was hoisted at the town-hall, terror and imprisonment were the order of the day, and prepared the triumph of the revisors, who wished to give strength to the party of the court. Surely it will be quite enough to read the *Patriot** of that time, to judge whether it be possible that Brissot, who denounced the

* Brissot's Journal.

affair

affair of the Champ-de-Mars, supported the people, and attacked the revisors, could at the same time have been their accomplice. This accusation is absurd in the extreme! But every thing is so from one end to the other of this work of iniquity. I will not enter here into the question of the war, which was the signal of the great division that took place among the patriots. Robespierre, fiery, jealous, greedy of popularity, and inclined to domineer, both by his nature, and the high opinion he entertained of his own merit, put himself at the head of the party that opposed the declaration of hostilities. It would be worth the trouble to examine the speeches on the subject: to me it appeared that the mass of enlightened persons were in general for the affirmative, and consequently of Brissot's opinion. Certain it is that the court was very repugnant to the measure, and that the king was in a manner overruled by his council. He had every thing to gain by delay: the enemy were making their preparations at their ease, and our inaction would have delivered us into their hands, a defenceless prey. Robespierre could not forgive Brissot this triumph. The ice was broken, and from that moment it became his sole object to bring forward all the misfortunes that befel us, whether inevitable or not, as crimes against the partisans of the war. The exaggeration of passion became by degrees a system of refined calumny, artfully contrived, and obstinately persevered in. Brissot could no longer make the eulogium of any man, without its being construed into perfidy, if that man afterwards departed from the line of duty. Brissot was acquainted with several persons in the ministry by whom he was esteemed—here was another reason of jealousy and distrust. Those ministers, honourably dis-

graced

graced by the court, were recalled after the fall of the throne; and Briffot at that time was one of the few men in the affembly poffeffed of any talents, or exercifing any influence: Briffot confequently appeared an important perfonage to Robefpierre, who determined to ruin him, and had full leifure to effect his purpofe; for Briffot, conftantly confiding in the goodnefs of his intentions, could not prevail upon himfelf to go and enter the lifts at the Jacobins with an everlafting haranguer, who tired him to death. He defpifed the adverfary by whom he was overcome. But who could have believed the convention fo weak, or the people fo ftupid? Thofe only, who not fuffering themfelves to be hurried along by the current of daily events, recur frequently to the page of hiftory, meditate upon its contents, and compare the prefent with times paft. I never faw any man in place do fo fince the revolution; indeed they have hardly time to breathe, and to anfwer to the calls of each returning day, without an extreme and uncommon economy in the diftribution of their hours.

The letter of Genfonnè and his affociates to Louis XVI. cannot be conftrued into treafon, unlefs by the moft determined malevolence. It is true, nobody could at that time be fure of a fuccefsful revolution: the wifeft men were therefore defirous that the king fhould feel the neceffity of enforcing the conftitution, and refolve upon recalling, and retaining thofe minifters who were fincerely inclined to execute the laws. They had given proofs of their patriotifm, and the application for their recal was not a ftep directed by private intereft, but the expreffion of the general will. Roland, for his part, knew nothing of the letter until a late period, and probably would never

never have heard of it if it had not become public. But let us attend to the charges brought against him in these articles of impeachment, which will reflect everlasting disgrace on the age and nation, that could either applaud them, or even suffer them to pass, without the strongest marks of reprobation.

"The very day after the 10th of August," say these articles, "Genſonné and his faction posted up libels re-
"flecting upon those who had contributed to the fall of
"the throne, upon the Jacobins, upon the council-ge-
"neral of the commune, and upon the people of Paris.
"The pens of Louvet, Briſſot, and Champagneux, were
"set to work; enormous packets of those libels were
"seen at Roland's house, and all his servants were em-
"ployed in dispersing them."

I have read this passage twice, without being able to conceive how any one could dare to write it. Genſonné never to my knowledge posted up any thing: Louvet was editor of the *Sentinel*, of which complete collections exist: it was of great service to the revolution, and is an everlasting refutation of these assertions; for it breathes nothing but liberty, great and wise principles, the hatred of tyranny, and the love of equality. Roland has perhaps contributed as much as any body to reconcile men's minds to the revolution; his circular letters exist; let them be read; and let any one be pointed out, that is not even excellent. Champagneux never dispatched any papers but those printed by order of the assembly; nor was any alteration ever made in them; the contrary supposition is as absurd as it is abominable. In the first place, it was impossible, for it was not Roland who had them printed, but the authors at

Baudoins,

Baudoins, from whom the minister used to demand a certain number of copies: secondly, it was useless; for supposing that he made a selection, he was free to send off a smaller number of those which he deemed the least deserving of attention: and, lastly, if there had been the smallest breach of faith, the persons interested would not have waited a year to make their complaints, and demonstrate the deceit. What then can be intended by this ridiculous passage?—I have divined it; and it is a matter which demands some explanation.

In revolutionary movements, the most active people are not always the most blameless: how many beings come forward only that they may appear of some consequence in the world! Their services, however, are not to be despised; but when once the point in view is gained, it becomes necessary to lose no time in re-establishing order to avoid the dissolution of the social body. The commune formed on the 10th of August had contributed to the fall of the tyrant: they did well; but several of its members had been guilty of various excesses; a great deal of pillage and robbery had taken place at the *Tuileries* and elsewhere; considerable sums had been given to the commune for the purchase of corn; and it was the duty of the minister of the home department to demand their accounts, and to transmit them to the legislative body. Roland then pressed the commune to give in their accounts; but the commune being little disposed, and still less able, to comply, the minister, with a view to justice, and to avoid sharing in the blame, made his report to the assembly accordingly. If the assembly had possessed sufficient energy, it would not have waited for such an opportunity, or at least would have

have laid hold of it, to conſtitute a new commune, a political operation equally juſt and neceſſary. But Danton, who made uſe of the commune, was miniſter: he had partiſans in the aſſembly; and contrived to keep his tool. Roland remained then in a difficult ſituation; liable to accuſation if he did not demand theſe accounts, and ſure to be hated if he did. His upright character did not permit him to heſitate; his auſterity perhaps gave ſtill greater ſolemnity to the demand; and when he was required to repreſent the ſtate of Paris to the aſſembly, he gave no quarter to the errors, the follies, and the faults of the commune. They were in great number; and the commune conſequently became his enemy. Thus did he acquire the hatred of that active body, who among the populace had the reputation of being the patriots of the 10th of Auguſt, and the exterminators of tyranny. Add to the commune all thoſe excited by the plunderer, Danton, againſt a colleague whoſe auſterity was a conſtraint upon him, and who had beſides denounced the September maſſacres, another exploit of a part of the commune, Santerre, &c. Add alſo thoſe whom the jealous Robeſpierre ſet againſt Briſſot's connexions, and you will have altogether a very conſiderable number, either of guilty men who felt the neceſſity of getting rid of their watchful denunciator, or of extravagant patriots prepoſſeſſed in favour of the heroes of the 10th of Auguſt, without ſeeing to the bottom of the buſineſs, or of people intereſted in ſupporting them, or of the ignorant whom they impoſed upon, with a few envious popular leaders, well ſkilled in contriving the overthrow of a man in poſſeſſion of the public eſteem. Such was the origin of a party, which was increaſed by all the

new-

new-comers to the convention, too little acquainted with Paris, and public affairs, to form a right judgment of things, and by all those whose vanity was hurt by the superiority of the distinguished members, with whom Roland naturally became intimate, because men of equal capacity are ever fond of one another's company. Had I more time, I could follow this party through all its ramifications, and indicate all its enterprises; but this is enough to put others in the way of coming at the truth.

It now appears clearly, that the party at present predominant, of which Amar is the organ, bestows the appellation of *libel* upon those writings in which Roland exhibited the state of Paris, called for the accounts of the commune, held up the massacres of September to public indignation, and recommended the establishment of order by way of reconciling all hearts to the revolution; which is somewhat more difficult than killing people, according to the practice of these gentlemen. They do not point out these pretended libels, for that would be burning their fingers; but they speak of libels in general, and the public believing there must needs be some foundation for a charge so boldly brought forward, applaud the declamation, and think themselves avenged when their own champions are put to death.

The understanding kept up with the Prussians is a piece of extravagance which one knows not how to characterize, and Brunswick must surely laugh at seeing people accused of being his friends who attacked him with so much vigour. It will suffice to read the letter in which it is pretended that Roland confesses the existence of a plan for quitting Paris, to form a judgment of the matter, especially as to the intention of opening a pasa paſſage for Brunſwick. I know, that on the ſuppoſition of the Pruſſians approaching very near Paris, the queſtion, what would be proper to do, or whether it would be expedient to ſend away from that town the national repreſentation, in which the whole empire was intereſted, was once debated; but the diſcuſſion was ſlight, and hypothetical, more ſo indeed than it ought to have been; nor did any one of the miniſters threaten his colleagues. It was Danton, who, after the event, thought of bringing forward the denunciation, by way of making a merit of it to himſelf, and of injuring Roland. I recollect thoſe matters perfectly, having heard my huſband mention them on the breaking up of the council, which was then held at his hotel. As to the great movement of the people of Paris, it is well known that it ſerved as a veil for the maſſacres of the month of September, and that it was Kellerman's action on the 20th of that month that ſaved the republic.

It is not leſs ridiculous to hear the government of that time accuſed of ſtarving the people. Never during Roland's adminiſtration were proviſions ſo ſcarce, and difficult to procure, as they are become ſince: his anxiety on that head was extreme, and any one may recur to what he ſays of the bad adminiſtration peculiar in that reſpect to the commune of Paris.

It is an infamous and abſurd calumny to aſſert that Roland employed the ſums given him to purchaſe proviſions, in the pay of hireling writers. In the firſt place, thoſe ſums never paſſed through his hands, nor could he diſpoſe of them otherwiſe than by orders upon the treaſury indicating the purpoſes for which they were wanted. Secondly, he gave an account of thoſe monies; he did

ſo

so every month, and repeated it on his going out of office, the whole accompanied by sufficient vouchers. Of these accounts he never ceased to call for a report; and they were accordingly examined; but as no fault could be found with them, the Mountain would never suffer a report to be made. Those who doubt it need only ask *Dupin*, a deputy and one of the commissioners charged with their examination; they need only ask *Saint-Aubin*, a commissioner of accounts, by whom the commissioners of the Convention were assisted in their labours, which lasted two months, and in which they proceeded with great rigour and a desire of finding fault, but without success. In the third place, no more than one hundred thousand livres (£4167) were given to Roland to pay for compositions and printing, out of which in six months he only spent thirty-four thousand (£1417), of which he likewise gave an account: the rest remained in the public treasury, as appears by the statement of what had been disbursed.

It requires a degree of malignity scarcely credible to advance such scandalous falsehood! Roland never established any new offices in his department; he only assigned to particular clerks the care of forwarding the papers he was charged to send off; nor did he ever give to any thing the name of *formation of public spirit*: his enemies began by inventing the chimera, and afterwards baptized it as they thought proper. As to me, I never interfered, much less did I direct any thing: I defy the proof of it. Roland had nothing to do with his colleagues in the department of finances; nor did his colleagues ever interfere in forwarding papers. It is impossible to mention a single paper dispatched by Roland himself, which did not tend to attach the people to the 10th of August, instead of inducing them to cast an odium on the events of that day. Roland had no command over the administration of the post-office to get any thing intercepted; nor, if he had, would the administrators ever have been able, without courting their own ruin, to engage in so odious a manœuvre. If they had only attempted it, how severely would they have been punished; they, who have been so much persecuted, and whose places have been taken from them, though their persons have not been touched?

It is false that Roland ever suppressed any thing which he was directed to forward: I have seen him send off the speeches of Marat. It is equally false that any thing was or could be mutilated, as I have said before: I have shewn that it was no less impossible than improbable, that the denunciation would not have been delayed till this time, if only a single instance of the kind had occurred; and that even now, when they have the impudence to advance it, they neither can nor dare cite a fact. But what an excellent precaution was that of accusing Roland and the Moniteur of making the mountaineers *appear like madmen* in the eyes of the whole republic, by the misplacing of a word! Not being able to annihilate history, they wish to bring its materials into discredit! O my God! if nothing were to remain but their calumnies and their conduct, the atrocity of their falsehoods would nevertheless appear. For a few years truth may be reduced to silence; but it cannot be extinguished: the very efforts made to annihilate it operate a contrary way, and serve to give evidence of its existence.

The

The discovery of the iron door is also brought forward against Roland as a crime; and nothing is more easy by way of accounting for the want of proof against the pretended Briffotine faction, than to suppose that he suppressed a part of its contents. But Roland had witnesses, and Roland did not contradict himself. A locksmith of the name of *Gamin*, living at Versailles, gave information of his having been employed by Louis XVI. to make a little hiding-place in his apartment at the Tuileries; but did not know what it might contain. Roland was charged with the inspection of the Tuileries: the palace and every thing belonging to it were intrusted to his care. Taking with him *Gamin*, and *Heurtier* a respectable architect, he repaired to the king's apartment, where, in a passage between two doors, Gamin lifted up a pannel of wainscot, and discovered a little iron door, which Roland ordered him to open. It served to close a hole in the wall in which several packets of papers were found. Roland called a servant, ordered a napkin to be brought, took out the packets, without untying them, cast his eyes upon the indorsements, which announced a correspondence with the generals and several other persons, put them in the napkin in the presence of Heurtier and Gamin, gave the parcel to his servant, and repaired to the convention, where he deposited them in a formal manner. As he was passing through the apartments he met a member, who asked him what he had there.—'Things of consequence,' answered he, 'which I am going to carry to the convention.'—It remains to be said, that when the minister of the interior was made responsible for the palace, and every thing it contained, the convention appointed a committee of some of its members to examine all the papers printed or in manuscript, which were there at the time of the assault, and which had been collected together. The members of the committee were angry that the minister had not sent for them to be present at the discovery. But Roland thought nothing could be more natural, upon Gamin's information, than to repair to the place; and, upon finding the papers, to submit them to the inspection of the convention. He conducted himself like a man whose conscious rectitude renders him incapable of distrust; though certainly very unlike an artful man of the world, who foresees all possible events, and takes care not to hurt the vanity of others. Roland was guilty of no real fault on this occasion; but he discovered great want of prudence and caution. Add to this, that among the members of the commission at the palace was one *Calon*, a person whom Roland despised, and with whom he sometimes had disputes, because the commissioners wished to exceed their powers, and to turn every thing topzy-turvy at the palace when they pleased, while Roland, naturally rigid, and deriving a right to resist from his responsibility, frequently opposed their proceedings. To give a good idea of this Calon, it will suffice to say, it was a matter of public notoriety, that he had set up a coffee-house and tavern close to the assembly, in partnership with a woman whom he kept.

It is now easy to see the origin of all the outcry about the iron cabinet, and to conceive how eagerly Roland's different enemies availed themselves of appearances to throw suspicion on his conduct, and how many little passions concurred in raising doubts concerning that circumstance.

cumſtance. Of what value is it ſince become to thoſe, who, wiſhing to accuſe Roland's friends in the convention of a conſpiracy, find it ſo convenient to make the world believe that the cabinet contained papers which the miniſter concealed! But recollect dates, calculate facts, and by attending particularly to the one in queſtion, you will ſee, if Roland had meant to convey any thing away, he would firſt have repaired in ſecret to the place, after which he would have called witneſſes, and obſerved every neceſſary form in the diſcovery. His rapid and incautious way of proceeding, by expoſing him to blame, muſt prove his innocence to every reflecting mind. *Heurtier* exiſts; he is a man advanced in years, and generally eſteemed; and *Gamin* exiſts alſo: they took minutes of all that paſſed, which will not be loſt to hiſtory any more than theſe details. I ſhall make no remark on the charge in which Roland is accuſed of favouring the partiſans of ariſtocracy, and of receiving the emigrants with open arms. Roland in his adminiſtration was juſt, impartial, and ſevere: he received nothing but the law with open arms: it was the object of all his attention, and the guide of all his deciſions. It muſt no doubt appear as ſtrange to ariſtocracy to be put under the protection of ſuch a patron, as it muſt to Brunſwick to hear himſelf ſtyled Roland's friend: but theſe are follies which will not long prevail. True it is that the republic once eſtabliſhed, Roland wiſhed to attach its very enemies to it by an equitable form of government: he wiſhed for good laws inſtead of blood. Thoſe principles inſpired with a kind of confidence the perſons who, without being fanatics in the cauſe of royalty, were however far from being republicans,

republicans. They felt their prejudices give way, and acknowledged that the minister of the Interior, although a patriot, appeared to be an honest man. The jealous noted down these confessions, that they might represent Roland as a partisan of aristocracy; a title by which they have since distinguished every friend of reason and humanity.

I should be glad to know how Roland, who, under the old government, had stood in the way of his own promotion by supporting the liberty of commerce, on which subject his opinions were considered as crimes; who had professed his principles in works published from fifteen to twenty years before; who, faithful to those principles at the time of the revolution, had taken such a decided part in its favour as to attract the enmity of all the aristocracy of Lyons; who, elevated to the ministry, had there conducted himself with the greatest firmness and energy; who had dared to write a letter to the king, which the partisans of the throne have not yet forgiven him; who, recalled to the administration of public affairs by the insurrection of the 10th of August, was interested in defending it both by his interest and his glory; how, I say, could Roland seek to decry it; to favour the royalists who hated him, or would have looked upon him with eyes of distrust; and to restore aristocracy, of which he had drawn upon himself the hatred, and which at this very moment is rejoicing at the persecution he undergoes? What could he have in view? He had reached the highest elevation then attainable, and enjoyed great consideration: both ambition and self-interest could seek for nothing more than to remain in place; and if he had listened to them he would
have

have soothed men's passions, flattered the different parties, and have been upon his guard against giving offence. The care of not making enemies is the strongest characteristic of the ambitious man, already arrived at eminence in a republic; while Roland, on the contrary, rigorously denounced the abuses he could not repress, never flattered any man, nor ever gave way to the violence or to the prejudices of the times. This is the conduct of a sincere and courageous man, and not that of a hypocrite.—Let us now return to the members of the Convention, to whom the same reasoning will apply.

The electoral body of Paris was evidently at the command of Robespierre and Danton: its nominations were entirely their work. It is notorious that Robespierre made an harangue against Priestley, and in favour of Marat: it is notorious that he brought forward his brother: it is equally known that Danton, laying aside his ministerial functions, repaired to the hustings to exercise his sway; nor is it forgotten, that these leaders of the electors were the means of getting d'Orleans returned. (Here I ask, by the way, Why he was not waited for at the trial of the deputies with whom he was confounded in the articles of impeachment, and to whom he was assigned as an accomplice?) Among the Parisian delegates to the Convention were seen the members of the famous Committee of Vigilance *(surveillance)*, that directed the massacres of September, and advised the departments to imitate so good an example, in a circular letter, which is well known, and which Danton forwarded under his own cover. There were also seen men accused of robberies, whom the council-general, composed in part of new members, has since thought it indispensable to denounce, although sitting in the Convention, where they still remain on the summit of the Mountain (Sergent and Panis). The *constituents*, repairing to the Convention, and acquainted with Paris, the revolution, and all the men of any note, were uneasy at this Parisian deputation, indignant at the events of the 2d of September, disposed to distrust the former, and to punish the authors of the latter. That disposition would not have escaped the persons interested, even if the *constituents* had endeavoured to conceal it, which they did not. But the Convention opened before it was complete, and the Parisian members formed a party, which was reinforced by all the ignorant and weak, as fast as they arrived: it had collected a considerable number by the time the whole Convention had assembled, and all the *constituents* were arrived. I need not say, that I give this appellation to the members who had belonged to the assembly of 1789, and who, for the most part, seated themselves on what was called the right side of the Convention.

The agitation of Paris, the conduct of the commune, the weakness of the department*, the high tone of its deputies, and the tyranny of the galleries, suggested the idea of a departmental guard, as the first step to insure the liberty of the national representation, to remind the Parisians that they were not its masters, and to prevent the departments from forgetting the necessity of maintaining an equilibrium for the common advantage. In Buzot's

---

* Department means here the directory of the department of Paris, which made some feeble attempts to check the presumption of the Commune. *Transl.*

report

report on the subject may be seen the principal reasons in favour of the proposition. It was a gauntlet thrown down as the signal for combat. The Parisian members felt they were in danger of losing their ascendance, and as some of the number were criminals, who could only be saved by maintaining it, every effort was made to parry so fatal a blow. From that moment it became a war of extermination, and as such they carried it on; but their adversaries were not sufficiently aware of the danger; they were not ready to coalesce, because they did not imagine that truth stood in need of a party; they neglected the Jacobin club, because the Jacobins gave them a bad reception; and they did not intrigue, because they had neither money nor cunning for the purpose. About forty of them used indeed to meet and converse at Valazé's, whence there proceeded much courage to support principles, and brave clamour, and much devotion to the public good; but never any measures, unless in the shape of motions, which were imputed to them as crimes. They wished to work on the constitution in the best way they might be able, since it was in vain to hope by further skirmishing to get possession of higher ground. The leaders of the Parisian deputation were desirous, on the contrary, to entangle the Convention in a trial, that they might keep up the heat of the public mind; make a merit of the death of a man already tumbled from the throne, and incapable of doing mischief; and retard a constitution, of which the completion would have restored order, and set bounds to their power. But, it may be said, these are the men who have made one since the 2d of June—Yes, and these are the men who prevented it before, as the journals of the time will shew; and the

proof

proof that they care no more about it at prefent is, that after having got it accepted, they have fufpended its execution, by declaring that France remains in a ftate of revolution; fo that the departments, which were only induced to accept it by laffitude, enjoy no greater repofe than before. Never, indeed, did they fuffer fo much agitation and mifery of every kind. It is eafy for any man who has attended the fittings of the Convention, to fay whence all the fcandalous fcenes proceeded. When the members of the right fide reafoned, they were accufed: if they attempted to defend themfelves they were called to order, loaded with abufe by the galleries, and even fpit upon: if, indignant at this treatment, they appealed to their conftituents, they were called confpirators, and clubs and piftols were held up in their faces; and yet, now they are on their trial, it is faid they governed. What have they done at their own pleafure?—Nothing whatever: they could not then be either in poffeffion of power, or leading men in the Convention. Their fpeeches in the king's affair fufficiently prove their good fenfe, and their defire of eftablifhing a republic by wifdom rather than blood. I fhall not enter into an examination of thofe fpeeches: it is neceffary to read them to form a judgment of their merit. All thefe things will no doubt be appreciated by pofterity without partiality: it will fee, that forgetting themfelves, they calculated for its advantage; it will honour their memory, and ftrew flowers upon their graves; a vain and tardy homage, which cannot reftore life to thofe who have loft it; but of which the hope affords confolation to thofe who devote themfelves to deftruction for the good of their country.

The

The murder of le Pelletier is still a kind of mystery; but I shall never forget two facts, which I will mention here: the first is, that all the members, at present proscribed, were afflicted beyond measure at that event. I saw Buzot and Louvet shed tears of rage, persuaded that some bold mountaineer had done the deed with a view of ascribing it to the members of the right side, and of exciting against them the revolutionary fanaticism of the people. The second is, that Gorsas, expressing this opinion in tolerably clear terms, added, that either the assassin would never be discovered at all, or that he would be found dead. It is certain that a Parisian Mountaineer, dispatched with another person in pursuit of Paris, did not overtake him till he came to an inn in Normandy, where they said that he had blown out his brains. It is certain also, that the Mountain made a kind of saint of le Pelletier, who certainly little expected such an honour. A man of a weak mind, and great opulence, he had gone over to them through fear, like Heraut-de-Sechelles, and other *ci-devant* nobles of the same character; and was only of use to them by the manner of his death. Its effect was such as the right side had foreseen; and this is an additional reason for being satisfied that the fugitives are not the authors of that of Marat, even if it were not absurd to suppose, that courage like Charlotte Corday's could be assumed at any man's bidding. Besides, considering the circumstances of the times, and their intention of coming to Paris, their having any share in the immolation of Marat would have been a most dangerous act of folly. To this we may add, that men, abhorrent of blood, endeavouring to repress murder, pillage, and all other excesses, and bold

enough

enough to defy their adversaries to their faces, are not likely to have recourse to such means; while they are natural enough to Danton, who drew up the lists of the massacres of September at his own house, and dispersed the eulogium of them under his own covers, as well as to his coadjutors, the members of the Committee of Vigilance, who were the directors of that bloody business.

It is necessary to study the sittings of the Jacobins in all these conjunctures, to see how the 10th of March was prepared, and to be acquainted with that day's conspiracy, which first miscarried, and was afterwards resumed, to be able to set a just value on the audacious charges which attribute our misfortunes to the wise statesmen about to be sacrificed.

It is truly curious to see how Amar, the reporter, confounds dates, facts, and personages. He makes the war of la Vendee the work of *the right side,* of the pretended faction in which he includes Roland.—Now the troubles in la Vendée did not begin till two months after he had gone out of office; and certainly at that period the Brissotines were not the leaders of the Convention: it cannot then be their fault if efficacious measures were not taken to appease those disturbances. I will go further: I will venture to affirm, that with Roland's activity, and his vigilant correspondence, the troubles in la Vendée would never have had time to get to any head: it was Garat's want of energy that encouraged their growth. I know from his first clerk, that in the beginning of the civil war, that weak minister was strangely tardy in his proceedings. Champagneux pointed out to him the rapid means proper
to

to be employed; but Garat, always uncertain how to act, adopted no plan, and suffered a spark to kindle a conflagration.

Amar pretends that the fugitives, after their proscription, attempted to assemble in la Vendée. What was there then to prevent them, if so inclined? They would now be in safety, instead of wandering as forlorn adventurers. They are every moment in danger of losing their lives, which they might insure by going over to the English, whose agents they are said to have been.— What is it then that hinders them?

Abominable calumniators, to be compared with the madmen who condemned Socrates, with the jealous wretches who ruined Phocion, with the intriguers who banished Aristides, and with the villains who murdered Dion, you say to the people: Here is liberty, and you violate it in the persons of their representatives; you pretend to give them a constitution, and you will not permit them to enjoy it; you proscribe, imprison, or bring to trial, two hundred members of the convention; and you say that they over-awed you, that they were a faction: what then are you? You who despise all rights, who set yourselves above all authority, who abuse every species of power, who govern by the sword, who preach up nothing but terror, and who have imposed upon groaning France the most execrable tyranny!—What did these men, whom you accuse of so many crimes, without proving any, get in the honourable struggle they sustained with intrepidity against villany and blind delusion, in the midst of mortifications without number, and of dangers which they were aware of, which they predicted, which you collected over their

heads,

heads, and with which you have overwhelmed them?—*They made a trade of their opinions concerning the colonies.*— The rich planters hated them: they did not pay them then; or, if they did, where are their bills? Were not they the persons who obtained a decree to oblige every member to furnish an account of his fortune, and to assign the reasons of its increase since the revolution? You did not enforce its execution, and you have since pretended not to remember it, by lately passing another of the same purport, and of which the effect will be the same. You bring Perrin to trial: why then do you keep Sergent among you, and why do you not make Danton regorge his ill-gotten wealth? The day perhaps will come; for it is natural that you should destroy one another at last, and for that purpose make use of your own hands. But how happens it that the wives of the *rich members* you have proscribed are so pinched by poverty?

Guadet's wife, suckling a child born in these disastrous times, guarded since her husband's departure by a *gendarme*, who makes a mockery of her tears, and watched by a barbarous porter, the president of the section, who will not suffer a parcel to be carried out, only subsists upon the produce of a few effects; watches, silver spoons, and linen, which she disposes of by stealth. The wife of Gensonné, dying of grief and of disease, depends upon the secret assistance of a few friends to provide for the support of two charming children. Brissot's wife, confined at first in ready furnished lodgings, because her door was sealed up, was afterwards dragged to the *Force*; where she would be still, as she has been for five days, upon bread and water, and be lying upon straw, if a friendly hand had not afforded her some relief. The wives of Petion and Roland, fellow prisoners at Sainte Pelagie, are obliged to borrow, to pay the trifling sums to which they limit their expences. And you, *Chabot*, where did you get the money, that you call the fortune of your bride? And you ——— but recrimination, however just, is unworthy of the cause of those celebrated men, who are now kept standing, by tyranny, at the bar of a sanguinary tribunal, the composition of which would make us laugh, if it did not transport us with horror. And these men, not yet under sentence, are crowded into a single room of the prison, to the number of twenty-nine, with one bed for every five! O France! you suffer this treatment to be inflicted on, I will not say your children, but your fathers in liberty, and your champions, and yet you talk of a republic!

I have not courage to dwell on the particulars of these abominable charges, after the public reading of which an advocate for the prisoners was heard to observe, that not one of the written documents on which they were founded had been communicated to him, as the law directs. On his request that the tribunal would take the matter into consideration, the president whispered for a moment to somebody on his right, and then answered in a faltering voice, that the immense number of these papers rendered their communication difficult; that besides a great many of them were sealed up at the houses of the accused; that they should be sent for, but that the trial in the mean time must go on. —Thus did they draw up the charges upon the strength of papers that had never been seen, and which are supposed to be at the houses of the accused; and thus do they proceed to judgment without communicating those they pretend to have in their poſſeſſion, under the pretence of their being too numerous—and this is not an impoſture!—Good heavens!—Never could I have believed theſe things if I had not been preſent. Called upon to attend at the trial as a witneſs, I was one of the auditory at the opening of the buſineſs: I imagined it was their intention to take advantage of the truth I might have the courage to tell, to effect my ruin.—After the reading of the charges I withdrew, and waited for my turn to be called: it did not come; and I was carried back to my priſon: this is the third day, and nobody has been ſent for me. I paſſed the hours of expectation on the firſt in the office of the clerk of the court, where I ſpoke with energy and freedom to all who happened to be there. Have they conſidered this energy and freedom might have an effect upon the audience; that it is better to avoid it; to diſpatch the deputies firſt; and then to ſend for me on my own account, without making me an intereſting acceſſory at the trial of others?—I am afraid ſo.—I am deſirous of deſerving death, by bearing witneſs in their favour while they are alive, and I dread loſing the opportunity. I am upon thorns; I wait for the meſſenger as a ſoul in pain waits for its deliverer; and have only written the above obſervations to beguile my impatience.

October 25.

MY LAST THOUGHTS.

To be, or not to be, that is the question.
It will soon be resolved in regard to me.

Is life a property which belongs to us? I think it is; but that property is given us upon conditions in regard to which alone we are liable to error.

We are born to seek happiness for ourselves and to contribute to that of others: the social state extends this destination, as well as all our other faculties, without creating any thing new.

As long as we have a field before us in which we can practise virtue, and give a great example, it becomes us not to quit it; for courage consists in continuing our career in spite of misfortune. But if malevolence mark out the limits of that career, we are free to stop short of them, especially when the fortitude with which we might undergo the last efforts of its rage can be conducive to no advantage. When I was put in confinement, I flattered myself that I should contribute to my husband's glory, and help to enlighten the public, if brought to trial. But it was then I should have been tried, and our persecutors were too dexterous to take so bad a time. They were circumspect as long as they had any thing to fear from those, who, having fled from their violence, inspired the departments with zeal in their defence. But now that terror holds its iron sceptre over a subjugated world, insolent guilt no longer delays its triumph; it deludes, it oppresses, and the gaping multitude wonders at its power. An immense city, fed upon blood and falsehood, furiously applauds abominable proscriptions, on which it stupidly imagines its salvation to depend.

Two months ago, I aspired to the honour of ascending the scaffold; the victim was then allowed to speak, and the energy of a courageous mind might have been serviceable to the cause of truth. Now all is lost!—This generation, rendered ferocious by infamous preachers of carnage, looks upon the friends of mankind as conspirators, and considers as its champions those abject wretches, who cover their vile passions and their cowardice with the mask of frantic enthusiasm. To live in the midst of it, is basely to submit to its horrible government, and to give room for the commission of new atrocities.

I know that the reign of the wicked cannot be of long duration: they generally survive their power, and almost always undergo the punishment they deserve.

Unknown and overlooked, I might in solitude and silence have withdrawn myself from the horrors which rend the bosom of my country, and have waited in the practice of domestic virtues, for the period of its misfortunes. But a prisoner, and marked out as a victim, I shall only, by prolonging my existence, afford a new gratification to tyranny.

Let us deceive it then, since it is not to be overthrown.

Forgive me, respectable man, for disposing of a life which I had devoted to you: your misfortunes would have attached me to it, if I had been permitted to alleviate them. But I am robbed for ever of the power of doing so, and you lose nothing but a shadow, an useless object of affliction and inquietude.

Forgive me, my dear child, young and tender girl,
whose

whose sweet image is impressed on my maternal heart, and staggers my resolution. Oh! certainly, I would not have deprived you of your guide, if it had been possible that they would have let her remain with you: the cruel wretches! have they any pity upon innocence!—But do what they will, they cannot rob you of my example; and I feel, and I will venture to say, upon the very brink of the grave, that it is a rich inheritance.

All you, whom heaven in its bounty gave me for friends, direct your attentions towards my orphan. A young plant violently torn from her native soil, she would have withered perhaps, or have been bruised by the hand of the spoiler; but you placed her in a kindly shelter, and beneath a reviving shade: there may she flourish, and may her beauty and her virtues repay your care! —Do not grieve at a resolution which puts an end to my sufferings: I can bear adversity: you know me, and you will not believe that weakness or fear have prompted my decision. If any one could assure me that before the tribunal at which so many just men are arraigned, I should be allowed to point out our oppressors, I would appear there with pleasure; but experience has too well shewn that the vain formality of judgment is only an insulting parade in which they take care to refuse the victim the privilege of speech *. Shall I then wait till it please my executioners to indicate the hour of my death, and to enhance their triumph by the insolent clamours to which I shall be exposed. Most certainly I should be able to brave them, if my fortitude could instruct

* Look at Gorsas; he is condemned; he is about to die; he is in their hands; they forbade him to speak: such is the fate of the courageous apostles of liberty!

the stupid populace; but they are no longer capable of feeling any thing, except the savage delight of seeing the blood of others spilt, while they run no risk of shedding their own.

The time foretold is come, when their cries for bread are appeased with dead bodies: their degraded nature is regaled by the spectacle, and the gratification of this brutal appetite will render the scarcity of bread supportable, until it shall exceed the sufferance of nature.

Perhaps, some one may say, these dominators of the present day, who sacrifice every thing to their fears, may not extend their fury so far as you.—Why, do you not see that they have purposely provided the means of doing so by comprising me in the absurd indictment against the republicans whom they detest?

Shall I then hold my existence subject to their pleasure, until the fancy shall take them, of first bringing me forward in my turn upon the stage, and then commanding the *exit* of so formidable a witness of their villainy?— Yes, formidable, for long ago my eyes read the secret of their hearts; my soul abhorred them; and my courage set them at defiance: they know it: they must then be determined on my ruin.

But the chances of a new revolution; the approach of the foreign armies!—What signifies it to my safety?— I should like as little to owe it to the Austrians, as to receive death from the French at present in power. They are alike the enemies of my country, and I desire nothing from any of them but their honourable hatred.

Oh! if those pusillanimous beings, those men unworthy of the name, whose weakness assumed the disguise of prudence, and ruined the estimable *twenty-two*,
if

if they had poffeffed my courage, they would have redeemed the firft faults of their conduct; they would have provoked on the fecond of June, by a formal oppofition, the imprifonment to which they have juft been configned. Their refiftance would then have enlightened the uncertain and timid departments; it would have faved the republic; and if they had been doomed to perifh, it would have been with as much glory to themfelves, as utility to their country.

The cowards, they entered into a compromife with guilt!—It was decreed that they fhould fall in their turn; but they fall inglorioufly, unpitied by any, and with nothing to hope for from pofterity, but its perfect contempt. Why, in this laft conjuncture, rather than obey their tyrants, defcend to their bar, walk out of the affembly like a timid flock marked for flaughter by the butcher, and fubmit to be taken into cuftody—why did they not do themfelves juftice by falling upon the monfters, and expunging them from the face of the earth?

Divinity, fupreme being, foul of the univerfe, principle of every thing great, good, and happy, thou in whofe exiftence I believe, becaufe I muft needs emanate from fomething better than what I fee around me, I am about to be reunited to thine effence!—I invoke the kindnefs of all thofe to whom I was dear in favour of that good fervant, whofe uncommon fidelity made her a pattern in her way. The excellent woman! How many tears has her attachment for me made her fhed during the laft thirteen years. How many fecret forrows has fhe fhared in filence, which but for her affectionate attentions I fhould not have known that fhe perceived! What activity in my afflictions! What devotion in my misfortunes!

misfortunes!—If the chimæras of the metempsychosis had any reality, and if our wishes could have any influence upon the changes we should then undergo, I should be glad to return to the world in another shape, that I might take care of her in my turn, and administer comfort to the old age of so kind and worthy a creature! O my friends! discharge the debt I owe her; it is the most grateful tribute you can pay to my memory.

As to my property, I find in the resolution I have taken, the advantage of securing it to whom it belongs: it will descend to my daughter, who, even if they should seize upon her father's fortune, would have a right to claim every thing of mine on which the State has put its seals: she can claim besides twelve thousand livres (500*l.*) which were my portion, as will appear by the marriage contract, executed in February 1780, at Durand's, a notary, resident at Paris, in the *Place Dauphine*. Moreover an estate, a little wood and a meadow, bought by me, in pursuance of the power given me by the *written law* * according to which I was married, from monies arising from sundry sums that came to me in my own right, by inheritance or reimbursement, as will appear by the contract executed at Dufresne's, notary, *Rue Vivienne*, in 1791, and by a deed of which duplicates exist in my apartment at Thésée, and at Villefranche; the whole amounting to thirteen or fourteen thousand livres. [From £540 to £580.]

---

* The written law *(le droit écrit)* is the old Roman law, which was retained in several parts of France till the fall of the ancient despotic system. It was so called in contradistinction to the traditionary customs, or common law, which prevailed in other places. Hence the provinces of France were divided into *Pays de droit écrit* and *Pays Coutumier*.—Transl.

I have

I have besides a thousand crowns in paper, which shall be pointed out. I desire that enough may be taken out of that sum to buy my daughter the harp on which she plays, and which I hired from Koliker, a musical instrument-maker, *rue des Fossés-Saint-Germain-des Prés*: he is an honest and fair-dealing man, and will perhaps abate something of the hundred crowns (£12. 10s.) he asked for it. At any rate I should rather choose it to be laid out in that way than kept in paper. Virtues are the first of treasures: but they are employed to better advantage by the help of talents. No body can tell the relief that music affords in solitude and misfortune, nor from how many seductions it may be a preservative in prosperity. Let the teacher of the harp be kept a few months longer: by that time, if circumstances will not admit of further expence, the dear little girl, by making good use of her time, will know enough for her own amusement. Among the things sealed up is an excellent forte-piano, bought out of my savings, and for which the receipt was consequently made out in my own name, as will appear by examining the papers: let it by all means be claimed. As to drawing, that is the essential article to which her application, care, and attention, ought to be directed.

I have found means to get a letter written to her uncle and godfather, and I hope if he be at liberty, that he will take the necessary steps to secure for my child all that belongs to her. In that case, not being left destitute herself, she ought to provide for our maid Fleury; and this is what I beg those who may watch over her conduct to prevail upon her to do.

My venerable relations, the Besnards, *rue et ile St. Louis,* lodged some money in my husband's hands, of which we used to pay them the interest. As they may be ignorant of the forms to be observed in establishing their claim, the necessary information should be given to those respectable old people. They should now and then also see their great-great niece, who stands them in the stead of a child, and who will soon be their only hope.

I never had any jewels; but I possess two rings of very moderate value, which were left me by my father; I intend them, as memorials, the emerald for my daughter's adoptive father, the other for my friend Bosc.

I have nothing to add to what I lately expressed to the generous woman who has the goodness to be a mother to my child: the services which she and her husband render me, inspire a sentiment which I shall carry with me to the grave, and which words cannot express.

May my last letter to my daughter fix her attention upon that object which appears likely to become her particular pursuit; and may the remembrance of her mother attach her for ever to those virtues which afford us consolation in every circumstance of distress.

Farewell, my dear child, my worthy husband, my faithful servant, and my good friends; farewell, thou sun, whose resplendent beams used to shed serenity over my soul while they recalled it to the skies: farewell, ye solitary fields which I have so often contemplated with emotion; and you, ye rustic inhabitants of Thezée, who were wont to bless my presence, whom I attended in sickness, whose labours I alleviated, and whose indigence

gence I relieved, farewell; farewell peaceful retirements, where I enriched my mind with moral truths, and learned in the silence of meditation to govern my passions, and to despise the vanity of the world.

TO MY DAUGHTER.

October 18, 1793.

I do not know, my dear girl, whether I shall be allowed to see, or to write to you again. REMEMBER YOUR MOTHER. In these few words is contained the best advice I can give you. You have seen me happy in fulfilling my duties, and in giving assistance to those who were in distress.—It is the only way of being happy.

You have seen me tranquil in misfortune and in confinement, because I was free from remorse, and because I enjoyed the pleasing recollections that good actions leave behind them. These are the only means that can enable us to support the evils of life, and the vicissitudes of fortune.

Perhaps you are not fated, and I hope you are not, to undergo trials so severe as mine; but there are others against which you ought to be equally on your guard. Serious and industrious habits are the best preservative against every danger; and necessity as well as prudence command you to persevere diligently in your studies.

Be worthy of your parents: they leave you great examples to follow; and if you are careful to avail your-

self

self of them, your existence will not be useless to mankind.

Farewell, my beloved child, you who drew life from my bosom, and whom I wish to impress with all my sentiments. The time will come when you will be better able to judge of the efforts I make at this moment to repress the tender emotions excited by your dear image. I press you to my heart.

Farewell, my Eudora.

TO MY FAITHFUL SERVANT FLEURY.

My dear Fleury, you whose fidelity, services, and attachment, have been so grateful to me for thirteen years, receive my embraces, and my farewell.

Preserve the remembrance of what I was. It will console you for what I suffer: the good pass on to glory when they descend to the grave. My sorrows are about to terminate; lay aside yours, and think of the peace which I am about to enjoy, and which nobody will in future be able to disturb. Tell my Agatha that I carry with me to the grave the satisfaction of being beloved by her from my infancy, and the regret of not being able to give her proofs of my attachment. I could have wished to be of service to you—at least let me not afflict you.

Farewell, my poor Fleury, farewell!

Friday,

Friday, 24 *October*.

You cannot imagine, dear Jany, all the vexation I have suffered at not being able to write to you at my ease, nor even to read your letter at leisure: I perceived that I had an officer close at my heels, and was afraid on your account. I am like a person infected with the plague. I have no longer any thing to lose, but I am frightened out of my wits for those who accost me; insomuch that yesterday at the court of justice, I was in doubt whether I should return the salute of a man whom I recollected, and whom I thought highly imprudent for shewing me politeness in public.—I was present at the reading of those articles of impeachment, a prodigy of delusion, or rather a masterpiece of perfidy. As soon as they had been read, the advocate, Chauveau, observed in terms of great moderation, that, contrary to all form of law, the documents on which they were founded had not been communicated to the prisoners' counsel. He therefore begged the tribunal to take the matter into consideration, and give orders for their delivery. After a moment's whispering, the president made answer, in a faltering voice, that the papers in question were for the most part sealed up at the houses of the accused; that orders would be given to proceed to the removal of the seals, and that in the mean time the trial would begin. Yes, Jany, I heard this very distinctly with my own ears! I looked about to see if it were not a dream, and I asked of myself whether posterity would believe these things if they should come to its knowledge?— Well, the people felt nothing of all this; they did not

perceive

perceive the atrocity of such conduct; the absurdity of bringing forward a charge and of withholding the vouchers of its truth; the stupidity of pretending that those vouchers are at the houses of the accused, of whose papers as yet no inventory has been taken; and the folly and impudence of confessing it. The president muttered a few words besides concerning the immense number of the other papers, and the difficulty of communicating them; but that was neither more just, nor less absurd. The witnesses were then sent out of court, that they might be called in their turns to make their deposition: my time is not yet come, but probably may to-morrow. I can peceive nothing, in these proceedings, but the intention of taking advantage of the truths I may have the courage to tell, to effect my ruin, which, considering the villains I have to deal with, and my contempt of death, is by no means difficult. Perhaps then we are doomed to meet no more. My friendship bequeaths to you the care of my memory. If I could think of any thing more conformable to the generosity of your sentiments, which I have known too late, I would charge you with it: but why, my dear Jany, known too late? It was Providence that conducted every thing: had I earlier known your worth, my affection for you would have involved you in my misfortunes. You will dispose of every thing for the best. A fall out of the window may be supposed, and those who will not believe it may be sent to see. As there are many workmen, masons and others, nothing is more easy than to imagine, that one of them, or somebody disguised like one of them, stole, at a certain hour under my window, and received the parcel.—This idea is indeed a very good one,

one, and carries with it an air of probability. The *portraits, anecdotes,* and other detached pieces, should be presented to the public as materials to be worked up in better times. The little *depot* ought not to be neglected: it should be added to the mass. ——

The being summoned as a witness previously to the being judicially accused, forces me to adopt a different mode of proceeding from that on which I had determined when I gave you my will, and for which I had already made my preparations: I will then drain the bitter cup to the last drop. Farewell, Jany, farewell!

———

Your letter, my dear Bosc, was highly welcome: it discovers to me your whole heart, and the full extent of your attachment: they are both as uncommon, in my estimation, as they are dear to me. We do not however differ so much as you imagine; we did not understand each other perfectly. It was not my intention to depart at that moment, but to procure the means of doing so when I should deem it fitting. I was desirous of rendering homage to the truth, as I have it in my power to do, and then to make my *exit* just before the last ceremony. I thought it noble to deceive the tyrants. I had long ruminated on the project; and I swear to you, that it was not inspired by weakness. I am perfectly well; my head is as cool, and my spirit as unbroken, as ever. True it is, however, that the present trial embitters my sorrows, and inflames my indignation.

nation. I thought that the fugitives alfo had been taken up. It is poffible that deep grief, and the exaltation of fentiments already terrible, might have matured in the fecret receffes of my heart a refolution, to which my mind did not fail to afcribe the moft excellent motives.

Called upon to give evidence in this affair, I thought it neceffarily called for a different mode of proceeding. I was determined to avail myfelf of the opportunity to reach the goal with greater celerity: I intended to thunder, and then to withdraw from their power. I thought the very circumftance would authorize me to fpeak without referve, and that I ought to have it in my pocket when going into court. I did not however wait for it to fupport my character. During the hours of expectation I paffed in the clerk's office, in the midft of ten perfons, *officers*, *judges* of the other fections, &c. and in the hearing of *Hebert* and *Chabot*, who came into the next room, I fpoke with equal energy and freedom. My turn to be heard did not come; they were to fetch me the fecond day: the third however is almoft over, and nobody has yet appeared. I fear thefe knaves perceive that I may poffibly furnifh an interefting epifode, and think that, after having fummoned me, it is better to reject my evidence.

I wait with impatience, and am now afraid I fhall not have an opportunity of acknowledging my friends in their prefence. You are of opinion, my dear Bofc, that in either cafe I ought to wait for, and not accelerate the cataftrophe: it is on this alone we are not perfectly agreed. It feems to me, there would be weaknefs in receiving the *coup-de-grace* from the hands of others, instead of taking it from my own; and in exposing myself to the insolent clamours of a brutal populace, as unworthy of such an example as it is incapable of turning it to account. No doubt it would have been right to do so three months ago; but now it will be lost on the present generation; and as to posterity, the other resolution, well managed, will have quite as good an effect.

You see that you did not understand me.—Examine then the matter in the same point of view in which it strikes me: it is not at all the same as that in which you see it. When you shall thus have maturely considered it, I will abide by your determination.

I hasten to conclude, that you may have my answer by the same conveyance: it is enough for me to have indicated what you will be able to investigate in the leisure of meditation —My poor little girl! Where then is she? Let me know, I beg of you: send me a few particulars, that my mind's eye at least may see her in her new situation. Affected by your cares, you think that I feel likewise the cruelty of all these circumstances. I understand that my brother-in-law is in confinement: no doubt the sequestration of his property is still in force, and perhaps he is in danger of banishment.

Consider that your friendship, which finds the task I impose upon it a painful one, may easily deceive you, as to what you can or ought to do in that respect. Try to think of the matter, as if it were neither you nor I, but two indifferent persons, in our relative situations, submitted to your impartial judgment. Attend to my fortitude; weigh my reasons; calculate coolly; and recollect how little a mob is worth that is capable of feasting upon such a sight.

I embrace

I embrace you tenderly. Jany will tell you what it is possible to attempt some morning, but take care not to run any hazard.

NOTES

On my Trial, and the Examination by which it began.

At the first moment of my confinement, I thought of writing to Duperret, to beg him to get some attention paid to my complaints. Without being intimate, I had observed in him that courageous disposition which prompts a man to stand forth without fear of consequences whenever he has it in his power to oblige; and he had inspired me with that confidence which arises in a revolution from a conformity of principles. I was not deceived: Duperret answered me with kindness and warmth; and added, to the expressions of his own sentiments, some intelligence concerning the state of public affairs, and the fugitive deputies. I thanked him; and, in replying to the passage that related to our friends, expressed my wishes for their safety, and for that of my country. A few days after, having printed the examination which I had undergone before an administrator of the police at the Abbey, I sent a copy to Duperret; and took that opportunity of testifying my contempt for the silly lies which Hebert had just told in speaking of me in his *Pere Duchesne*. The whole of our correspondence might amount to three or four short letters, including a note, in which I acquainted Duperret, as I acquainted

at

at the time several other persons, whom I supposed to take an interest in my welfare, with the sudden transformation of my enlargement from the Abbey, into a new confinement at Sainte-Pelagie. It is on this correspondence they mean to found an accusation against me, as having been connected, indirectly at least, with the rebels of Calvados. The very day of Brissot's execution I was removed to the *Conciergerie,* put into a noisome room, and forced to sleep in a bed without sheets, which a fellow-prisoner was good enough to lend me. The day after I was examined in the office of the tribunal, by judge David, accompanied by the public accuser, and in the presence of a man whom I suspect to be a juror. At first they asked me many tedious questions concerning Roland before the 14th of July, 1789; who was mayor of Lyons when he was municipal officer, &c.—I answered those questions by an exact relation of facts; but from that very moment I could perceive, while asking many particulars, they did not wish me to be circumstantial in my answers. Without any transition, I was asked, if during the Convention I had not been in the habit of seeing such and such members (and the proscribed and condemned were named); and if in their conferences I had not heard them mention a departmental force, and the means of obtaining it. I had to remark, that I had seen some of those members as friends, with whom Roland had been intimate from the time of the constituent assembly; others by accident, either as acquaintance, or because brought to our house by their colleagues; and that several of them I had never seen at all: that besides there had never been any secret councils or conferences at Roland's; but the conversation was public, and turned on matters which engaged the attention of the Assembly, and interested every body. The debate was long and violent before I could get my answers taken down. They desired me to confine myself to *yes* and *no*; accused me of being talkative; and told me I was not shewing my wit at the hotel of the Interior. The public accuser and the judge, especially the first, behaved with the positiveness and acrimony of persons persuaded that they had a great criminal before them, and impatient for her conviction. When the judge had asked a question, and the public accuser did not find it to his liking, he couched it in other terms, extended and rendered it complex and captious, interrupted my answers, and required them to be more concise: it was downright persecution. I was kept about three hours, or rather more, after which the examination was suspended, to be resumed, as I was told, in the evening. I am waiting for it. A determination to destroy me seems evident.—I will not prolong my life by any base subterfuge; neither will I lay bare my bosom to malevolence; nor facilitate, by a silly complaisance, the labours of the public accuser, who seems desirous of my furnishing him by my answers with matter for the indictment which his zeal meditates against me.

Two days after, I was sent for to be re-examined. The first question turned upon the pretended contradiction that existed between my letters to Duperret, and my having said I was not particularly intimate with him; whence it resulted, that I disguised the truth in regard to my political connexions with the rebels. I

answered

answered that I had never seen Duperret ten times in my life, and not even once in private, as it was easy to perceive by the first letter I addressed to him, when sending him a copy of that I had written to the Convention; that the subsequent letters were the consequence of the kind and explicit answer I had then received, &c. That at the period our little correspondence began there was no question of revolt and rebellion; and at that time I had no room for a choice in the assembly, where there was scarcely any person to whom I was known, or who would have undertaken the care of my interests.

Question. Who were the common friends of yourself and Duperret?

Answer. Barbaroux in particular.

Question. Was it known to you that Roland, before he entered into the administration, belonged to the Committee of Correspondence of the Jacobins?

Answer. Yes.

Question. Was it not you who took upon you to compose the letters it was his duty to draw up for the Committee?

Answer. My husband never borrowed my thoughts, although he may sometimes have employed my pen.

Question. Were you not acquainted with the office for the *formation of public spirit*, established by Roland to corrupt the departments; to bring to Paris a departmental force; to tear the republic to pieces, according to the plans of a liberticide faction, &c.; and was it not you who conducted the business of that office?

Answer. Roland established no office under that denomination; and I conducted the business of none. After the decree, passed at the latter end of August, or-

dering

dering him to disperse useful writings, he assigned to some of his clerks the care of forwarding them, exerting himself to the utmost in the execution of a law which tended to diffuse the knowledge and the love of the revolution. This he called the *patriotic correspondence*; and as to his own writings, instead of promoting discord, they all breathed a desire to concur in the maintenance of order, and of peace.

Here it was observed, it was in vain for me to attempt to disguise the truth, as it evidently appeared, by all my answers, I was desirous of doing; that upon the door of the very office was a ridiculous inscription, and that I was not so great a stranger to my husband's transactions as not to know it; that my endeavours to justify Roland would be equally ineffectual; and fatal experience had but too well shown the mischief that perfidious minister had done, by asperfing the most faithful representatives of the people, and by exciting the departments to take up arms against Paris.

To this I answered, that far from desiring to disguise the truth, I was proud of doing homage to it, even at the risk of my life; that I had never read the inscription in question; on the contrary, I had remarked at the time the report of it was in circulation, that it was not to be found in the printed lists of offices belonging to the interior department; and that, in answer to the injurious imputations upon Roland, I had only two facts to oppose: the *first* his *writings*, which all contained the best principles of morality and *politics*; the *second*, his forwarding all those printed by order of the National Convention, even the speeches of the members

bers of that assembly, who passed for the most violent in opposition.

Question. Do you know at what time Roland left Paris, and where he may be?

Answer. Whether I do or not, is what I neither ought or choose to tell.

It was observed, this obstinacy in constantly disguising the truth proved I thought Roland guilty; that I set myself in open rebellion against the law; that I forgot the duty of a person accused, whom it behoves above all to reveal the truth to justice, &c. The public accuser, who put the question, took care to accompany it, as he did every other he thought proper to ask, with insulting epithets, and expressions indicating anger. I attempted to answer; but he forbad details; and both he and the judge, endeavouring to avail themselves of the kind of authority given by their office, employed all means to reduce me to silence, or to make me say what they thought fit. Indignant at the treatment, I told them I would complain in open court of their unheard of and captious mode of examination; that I would not suffer myself to be brow-beaten; and that I considered the laws of reason and nature as superior to all human institutions: then turning round to the clerk, 'Take up your pen,' said I, 'and write.'

Answer. 'A person accused is answerable for his own actions, but not for those of others. If, during more than four months, Roland had not solicited in vain the passing of his accounts, he would not now be obliged to absent himself, nor should I, supposing me to be acquainted with it, be obliged to make a secret of his place of residence.—I know of no law which requires me to betray the dearest sentiments of nature.'

Here the public accuser exclaimed in a rage, that there was no end to my loquacity; and here closed the examination.

'How I pity you,' said I calmly. 'I forgive you even the disagreeable things you say: you think you have a great criminal before you, and are impatient to convict her. How unfortunate is the man who entertains such prejudices! You may send me to the scaffold; but you cannot deprive me of the satisfaction I derive from a good conscience, nor of the persuasion that posterity will revenge Roland and me, by devoting his persecutors to infamy.' Being desired to choose my advocate, I named Chauveau, and retired, saying to them with a smile, 'I wish you, in return for all the ill you mean to do to me, the same peace of mind I enjoy, whatever may be the reward attached to it.'

The examination took place in a room called the council-chamber, at a table with several persons sitting round it, who appeared to be there for the purpose of writing, and who did nothing but listen to what I said. There were many goers and comers; nor could any thing be less secret than the transaction.

DRAUGHT

DRAUGHT OF A DEFENCE INTENDED TO BE READ TO THE TRIBUNAL *.

THE charge brought against me rests entirely upon the pretended fact of my being the accomplice of men called conspirators. My intimacy with a few of them is of much older date than the political circumstances, in consequence of which they are now considered as rebels; and the correspondence we kept up through the medium of our common friends, at the time of their departure from Paris, was entirely foreign to public affairs. Properly speaking, I have been engaged in no political correspondence whatever, and in that respect I might confine myself to a simple denial; for I certainly cannot be called upon to give an account of my particular affections. But I have a right to be proud of them, as well as of my conduct, nor do I wish to conceal any thing from the public eye. I shall therefore acknowledge, that, with expressions of regret at my confinement, I received an intimation that Duperret had two letters for me, whether written by one or by two of my friends, before or after their leaving Paris, I cannot say. Duperret had delivered them into other hands, and they never came to mine. Another time I received a pressing invitation to break my chains, and an offer of services, to assist me in effecting my escape in any way I might think proper, and to convey me whithersoever I might afterwards wish to go. I was dissuaded from listening to such proposals

* Written at the *Conciergerie* the night after her examination.

by duty and by honour; by duty, that I might not endanger the safety of those to whose care I was confided; and by honour, because at all events I preferred running the risk of an unjust trial, to exposing myself to the suspicion of guilt by a flight, unworthy of me. When I consented to be taken up on the 31st of May, it was not with the intention of afterwards making my escape. In that alone consists all my correspondence with my fugitive friends. No doubt, if all means of communication had not been cut off, or if I had not been prevented by confinement, I should have endeavoured to learn what was become of them; for I know of no law by which my doing so is forbidden. In what age, or in what nation, was it ever considered a crime to be faithful to those sentiments of esteem and brotherly affection which bind man to man? I do not pretend to judge of the measures of those who have been proscribed: they are unknown to me; but I will never believe in the evil intentions of men, of whose probity, civism, and devotion to their country, I am thoroughly convinced. If they erred it was unwittingly; they fall without being abased; and I regard them as unfortunate without being liable to blame. I am perfectly easy as to their glory, and willingly consent to participate in the honour of being oppressed by their enemies. I know those men, accused of conspiring against their country, to have been determined republicans, but humane, and persuaded that good laws were necessary to procure the republic the good-will of persons who doubted whether it could be maintained; which it must be confessed is more difficult than to kill them. The history of every age proves, that it requires great talents to lead men to virtue by wise
   institutions,

institutions, while force suffices to oppress them by terror or to annihilate them by death. I have heard them assert, that abundance, as well as happiness, can only proceed from an equitable, protecting, and beneficent government; and that the omnipotence of the bayonet may produce fear, but not bread. I have seen them animated by the most lively enthusiasm for the good of the people, disdaining to flatter them, and resolved rather to fall victims to their delusion than be the means of keeping it up. I confess these principles, and this conduct, appeared to me totally different from the sentiments and proceedings of tyrants or ambitious men, who seek to please the people to effect their subjugation. It inspired me with the highest esteem for those generous men: this error, if an error it be, will accompany me to the grave, whither I shall be proud of following those whom I was not permitted to accompany.

My defence I will venture to say, is more necessary to those, who really wish to come at the truth, than it is to myself. Calm and contented in the consciousness of having done my duty, I look forward to futurity with perfect peace of mind. My serious turn, and studious habits, have preserved me alike from the follies of dissipation, and from the bustle of intrigue. A friend to liberty, on which reflexion had taught me to set a just value, I beheld the revolution with delight, persuaded it was destined to put an end to the arbitrary power I detested, and to the abuses I had so often lamented, when reflecting with pity upon the fate of the indigent classes of society. I took an interest in the progress of the revolution, and spoke with warmth of public

lic affairs; but I did not pass the bounds prescribed by my sex. Some small talents perhaps, a considerable share of philosophy, a degree of courage more uncommon, and which did not permit me to weaken my husband's energy in dangerous times: such perhaps are the qualities which those who know me may have indiscreetly extolled, and which may have made me enemies among those to whom I am unknown. Roland sometimes employed me as a secretary; and the famous letter to the king, for instance, is copied entirely in my hand-writing: this would be an excellent count to add to my indictment, if the Austrians were trying me, and if they should have thought fit to extend a minister's responsibility to his wife. But Roland long ago manifested his knowledge, and his attachment to the great principles of politics: the proofs of them exist in his numerous works, published during the last fifteen years.—His learning and his probity are all his own, nor did he stand in need of a wife to make him an able minister. Never were conferences or secret councils held at his house; his colleagues, whoever they might be, and a few friends and acquaintance, met once a week at his table, and there conversed in a public manner on matters in which every body was concerned. As to the rest, the writings of that minister, which breathe throughout a love of order and of peace, and which lay down in the most forcible manner the best principles of morality and politics, will for ever attest his wisdom, as his accounts will prove his integrity.

To return to the offence imputed to me, I have to observe that I never was intimate with Duperret. I saw him now and then at the time of Roland's administration;

stration; but he never came to our house during the six months that my husband was no longer in office. The same remark will apply to the other members, our friends, which surely does not accord with the plots and conspiracies laid to our charge. It is evident by my first letter to Duperret, I only wrote to him because I knew not to whom else to address myself, and because I imagined he would readily consent to oblige me. My correspondence with him could not then be concerted; it could not be the consequence of any previous intimacy, and could have only one object in view. It gave me afterwards an opportunity of receiving accounts from those who had just absented themselves, and with whom I was connected by the ties of friendship, independently of all political considerations. The latter were totally out of the question in the kind of correspondence I kept up with them during the early part of their absence. No written memorial bears witness against me in that respect, those adduced only leading to a belief that I partook of the opinions and sentiments of the persons called conspirators. This deduction is well founded: I confess it without reserve, and am proud of the conformity. But I never manifested my opinions in a way which can be construed into a crime, or which tended to occasion any disturbance. Now, to become an accomplice in any plan whatever, it is necessary to give advice, or to furnish means of execution. I have done neither; I am not then reprehensible in the eye of the law—there is no law to condemn me, nor any fact which admits of the application of a law.

I know that in revolutions, law, as well as justice, is

often forgotten; and the proof of it is, that I am here. I owe my trial to nothing but the prejudices, and violent animosities which arise in times of great agitation, and which are generally directed against those who have been placed in conspicuous situations, or are known to possess any energy or spirit. It would have been easy for my courage to put me out of the reach of the sentence I foresaw; but I thought it rather became me to undergo it: I thought that I owed the example to my country; I thought that if I were to be condemned, it must be right to leave tyranny all the odium of sacrificing a woman whose crime is that of possessing some small talents which she never misapplied, a zealous desire of the welfare of mankind, and courage enough to acknowledge her unfortunate friends, and to do homage to virtue at the risk of her life. Minds which have any claim to greatness are capable of divesting themselves of selfish considerations; they feel they belong to the whole human race; and their views are directed to posterity alone. I am the wife of a virtuous man exposed to persecution; and I was the friend of men who have been proscribed and immolated by delusion, and the hatred of jealous mediocrity. It is necessary that I should perish in my turn, because it is a rule with tyranny to sacrifice those whom it has grievously oppressed, and to annihilate the very witnesses of its misdeeds. I have this double claim to death from your hands, and I expect it. When innocence walks to the scaffold, at the command of error and perversity, every step she takes is an advance towards glory. May I be the last victim sacrificed to the furious spirit of party! I shall quit with joy this unfortunate earth, which swallows

lows up the friends of virtue, and drinks the blood of the juſt.

Truth! friendſhip! my country! ſacred objects, ſentiments dear to my heart, accept my laſt ſacrifice. My life was devoted to you, and you will render my death eaſy and glorious.

Juſt heaven! enlighten this unfortunate people for whom I deſired liberty. . . . . Liberty!—It is for noble minds, who deſpiſe death, and who know how upon occaſion to give it to themſelves. It is not for weak beings who enter into a compoſition with guilt, and cover ſelfiſhneſs and cowardice with the name of prudence. It is not for corrupt wretches who riſe from the bed of debauchery, or from the mire of indigence, to feaſt their eyes on the blood that ſtreams from the ſcaffold. It is the portion of a people who delight in humanity, practiſe juſtice, deſpiſe their flatterers, and reſpect the truth. While you are not ſuch a people, O my fellow-citizens! you will talk in vain of liberty: inſtead of liberty you will have licentiouſneſs, of which you will all fall victims in your turns: you will aſk for bread; dead bodies will be given you; and you will at laſt bow down your necks to the yoke.

I have neither concealed my ſentiments nor my opinions. I know that a Roman lady was ſent to the ſcaffold for lamenting the death of her ſon. I know that in times of deluſion and party rage, he who dares avow himſelf the friend of the condemned or of the proſcribed expoſes himſelf to their fate. But I deſpiſe death; I never feared any thing but guilt, and I will not purchaſe life at the expence of a baſe ſubterfuge. Woe

to

to the times! woe to the people among whom doing homage to disregarded truth can be attended with danger, and happy he who in such circumstances is bold enough to brave it!

It is now your part to see whether it answer your purpose to condemn me without proof, upon mere matter of opinion, and without the support or justification of any law.

---

18 *Brumaire.*

By authority of the criminal revolutionary tribunal established by the law of the 10th of March 1793, without appeal to the tribunal of annulment, and also in virtue of the power delegated by the law of 25 April of the same year, to the said tribunal sitting in the hall of justice at Paris:

The indictment drawn up by the public accuser against Mary-Jane Phlipon, wife of John-Mary Roland, aged thirty-nine years, born at Paris, and dwelling there, in the *rue de la harpe*, of which the tenor is as hereafter followeth:

Antony-Quintin Fouquier-Tinville, public accuser of the extraordinary criminal and revolutionary tribunal, (established at Paris, by a decree of the national convention, of the 10th of March, the second year of the republic, without appeal to the tribunal of annulment) by virtue of the power to him given by the second article of another decree of the convention of the 5th of April following, importing that the public accuser of the said tribunal is authorised to arrest, prosecute, and bring to judgment,

judgment, on the denunciation of the conftituted authorities and of citizens,

SHEWETH that the fword of the law has recently ftruck feveral principal chiefs of the confpiracy which exifted againft the liberty and fafety of the French people; but a great number of authors and accomplices of that confpiracy ftill exift, and hitherto have found means, by a cowardly flight, to avoid the juft punifhment of their crimes: of the number is Roland, ex-minifter of the home department, the principal agent of the confpirators. The flight of fome of them did not put a ftop to the correfpondence between thofe who remained at Paris, as well at liberty as in a ftate of arreft: they correfponded alfo with thofe who had taken refuge at Caen, and other cities of the republic. Roland on leaving Paris left behind him his wife, who, although put in confinement in a houfe of arreft, continued to correfpond with the confpirators who had retired to Caen, through the medium of another who remained at Paris. That intriguing woman, who is well known to have received, and affembled at her houfe the principal chiefs of the confpirators in fecret councils, of which fhe was the foul, received, although in prifon, letters from Barbaroux and others of the refugees at Caen; and always anfwered them in terms favourable to the confpiracy. Of this correfpondence the proof exifts, Firft, in a letter dated from Evreux, the 13th of June laft, written by Barbaroux to Lauze Duperret, in which he fays: " Do not forget the eftimable wife of Roland, and " try to give her fome confolation in her prifon, by " conveying to her the good news, &c." 2dly, in a letter, dated the 15th of the faid month of June, from

the

the said Barbaroux to the said Lauze Duperret, in which are the following passages. " You have no doubt executed " my commission in regard to Madame Roland, by trying " to convey to her some little consolation.—Make an ef- " fort to see her, and tell her, that the *twenty-two* proscrib- " ed, and all honest men, share her afflictions, &c. Here- " with you will receive a letter which we have written to " that estimable woman. I need not say that you alone " can execute this important commission; she must at all " events try to get out of her prison, and into some " place of safety, &c." 3dly, In a letter written by Lauze Duperret to the said wife of Roland, in which he says: " I have kept for several days three letters which " Barbaroux and Buzot inclosed to me, without having " it in my power to convey them to you; and what " is still more unfortunate, is, that at the moment I " might avail myself of the means you afford me, " the thing is become impossible, as they are in " the hands of Petion, to whom I thought it advise- " able to deliver them, supposing he had it more in " his power to forward them than any body else, and who " set off without being able so to do. I shall this very " day give notice of it to those citizens to whom I am " going to write by a safe conveyance, and shall in- " form them I have it now in my power to execute " their commands with more punctuality, &c." 4thly, In a note dated the 24th of June, written by the above wife of Roland to Duperret, in which she acquaints him she has been released from the abbey; that she thought she was going to return home; but that before she reached it she was taken up and conducted to Sainte-Pelagie. 5thly, and lastly, in three other letters written

by

by her in like manner to Lauze Duperret; the first dated June 6, the second without date, and the third June 24. In the second she says: " The accounts " I receive from my friends are the only pleasure I " am sensible of: you have assisted in procuring me " that pleasure: tell them my confidence in their " courage and knowledge of what they are capable " of doing for liberty, stands me in stead of every " thing, and consoles me in all my misfortunes; tell " them my esteem, my attachment, and my good " wishes, will follow them wherever they go. Barba- " roux's hand-bill gave me great pleasure," &c.

After the contents of the said letters there can be no doubt that the said wife of Roland was one of the principal agents and abettors of the conspiracy.

These things considered, the public accuser has drawn up the present indictment against Mary-Jane Phlipon, the wife of Roland, heretofore minister of the Interior, for having wickedly, and designedly, aided and assisted in the conspiracy which existed against the unity and indivisibility of the republic, against the liberty and safety of the French people, by assembling at her house, in secret council, the principal chiefs of that conspiracy, and by keeping up a correspondence tending to facilitate their liberticide designs.

Wherefore the public accuser demands, that a record be made, by the tribunal assembled, of the accusation brought by him against Mary-Jane Phlipon, the wife of Roland; and that in consequence he be ordered with his best speed, and by a serjeant *(huissier)* of the tribunal, bearer of the warrant, to take the said Mary-Jane Phlipon, wife of Roland, into custody, and to lodge her in the *houſe of arreſt* of the *Conciergerie* at Paris, there to remain in cloſe impriſonment; as alſo that the ſaid warrant be notified to the accuſed, and to the tribunal of Paris.

Done, in the cabinet of the public accuſer, this ſeventeenth of Brumaire, in the ſecond year of the French republic, one and indiviſible.

    (Signed)   A. Q. Fouquier.

The warrant iſſued againſt her by the tribunal, and the minutes of the delivery of her perſon in the houſe of juſtice of the Conciergerie, as alſo the declaration of the jury of judgment, importing:

That there has exiſted a horrible conſpiracy againſt the unity and indiviſibility of the republic, the liberty and ſafety of the French people:

That Mary-Jane Phlipon, wife of John-Mary Roland, is convicted of being one of the abettors or accomplices of that conſpiracy.

The tribunal, after having heard the public accuſer deliver his reaſons concerning the application of the law, condemns Mary-Jane Phlipon, wife of John-Mary Roland, ex-miniſter, to the puniſhment of death, in conformity with the law of the ſixteenth of December, one thouſand ſeven hundred and ninety-two, which has been read, and which is conceived in theſe terms:

" The National Covention decrees, that whoever ſhall propoſe or attempt to deſtroy the unity of the French republic, or to detach its integral parts to unite them to a foreign territory, ſhall be puniſhed with death."

Declares the property of the ſaid wife of Roland confiſcated fifcated to the ufe of the nation, in conformity with the law of the 10th of March laft, which has been read, and which is conceived in thefe terms: " The property of thofe who fhall be condemned to the punifhment of death, fhall be confifcated to the ufe of the republic: a provifion fhall be made for fuch widows and children as have no property of their own."

Orders the public accufer to fee that the prefent fentence be put in execution, within twenty-four hours, on the *Place de la Revolution* in this city, and to be printed and pofted up throughout the whole extent of the republic, wherever need may be.

Done, and pronounced in open court, the eighteenth of the month Brumaire, the fecond year of the French republic; prefent, citizens René-Francis Dumas, vice-prefident, performing the functions of prefident; Gabriel Deliegé, Francis-Jofeph Denifot, and Peter-Noel Subleyras, judges; who have figned the minutes, with Wolff, clerk of the court.

Collated.

A true copy, delivered by the underfigned.

PARIS, fecretary *(Greffier.)*

Such was the fentence that fent to the fcaffold, at the age of thirty-nine, a woman, whofe energetic difpofition, feeling heart, and cultivated mind, rendered her the delight and admiration of all who knew her. Her death reflects equal glory on her fex, and difgrace on her executioners.

It is not my province to draw her character: her writings exprefs it; her conduct is her teftimony; and history will revenge the injustice of her contemporaries.

The sentence was preceded for form's sake, and according to the custom of that horrible tribunal, by a mock trial *(débats)*, in which madam Roland was not allowed to speak, and in which hired ruffians vomited forth the most atrocious calumnies before other ruffians, the execrable tools of Robespierre, so unworthily honoured with the title of judges and jurors. I have not been able to procure a detail of the proceedings, which, as is well known, must not be taken in writing: but I know that only one person paid a tribute to truth, and that he was some time after sent on that account to the scaffold. I mean the worthy Lecocq, who for eight months only had lived with Roland as a servant, and whose excellent qualities deserved a better fate.

Madam Roland did not deceive the expectations of her friends. She was conducted to the scaffold with all the calmness of a great mind, superior to the idea of death, and possessing sufficient power to overcome the natural horror of immediate dissolution. To exhibit a picture of her last moments, I cannot do better than borrow the elegant and impressive pen of Roiuffe. The following is the account he gives of them in his work intituled *Memoires d'un détenu, pour servir à l'histoire de la tyrannie de Robespierre*; a work which will furnish history with more than one important delineation, and which will never be read without emotion.

"The blood of the *twenty-two* was still warm when madam Roland was brought to the *Conciergerie*. Well aware of the fate that awaited her, her peace of mind continued undisturbed. Though past the prime of life, she was still a charming woman: she was tall and of elegant make; and her countenance was expressive; but her misfortunes and long confinement had left traces of melancholy on her face, which tempered its natural vivacity. She had the soul of a republican in a body made up of graces, and fashioned by a certain courtly style of politeness. Something more than is generally found in the eyes of women beamed from hers, which were large, dark, and full of softness and expression. She often spoke to me at the grate with the freedom and energy of a great man. This republican language, from the mouth of a pretty French woman, for whom the scaffold was preparing, was one of the miracles of the revolution to which we were not then accustomed. We all stood listening round her, in admiration and astonishment. Her conversation was serious without being cold; and she expressed herself with a choice of words, a harmony and cadence, that made her language a kind of music with which the ear was never satisfied. She always spoke of the members, who had just been put to death, with respect; but she spoke of them at the same time without feminine pity, and even reproached them with not having adopted measures sufficiently energetic. She generally styled them *our friends*, and often sent for Claviere to converse with him. Sometimes her sex would recover the ascendance; and it was easy to see, that the recollection of her daughter and her husband had drawn tears from her eyes. This mixture of natural softness, and of fortitude, rendered her the more interesting. The woman who waited on her, said to me one day, '*Before you she calls up all her courage; but in her own room she sometimes stands for hours together, leaning against her window and weeping.*' The day she was sent for to be examined, we saw her pass with her usual firmness; but when she returned the tears were glistening in her eyes: she had been treated with so much harshness, and questions so injurious to her honour had been asked her, that her tears and her indignation had burst forth together. A mercenary pedant coldly insulted this woman, celebrated for the excellence of her understanding, and who, at the bar of the National Convention, had reduced her enemies to silence, and forced them to admire the easy graces of her eloquence. She remained eight days at the *Conciergerie*; and in that short time rendered herself dear to all the prisoners, who sincerely deplored her fate.

The day she was condemned, she was neatly dressed in white; and her long black hair flowed loosely to her waist. She would have moved the most savage heart, but those monsters had no heart at all. Her dress, however, was not meant to excite pity; but was chosen as a symbol of the purity of her mind. After her condemnation, she passed through the wicket with a quick step, bespeaking something like joy; and indicated by an expressive gesture, that she was condemned to die. She had, for the companion of her misfortune, a man whose fortitude was not equal to her own, but whom she found means to inspire with gaiety, so cheering and so real, that it several times brought a smile upon his face.

At the place of execution, she bowed down before the statue of Liberty, and pronounced these memorable words:

words: *O Liberty, how many crimes are committed in thy name!*

She often said, that her hufband would not furvive her; and foon after we learned in our dungeons, that the virtuous Roland had killed himfelf on the public road, thereby indicating his wifh to die irreproachable in regard to courageous hofpitality.

My heart, though fuffering many cruel torments in that horrible abode, felt nothing more feverely than the pang occafioned by the death of that celebrated woman.—The remembrance of her murder, added to that of my unfortunate friends, will make my mind a prey to inconfolable forrow to the laft period of my exiftence.

END OF THE SECOND PART.

SUPPLEMENT*.

The Examination of Citizeness Roland at the Abbey, taken from Duláure's paper called the Thermometre du Jour, of the 21*st and* 22*d June,* 1793.

I consider it as an indispensable duty, whatever may be the prejudices of the public, to afford to persons accused the means of making known their justification. This induces me to publish the examination of madam Roland. None but cowards, and men strangers to equity, can blame this conduct. DULAURE.

The 12th of June, Louvet, an administrator of the police, repaired to the Abbey to examine madam Roland.

Question. Are you not acquainted with the troubles which agitated the republic during and after the administration of citizen Roland, your husband?

Answer. Those things were known to me, as to every one else, by conversations and the public papers.

Observed. This negative manner of answering a question is not satisfactory, newspapers not giving that intimate knowledge which I must certainly have had of public affairs.

* This piece probably was inserted in the part of the Historical Memoirs which was burnt. It has been thought proper to give it here by way of supplement.

Answer.

Answer. I was not bound to acquire any such knowledge, since as a woman I had no business to interfere in them.

Question. Had you no knowledge of a plan for a federative republic, and for detaching the departments from Paris?

Answer. I never heard of such a thing: I can say, on the contrary, that Roland, and all the persons I was in the habit of seeing, constantly spoke in my presence of the expediency of maintaining the unity of the republic, as tending to give it greater force; of the consequent necessity of preserving an equilibrium between all the departments; of their wish that Paris might do nothing to excite the jealousy of the rest; of their desire to see *justice* and *liberty* prevail throughout France, and to concur in the maintenance of them.

Observed. That if those persons spoke of *justice* and *liberty* without *equality*, their principles were reprehensible.

Answer. In my opinion, as well as in that of the persons in question, *equality* is the necessary consequence of *justice* and *liberty*.

Question. Who were the persons that composed Roland's society and yours?

Answer. His old friends, and those with whom he had business to transact.

Observed. That it would be desirable to know the names of the citizens and persons of my own sex with whom I was in the greatest habits of intimacy.

Answer. Those with whom I was most intimate are generally

generally known, and most assuredly nobody came to my house in secret.

Observed. That I could certainly name those who the most frequently visited the minister, and formed his private parties.

Answer. As a man in office, Roland sometimes received a hundred persons in a day, not one of whom I saw. As to myself, I never had any extensive circle of visitors; but sometimes gave a dinner to my husband's colleagues, and to the persons with whom they were in any way connected.

Question. Had you no knowledge of writings sent to the departments to provoke them to rise against Paris?

Answer. I never heard of such a thing.

Observed. That Roland while minister had however formed offices *of public opinion* in the departments, and it appeared that sums of money were set apart for the purpose.

Answer. The first part of the observation appears to me absolutely destitute of foundation. As to the second, every body knows the minister of the Interior was allowed a sum of money in order to disperse useful writings; and as Roland has given in his accounts, it is easy to see what writings were sent to the departments.

Question. Can you not name those writings? You must certainly know what they were.

Answer. The accounts being public, and having been posted up, any one may recur to them for a more exact list of those writings than I am able to give. As to to their contents, it belongs to the public, and not to me, to decide upon their merit.

Obſerved. That Roland could not have given in his accounts, ſince he ſo earneſtly ſolicited permiſſion to do ſo, when deſirous of leaving Paris.

Anſwer. Not wiſhing to ſuppoſe the perſon who examines me has any bad intention, I can only attribute the preſent obſervation to an extreme ignorance of facts. Roland not only delivered a monthly account to the convention, but on going out of office, gave in a general account, in which every thing was detailed in the moſt particular manner. What he ſolicited was the paſſing of thoſe accounts, that is to ſay, their inveſtigation by the commiſſioners of the convention, and ſuch a report of them to that aſſembly as they might appear to deſerve. The committee of public accounts in conſequence impoſed this taſk on ſeveral of its members.

I added, I knew that they had come repeatedly to the hotel of the Interior; that they had examined the minutes and vouchers; had been edified, as they needs muſt, by the adminiſtration of a man whoſe integrity and courage would long be the theme of praiſe; that it was Roland's moſt earneſt deſire, as well as mine, that the commiſſioners ſhould make their report, and that I begged all good citizens to join me in my endeavours to obtain it.

[I was interrupted in this anſwer: it was thought too long; and I was accuſed of being acrimonious. I obſerved, that I availed myſelf of my rights, and that there
was

was no acrimony in informing those who were ignorant of Roland's having given in his accounts, that he had done so long ago.]

Question. Among your acquaintance was there no friend of Dumouriez?

Answer. There was nobody intimate with him, to the best of my knowledge, among those I was in the habit of seeing.

Question. Have you had no connexion with traitors?

Answer. All the persons I was acquainted with, were so noted for their patriotism, that it was impossible even to suspect them of any intercourse with traitors.

Question. Do you know where your husband is?

Answer. I do not.

Question. Were you not privy to a plan for dissolving the popular societies?

Answer. Nobody in my presence ever disclosed such a plan, or opinions tending that way.

Here, after a confinement of twelve days, for which no motive had been assigned, ended my examination, without my being told of what I was accused or suspected, and consequently without my knowing on what facts I was to be questioned.

Confident that I had nothing to lose by telling the truth concerning my sentiments, and all the persons with whom I had been acquainted, I neglected to avail myself of my rights, and gave a plain and direct answer to every thing that was asked.

The examination was upon two sheets of paper: my signature was required at the end only. I demanded a copy, and was promised it the next day: nine are

however

however passed, and I have not yet received it, although I have sent to ask for it four times. But, on leaving the administrator, I committed to paper all that had passed. I am sure I have exactly related every thing that was said; and I sign *Roland*, formerly *Phlipon*.

End of the Supplement to the Second Part.

www.ingramcontent.com/pod-product-compliance
Lightning Source LLC
Chambersburg PA
CBHW020230240426
43672CB00006B/480